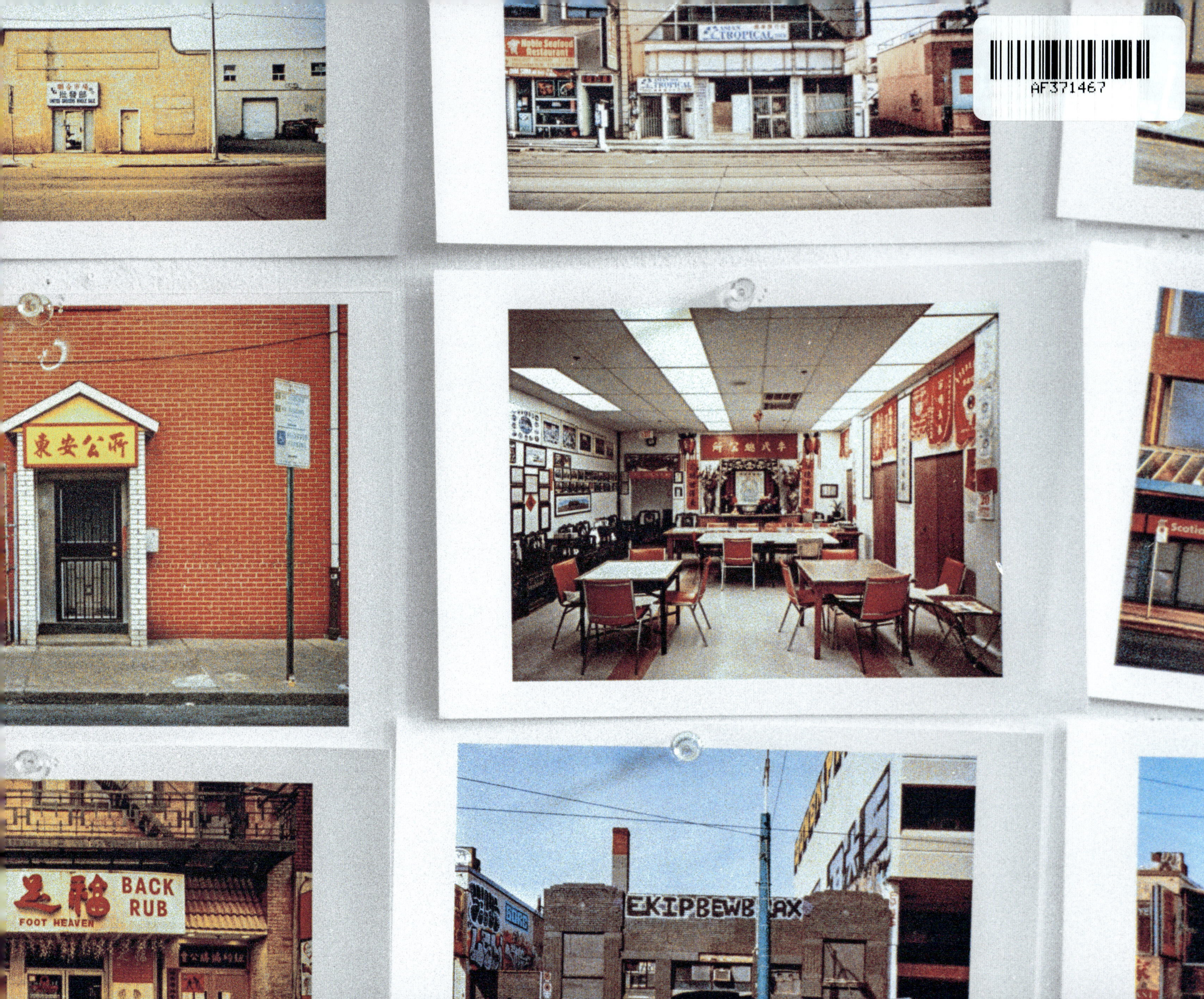
AF371467
Noble Seafood Restaurant
ASIAN TROPICAL
TROPICAL
Scotiaba
東安公所
BACK RUB
FOOT HEAVEN
EKIPBEWBRAX

CHINATOWNS
TONG YAN GAAI

Photographs by Morris Lum

WORK BOOK | DelMonico Books • D.A.P. New York

For Mom, Dad and Moi

INTRODUCTION

Lily Cho 曹美寶

The North American Chinatown holds a special place in the global cultural imaginary. It has become a stand-in for an idea of global Chineseness that extends well beyond Canada and the United States. Certainly for fans of popular martial arts cinema, the globality of the North American Chinatown is encapsulated in the way that the 1995 blockbuster film *Rumble in the Bronx* ushered Hong Kong actor Jackie Chan into global stardom alongside the deployment of Vancouver's Chinatown (where the film was shot) as a proxy for New York's Chinatown in the Bronx, which in itself was a proxy for Chinatown in general. The North American Chinatown has become a shorthand for concepts about Chineseness. It signals the ways in which diasporic Chinese communities have established distinct geographical spaces within cities that have historically been hostile to their presence.

For most of the twentieth century, Chinese migrants to North America have been subjected to forms of legal exclusion. In Canada, amendments to the head tax policies, formally known as the Chinese Immigration Act, 1885, meant that Chinese migrants, with few exceptions (such as members of the clergy and diplomats), were denied entry to Canada from 1923 until the law was finally repealed in 1947. In the United States, the Chinese Exclusion Act passed in 1882, with prohibition against Chinese migration in place until 1943. Successive waves of anti-Chinese sentiment shaped the daily life for North American Chinese communities long before and long after legal exclusion. In the twenty-first century, anti-Chinese racism, and anti-Asian racism more broadly, soared again during the COVID-19 pandemic. Throughout the long arc of racism against Asian communities in North America, Chinatowns have served as a place of both refuge and violence. They call attention to the persistence of these communities even as their very visibility has made them targets of racial violence.

The presence of Chinatowns has also been a way to talk about the resilience and persistence of Chineseness beyond China, and Morris Lum's method beautifully engages with this persistence. Through what I think of as a deeply committed longitudinal approach, Lum returns to these photographic sites multiple times over many years. He captures Chinatown as an idea that persists even as it changes. Look carefully and you will see some of these changes too. Once there was a restaurant, now there is a slim condominium tower. Once a pho restaurant and apartment complex residing next to one of the iconic gates into the community, now a gaping hole in the ground from which a golden yellow construction crane rises, itself a signal of the ambitions and hopes for a space that does and does not belong to the people who live and work there. Once a winding street of small business, now shutters, the only bright spots being a star-spangled flag and a school-crossing sign. Lum invites his viewers into acts of sleuthing and storytelling, to find for themselves the stories of community spaces changing and shifting, dying and being reborn.

This longitudinal view that Lum gives to his viewers does more than track the kinds of changes one might expect to find in any urban neighbourhood. *Chinatowns | Tong Yan Gaai* is not simply a lament about gentrification or the surrendering of racialized community spaces to the voraciousness of real estate development. Lum's project offers all of this, but it also gives its viewers a sense of the sedimentation that makes for the true life of a city and the cities within a city. Even in their naming, Chinatowns have declared themselves to be a space within a space. More than that, their sedimentation, the way that they hold within them layers upon layers of the history of a city, offers us a way to understand not just a city but our own relationship to memory and to ourselves. Freud famously thought of Rome as analogous to the human mind, where the city serves as a "psychical entity with a similarly long and rich past." For Freud, the way that all the different layers of Roman history could be seen from a mere shift in positioning—the Temple of Jupiter Capitolinus from one vantage point is the Palazzo Caffarelli from another; the Pantheon is also perceived as the seat of Agrippa's rule, through which we can glimpse the basilica of Santa Maria sopra Minerva—allows us to understand how histories coexist, buried, often intact, and layered. Lum's photographs make visible the complex sedimentation in cities that may seem less richly layered than Rome. The cities of Lum's focus—Boston, Calgary, Chicago, Edmonton, Los Angeles, Montreal, New York, Ottawa, Philadelphia, San Francisco, Seattle, Toronto, Vancouver, Victoria, and Winnipeg—hold multiple histories, layers of lived memory, and long trajectories of settlement that have sedimented. Lum's camera shifts our vantage points and, in so doing, unsettle what might have seemed solidly settled.

Of course, there will be histories that cannot be seen. The violence at the core of these histories cannot be fully captured by even the most perceptive and intuitive photographic eye.

Namely, the erasure of Indigenous history from North American Chinatowns, which is hard to see and hard to capture, because it is a history of violent erasure. Chinese migrants are settlers. Chinatowns are built on Indigenous land. The persecution experienced by Chinese communities layers tragedy over tragedy. Chinatowns and Chinese communities are not exempt from being complicit in the horrors of settler colonialism.

These photographs do insist, over and over, that Chinatown is not only a place for Chineseness. Vietnamese, Filipino, Japanese, Cambodian, and many other Asian communities can be found in any North American Chinatown, and the future of many Chinatowns has depended upon waves of Asian migration that are not solely Chinese. Lum captures the diversity of Chinatowns both in his photographs and in the subtitle for this project. The relationship between "Chinatown" and "Tong yan gaai" is not that of a simple translation. "Tong yan gaai" means something for early Chinese migrants and their descendants. These are the communities carved out of the history of the head tax and exclusion. It means something else in the late twentieth and early twenty-first centuries, when the People's Republic of China emerged as an economic superpower, accompanied by a rise of Chinese nationalism in diasporic communities, where the flourishing of Mandarin on the streets of Spadina, East Pender, Canal, Stockton, and the like functions as both a sign and a symptom of a new kind of Chinese ascendancy.

"Tong yan gaai" is a transliteration of the Cantonese name for Chinatown. To insist on this naming, as Lum does in his project, is to ask for a remembering of time when Chinese communities in North America were deeply connected to villages in southern China and Hong Kong. "Tong yan gaai" as a phonetic sign cuts right to the heart of the histories of migration that gave rise to Chinatowns in North America—the waves of late-nineteenth- and early-twentieth-century Chinese workers who built so much of North America and whose shared lingua franca was Toisan and Cantonese. *Tong Yan Gaai* remembers these histories but also recalls how these histories have become alien from Chinatown now and how this alienation simmers as tensions and connections that are grounded in the rise of Mandarin in the Chinese diaspora—and the importance of the many non-Chinese communities that have carved out a place in Chinatown.

Chinatowns have transformed the streetscapes of North American cities, but they are not just exteriors. There is an interior to every Chinatown. Lum's photographs insist that the sedimentation of memory and place demands an attention to more than the buildings and ceremonial gates that mark entry into these distinct cities within cities. Through the gates, past the doors of the restaurants and clan association buildings, there are rooms. Lum's camera shifts and moves us into these spaces of memory and history. Yet these spaces are alive with the work of what it means to sustain a community. Chairs stacked. Mahjong tables set for multiple games. Meeting tables at the ready. Lion dance equipment neatly stored. Here in the rooms of Lum's interior Chinatown, we are in situ, momentarily paused and ready for the next game, the next community celebration, the next dance.

Chinatowns | Tong Yan Gaai not only insists upon the endurance and persistence of Chinatowns; it also calls us to the profound vibrancy of these spaces. There is sometimes a curious tendency to talk about Chinatowns through a nostalgic frame that situates them as part of a past, one that has not yet happened. They are supposedly dying, or being gentrified out of existence, or erased by migration to the suburbs. Lum's photographs counter this tendency in so many ways. In part, his longitudinal approach shows how changes in habitation patterns, in demographics, in architecture, are not necessarily in and of themselves endings. But his project is not just one of historical documentation. It is also an aesthetic intervention. Look at these photographs. Soak in the deep saturation of the colour palette. Take in the light.

Chinatown is Chinese, and it is not. It is a place, and it is an idea. It is imagined, and it is deeply and dynamically real. It remains unchanged in that it accommodates constant change while still remaining recognizably Chinatown. Morris Lum's photographs capture these contradictions and complexities. These photographs do not fossilize Chinatown into a particular time even as they insist upon the endurance of Chinatown as a place.

導言

Lily Cho 曹美寶

北美唐人街在全球文化想像中佔據著獨特的位置。它早已成為全球華人性（global Chineseness）的代指，意涵遠超越加拿大與美國的範疇。對於主流武術電影觀眾而言，1995年的賣座大片《紅番區》正好體現了這種全球性：這部電影不僅讓香港演員成龍躍升為國際巨星，溫哥華唐人街（影片實際拍攝地）也被設定為紐約布朗克斯唐人街的替身——而布朗克斯唐人街本身又是唐人街通用意象的代身。北美唐人街已然成為關於華人性的諸多觀念的縮寫，標誌著華人離散社群如何在歷來對其存有敵意的城市中開闢出獨具一格的地緣空間。

整個二十世紀的漫長歷程中，移居北美的華人長期在法律層面受到排斥。在加拿大，《華人移民法》（Chinese Immigration Act, 1885）經多次修訂後，演變為徵收人頭稅的制度。自1923年起，除了少數例外（如神職人員與外交官），華人幾乎全面被禁止入境，直到1947年才正式廢除。在美國，1882年通過的《排華法案》（Chinese Exclusion Act）從根本上禁止華人移民，禁令持續至1943年。持續湧現的反華情緒，在法令施行前後的很長一段時間裡，都深刻地影響著北美華人社群的日常生活。進入二十一世紀後，針對華人的種族主義，以及更廣泛針對亞裔的歧視情緒，在COVID-19疫情期間再度激增。在亞裔社群長期承受的種族歧視歷史中，唐人街始終扮演著避風港與暴力現場的雙重角色。它們突顯了這些社群延續至今的堅韌與存續力——即便正是這份可見性，使其反而成為種族暴力的標靶。

唐人街的存在，長久以來一直是探討華人性如何在中國以外地區展現韌性與延續的切入點，而林耀基的創作方式正是對這種延續性的巧妙回應。他以我所理解的歷時性（longitudinal）實踐方式——一種長期且堅定投入的方式——多年重返那些拍攝地點，捕捉唐人街作為一個概念的持續存在，即便它的本身不斷在變化。細看之下，你也能辨識出這些轉變：曾經的餐館，如今變成狹長的公寓大樓；曾經是地標牌樓旁的越南餐館與公寓，如今是一個正在挖掘中的工地，金黃色的吊車高高升起，象徵著某種野心與對那片空間的期待——一個既屬於、又不屬於在那裡生活與工作的人們的空間；曾經佈滿小商舖的蜿蜒街道，如今鐵門緊閉，僅剩的亮點只有飄揚的星條旗與學區過街標誌。林耀基邀請觀者投入一場偵探式的探索與敘事行動，在影像中自行發掘這些社區空間的故事——如何變遷、流轉、凋零，繼而重生。

林耀基帶給觀者的這種歷時性圖景，遠不止於對城市社區變遷的常規追蹤。《Chinatowns｜唐人街 Tong Yan Gaai》並不只是對族裔社區空間仕紳化、或對城市開發貪婪壓力所做的退讓的哀嘆。林的作品固然涵蓋了這些層面，但更重要的是，它為觀者帶來了一種對沉積（sedimentation）的細緻感知——也正是這種沉積構成了一座城市的真實生命，以及隱含在城市之中的那些「城中之城」。唐人街，從命名開始，就已宣示它作為「空間中的空間」的地位。而正是這些沉積——歷史層疊的痕跡與交疊的時序——讓我們不僅得以理解一座城市，更得以重新思考我們自身與記憶之間、與自我之間的關係。

眾所周知，佛洛伊德曾以羅馬為喻，將其比作人的心智結構，視其為「一種同樣歷史悠久且延綿的精神性建構體」。對佛洛伊德而言，羅馬城錯綜交疊的歷史，只需改變觀看的位置便可一覽無遺——從某個角度看，是朱庇特神殿（Temple of Jupiter Capitolinus），從另一角度看，則是卡法雷利宮（Palazzo Caffarelli）；萬神殿（Pantheon）同時也被視為阿格里帕統治時期的象徵，透過它，我們得以一瞥背後的米涅瓦聖母大殿（Santa Maria sopra Minerva）。這種觀看方式讓我們理解：歷史是共時並存的、被掩埋卻未抹除的，層層堆疊且彼此交錯。林耀基的攝影作品亦讓我們得以看見，那些看似不如羅馬那般「層疊豐富」的城市中，其實同樣存在著複雜的沉積結構。他拍攝的城市——波士頓、卡加利、芝加哥、愛民頓、洛杉磯、蒙特婁、紐約、渥太華、費城、舊金山、西雅圖、多倫多、溫哥華、維多利亞與溫尼伯——皆蘊含著多重歷史、生活記憶的層次，以及長期聚居所沉澱出的軌跡。林的鏡頭轉換了我們的觀看視角，從而撼動了那些原本看似早已塵埃落定的既定認知。

當然，也有一些歷史是無法被看見的。即便是最具洞察力與直覺的攝影眼光，也無法完全捕捉構成這些歷史核心的暴力。具體而言，就是北美唐人街中被抹去的原住民歷史——這段歷史之所以難以被看見、難以被記錄，是因為它本身就是一種暴力抹除的結果。華人移民亦是定居者，唐人街則是建立在原住民土地之上的空間。華人社群所經歷的迫害，是一場悲劇疊加在另一場悲劇之上。但這並不意味著唐人街或華人社群能夠免於在殖民體制下所扮演的共謀角色；唐人街與華人社群亦未能置身於定居殖民體制的暴行之外。

這些攝影作品不斷重申一件事：唐人街不只是屬於「華人性」的地方。在任何一個北美唐人街裡，我們都可以看到越南人、菲律賓人、日本人、柬埔寨人，以及其他亞洲社群的身影。許多唐人街的未來，其實也仰賴這些非華裔的亞裔移民浪潮的加入與支持。林耀基不僅透過他的攝影作品，也透過這個項目的副標題，捕捉並強調了唐人街的多元樣貌。Chinatown 和 唐人街 Tong yan gaai 之間的關係，並不是單純的翻譯對應。對早期華人移民及其後代而言，Tong yan gaai 所指涉的是一段源於人頭稅與排華歷史的共同社群記憶。而到了二十世紀末與二十一世紀初，隨著中華人民共和國崛起為世界經濟強權，以及華人民族主義在離散社群中的興起，Tong yan gaai 又承載了另一層意義。此時，從士巴丹納街（Spadina）、東賓達街（East Pender）、運河街（Canal）、史塔克頓街（Stockton）等地不斷出現的普通話，不僅是一種崛起的象徵，也成了一種徵兆與症狀，代表著一種全新的華人優勢的興起。

Tong yan gaai 是 Chinatown 的粵語音譯。林耀基在他的項目中堅持使用這一命名方式，是一種召喚記憶的行動——回到北美華人社群曾與中國南方村落與香港擁有深厚聯繫的那段歷史。「Tong yan gaai」這個語音記號，直指支撐北美唐人街形成的移民歷史核心——那些在十九世紀末至二十世紀初來到北美、為基礎建設貢獻勞力的華工，他們的共通語言是台山話與粵語。這個名稱不僅是一段歷史的記憶，也提醒我們那段歷史與當下唐人街之間所產生的距離——而這種疏離感，

隨著普通話在離散華人社群中的興起，轉化為一種騷動的張力與交織的連結。同時，我們也應看見：在唐人街中逐步建立起自身空間的非華裔的亞裔社群，同樣構成這段歷史與當下不可忽視的一部分。

唐人街改變了北美城市的街景，但它們不只是外部空間。每一個唐人街都有其內部。林耀基的攝影作品反覆強調，記憶與場所的沉積要求我們關注的不僅僅是那些標誌這些「城中之城」的建築與牌樓。穿過這些牌樓、走進餐館與宗親會建築的大門之後，是一間間的房間。林的鏡頭帶領我們在這些承載記憶與歷史的空間中切換、穿梭。這些空間裡也充滿著維繫社群運作的種種物件：堆疊的椅子、多桌齊開的麻將、整備就緒的會議桌、收納妥當的舞獅裝備。在林所拍攝的唐人街內部空間中，我們彷彿身在其境，短暫停駐，準備迎接下一局麻將、下一場社區慶典、下一次舞獅登場。

《 Chinatowns ｜唐人街 Tong Yan Gaai 》不僅強調唐人街的延續與韌性，也喚起我們對這些空間深層活力的關注。人們有時傾向以一種懷舊的視角談論唐人街，彷彿它們屬於某個尚未真正來臨的過去：它們理應正在逝去，或因仕紳化而逐漸消失於視野，或被向市郊遷移的移民潮所抹去。林耀基的攝影作品在多方面反駁了這種觀點。某種程度上，他的歷時性實踐方式展現了居住模式、人口結構與建築風貌的轉變，而這些變化本身未必等同於終結。然而，這個項目不僅是歷史性的紀錄，更是一種美學上的介入。觀看這些照片，沉浸在飽和濃郁的色彩之中，感受光影的流動。

唐人街既是華人的，也不只是華人的。它既是一個具體的地方，也是一種概念的存在。它既出自想像，又真實且充滿活力。它之所以得以保持不變，是因為它能夠不斷地接納變化，同時仍保有唐人街那可被辨識的面貌。林耀基的攝影作品捕捉的，正是這些充滿矛盾又錯綜複雜的地方。這些照片並不將唐人街凝固在某個特定的時間點上，儘管它們堅定地指出唐人街作為一個地方的延續性。

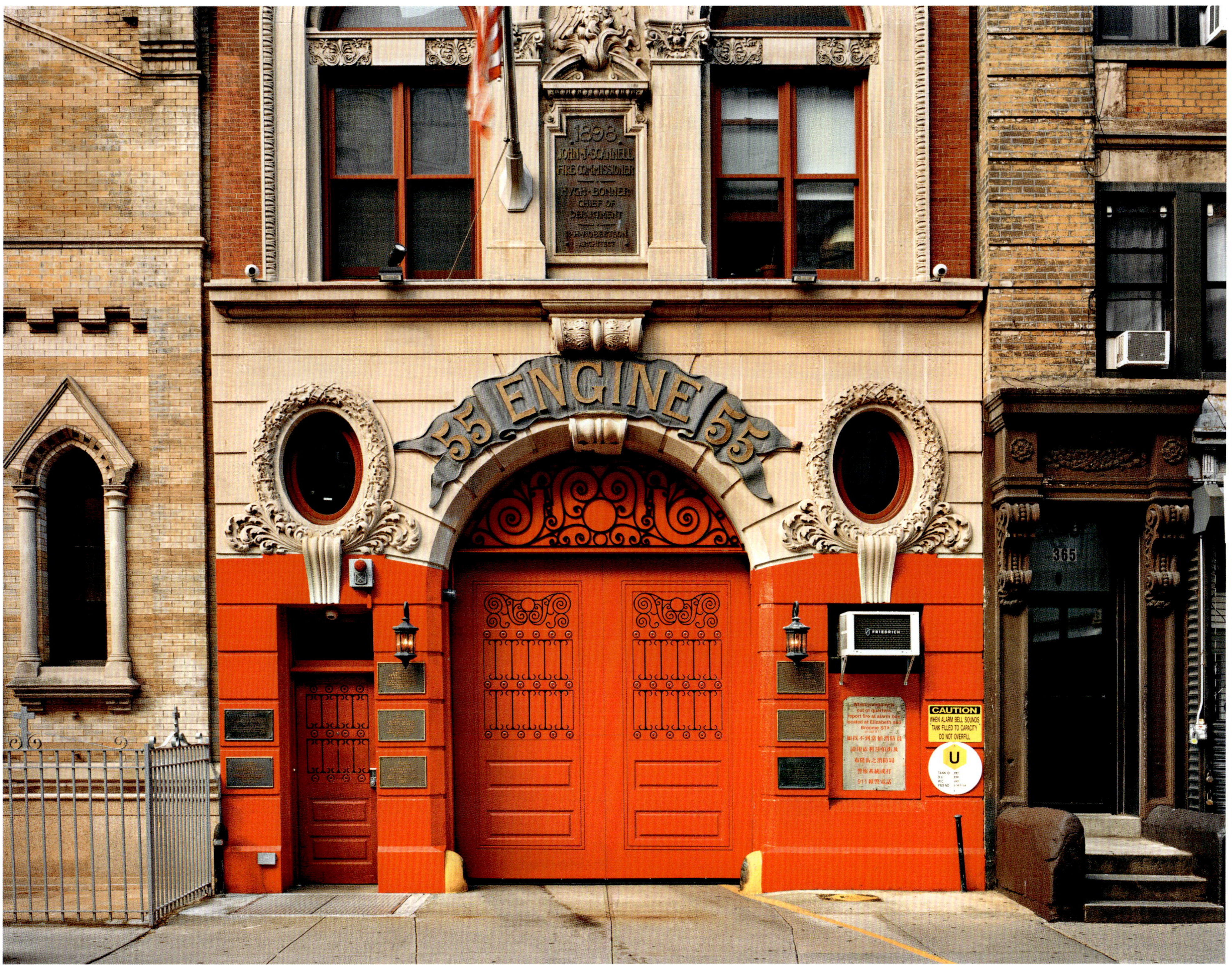

FDNY 55 Engine, Manhattan, 2019

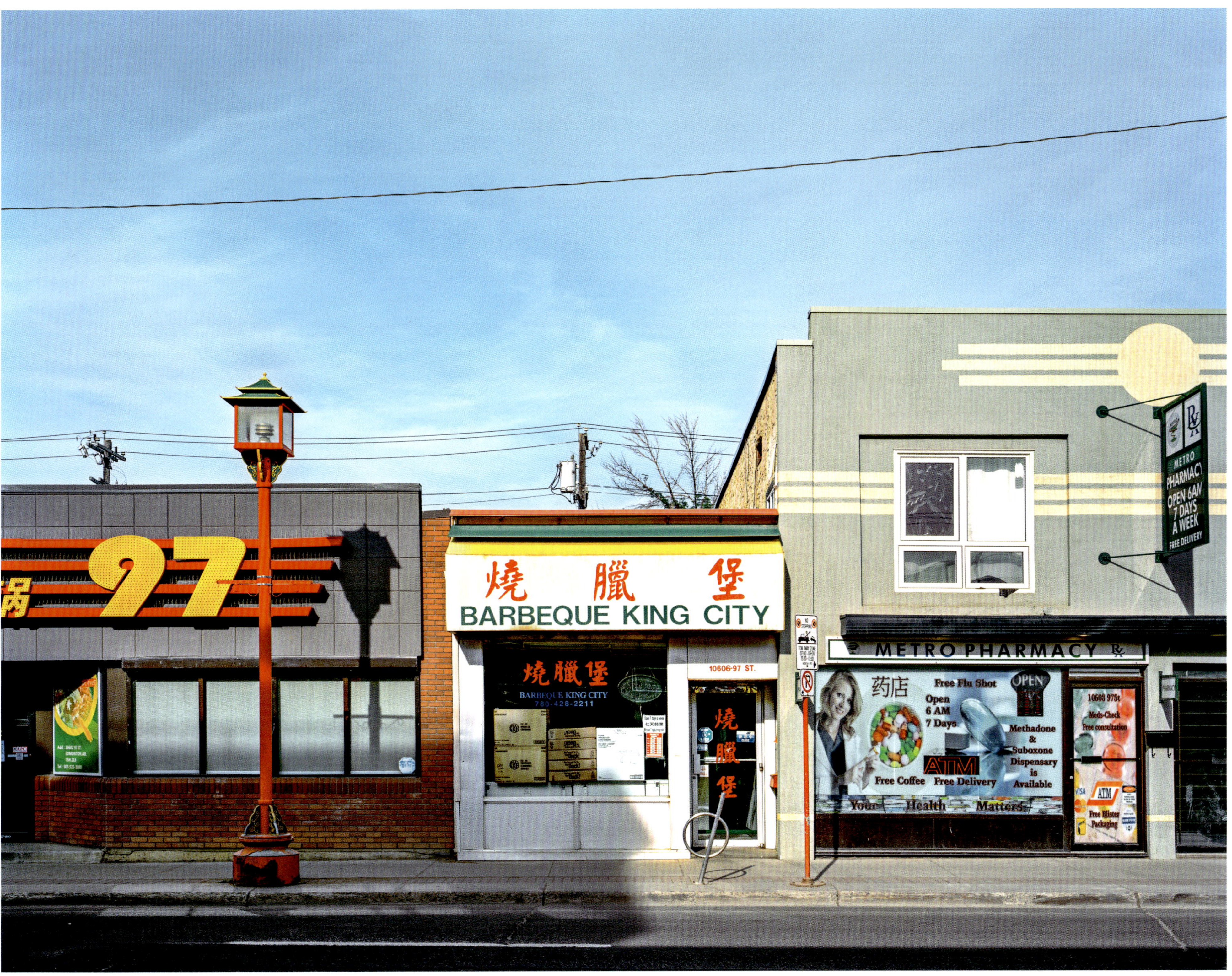

Barbeque King City, Edmonton, 2018

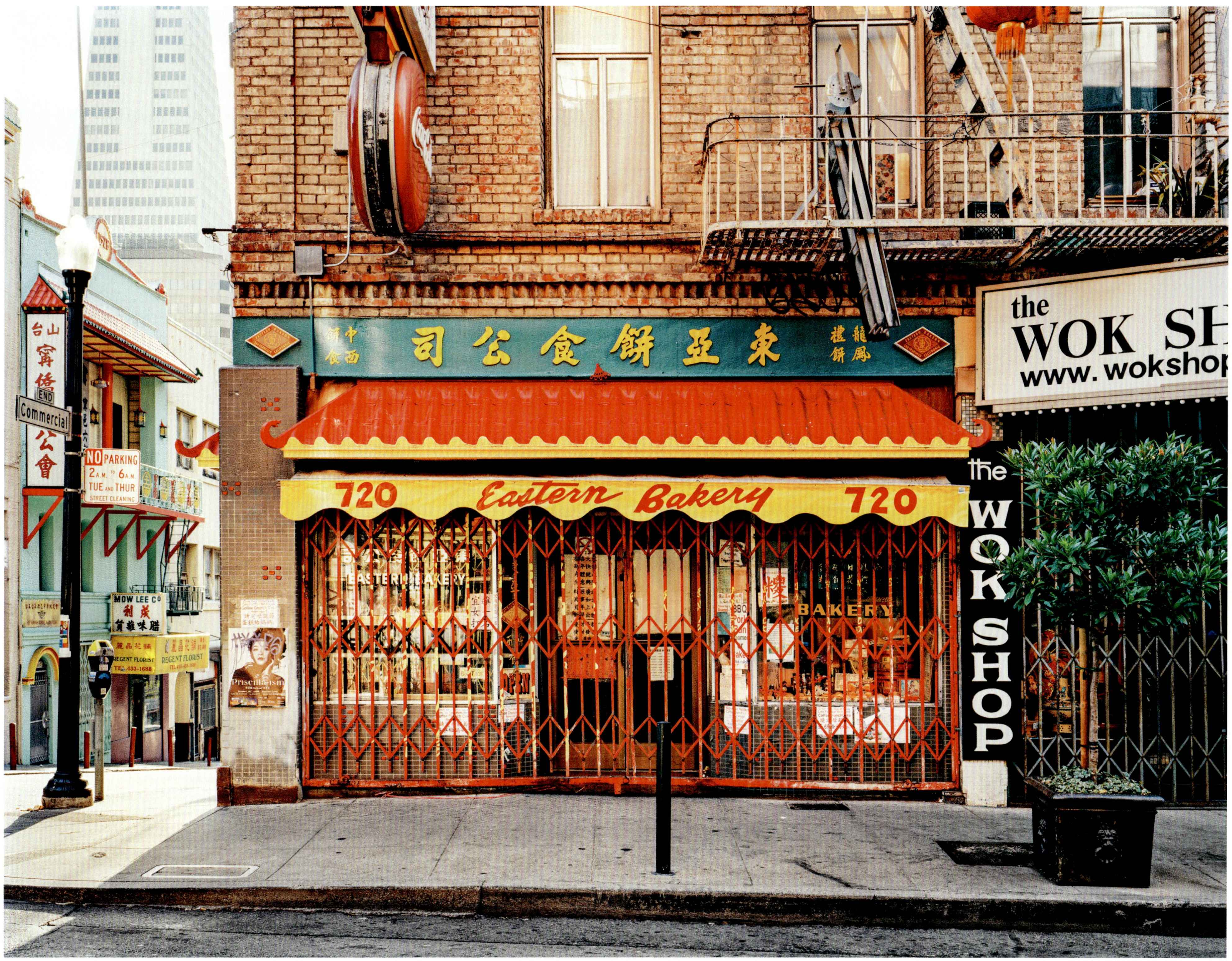

Eastern Bakery, San Francisco, 2017

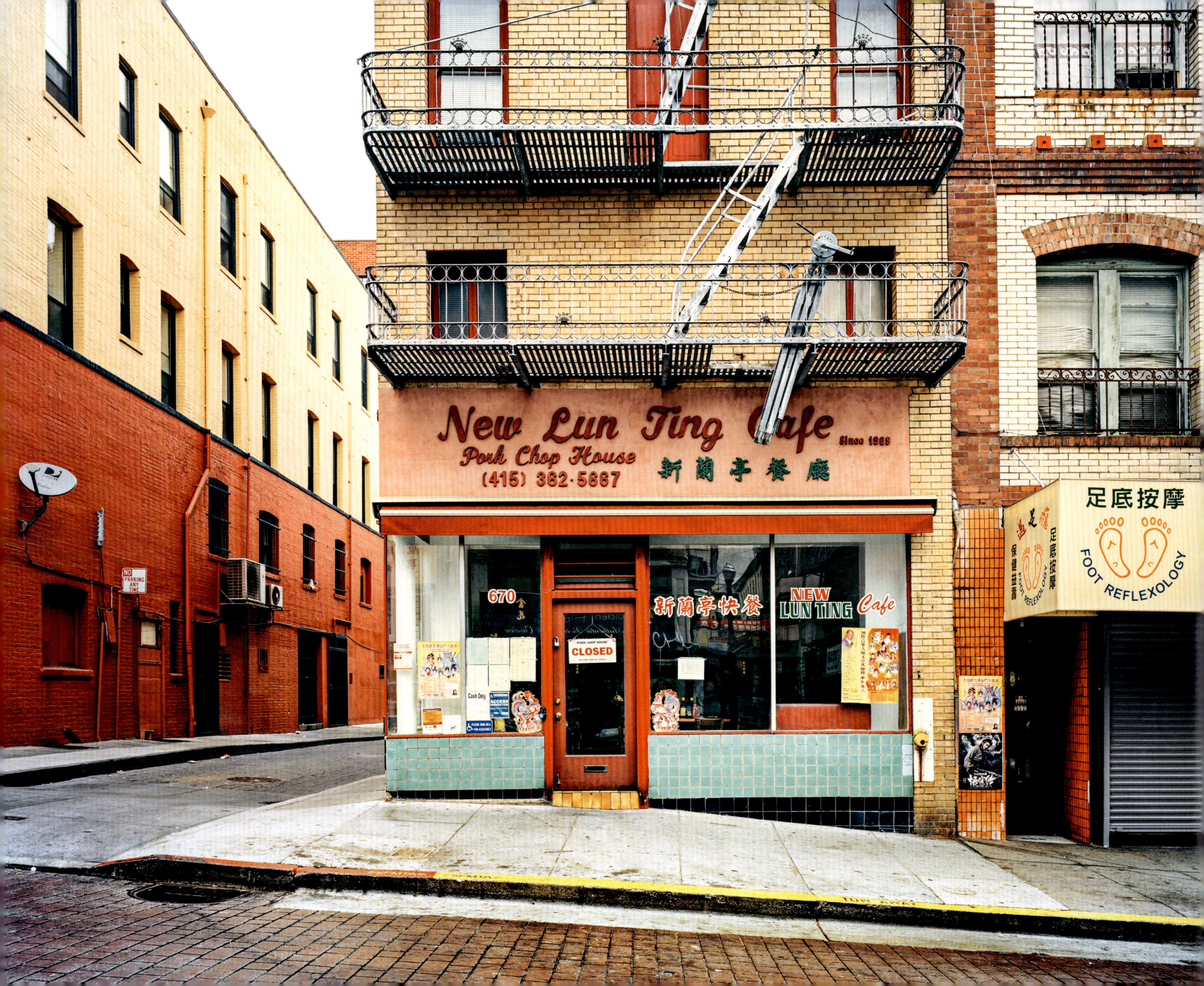

New Lun Ting Cafe
Since 1989
Pork Chop House
新蘭亭餐廳
(415) 362-5667
670
金
PORK CHOP HOUSE
CLOSED
Cash Only
PLEASE RING BELL FOR ASSISTANCE
新蘭亭快餐
NEW LUN TING Cafe
NO PARKING ANY TIME
足底按摩
FOOT REFLEXOLOGY
保證益青
FOOT REFLEXOLOGY
足底按摩
TOW AWAY

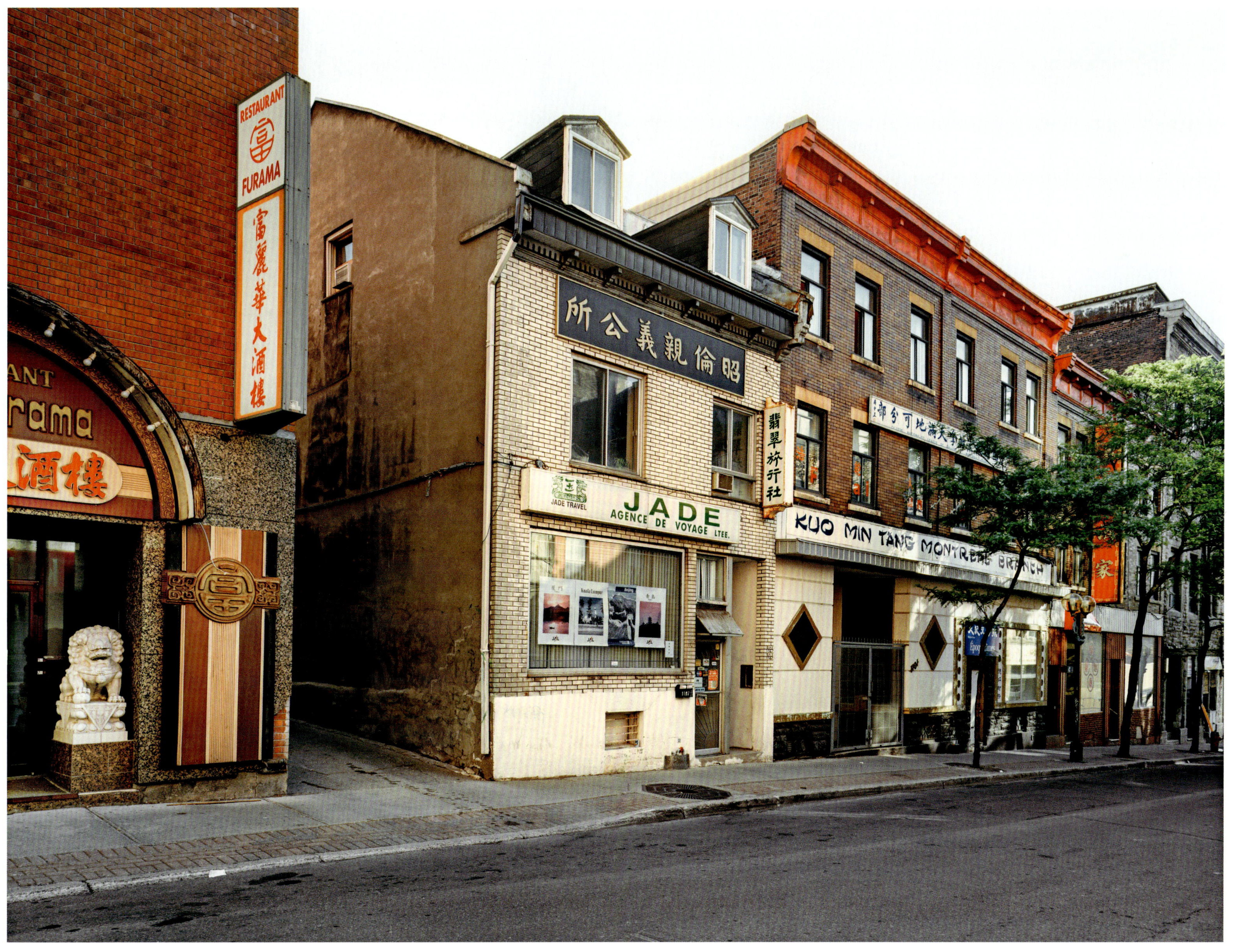

New Lun Ting Cafe, San Francisco, 2017

Jade Agence de Voyage Ltee., Montreal, 2014

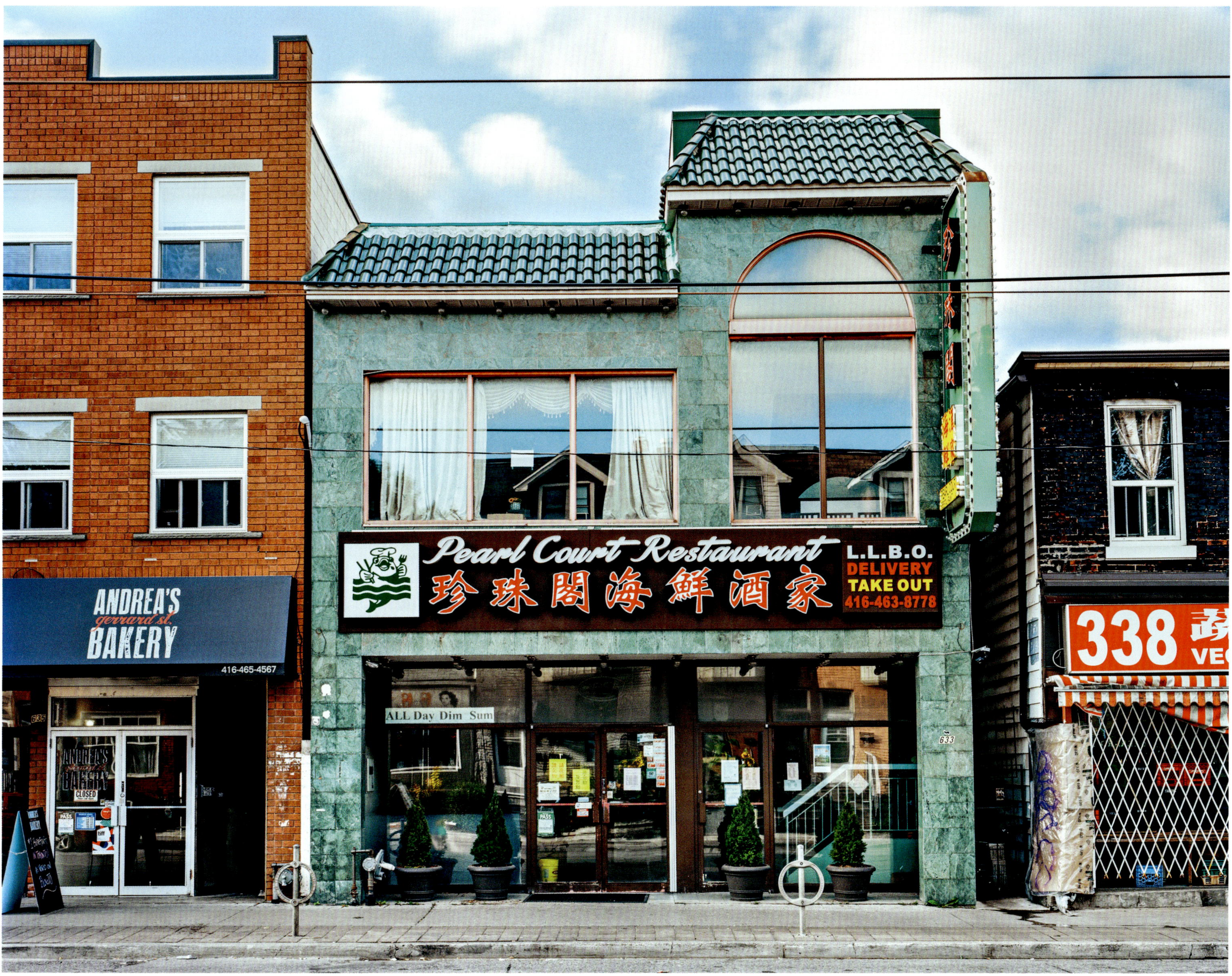

Pearl Court Restaurant, Toronto East Chinatown, 2017

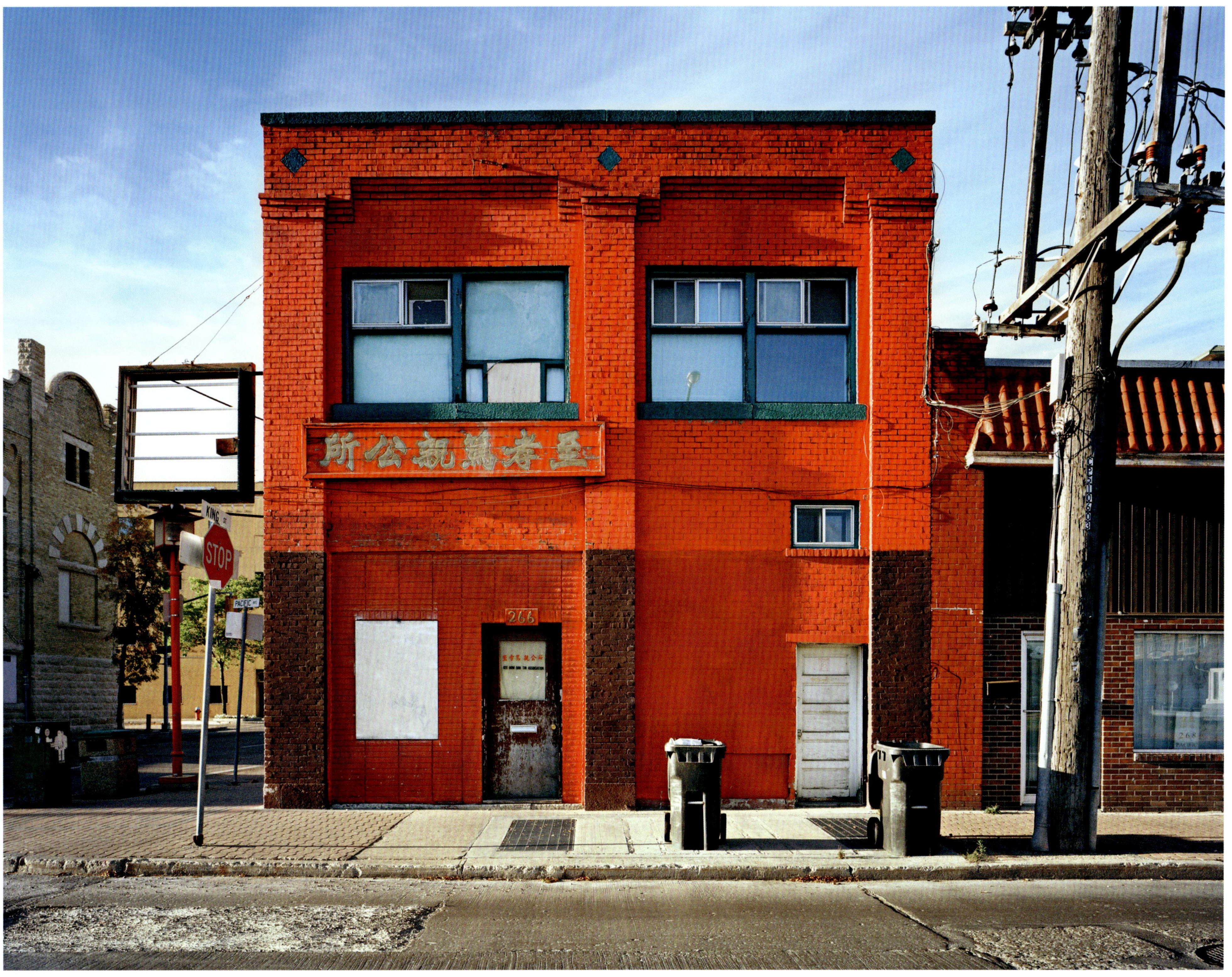

Gee How Oak Tin Association, Winnipeg, 2013

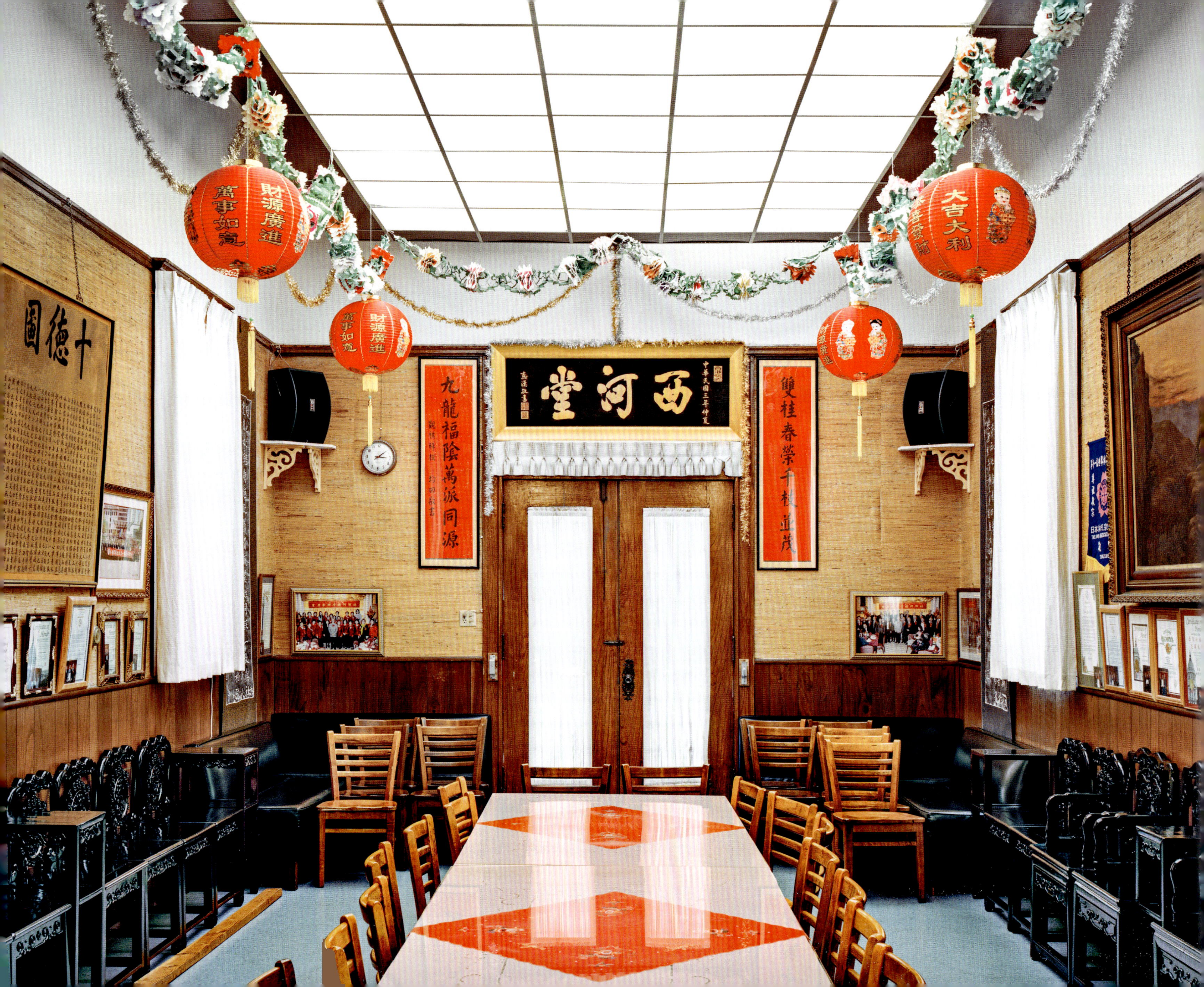

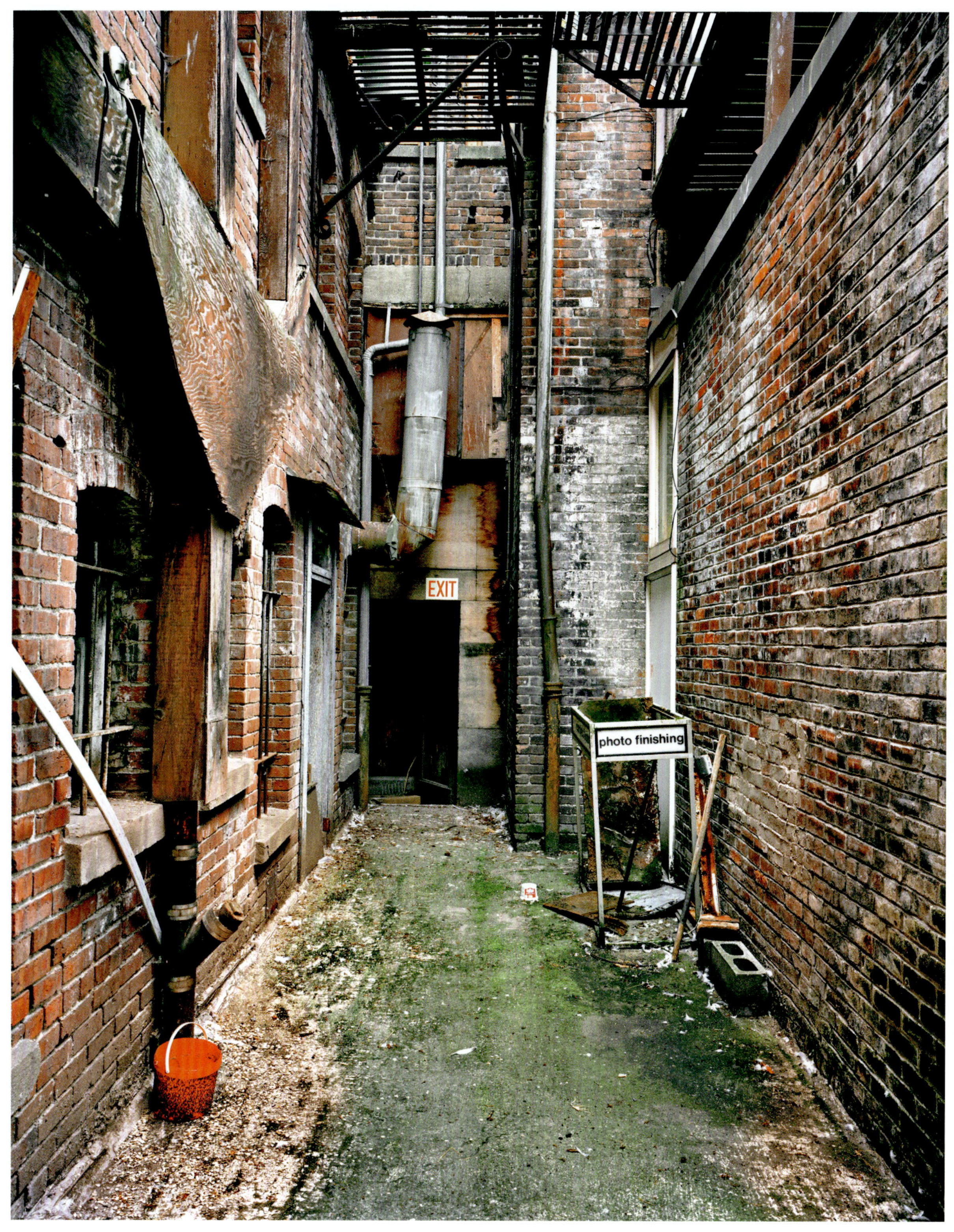

Lim Family Benevolent Society, San Francisco, 2017

Courtyard Behind Lee Block (East View), Victoria, 2014

Hong Kong BBQ Restaurant, Los Angeles, 2024

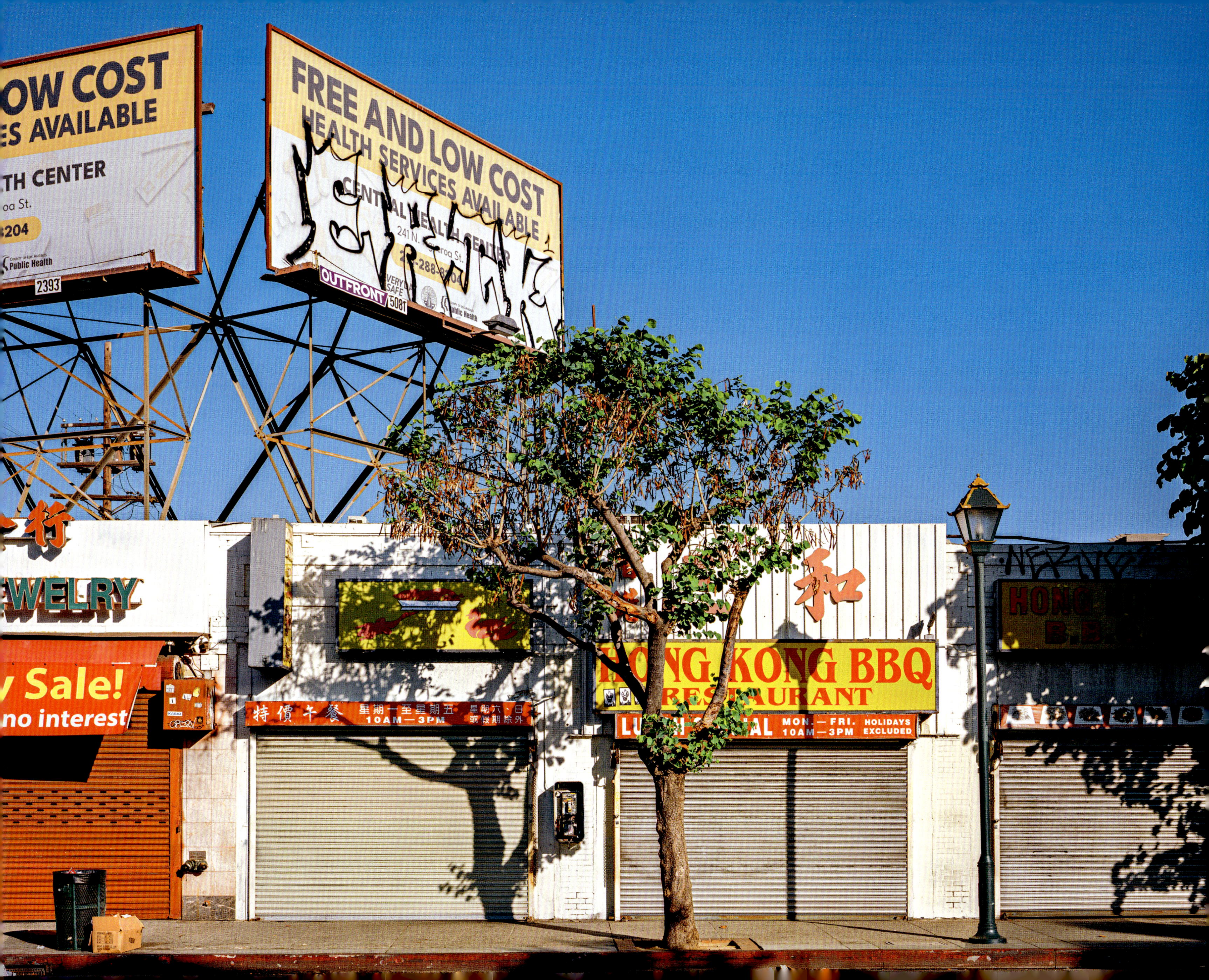
OW COST
ES AVAILABLE
TH CENTER
oa St.
204
Public Health
2393
FREE AND LOW COST
HEALTH SERVICES AVAILABLE
CENTRAL HEALTH CENTER
241 N. Figueroa St.
2 -288-
OUTFRONT
508
VERY
SAFE
Public Health
WELRY
y Sale!
no interest
特價午餐
10AM—3PM
星期一至星期五
星期六、日
或假期除外
HONG KONG BBQ
RESTAURANT
LU   AL
MON.—FRI.
10AM—3PM
HOLIDAYS
EXCLUDED
HONG
B
NE

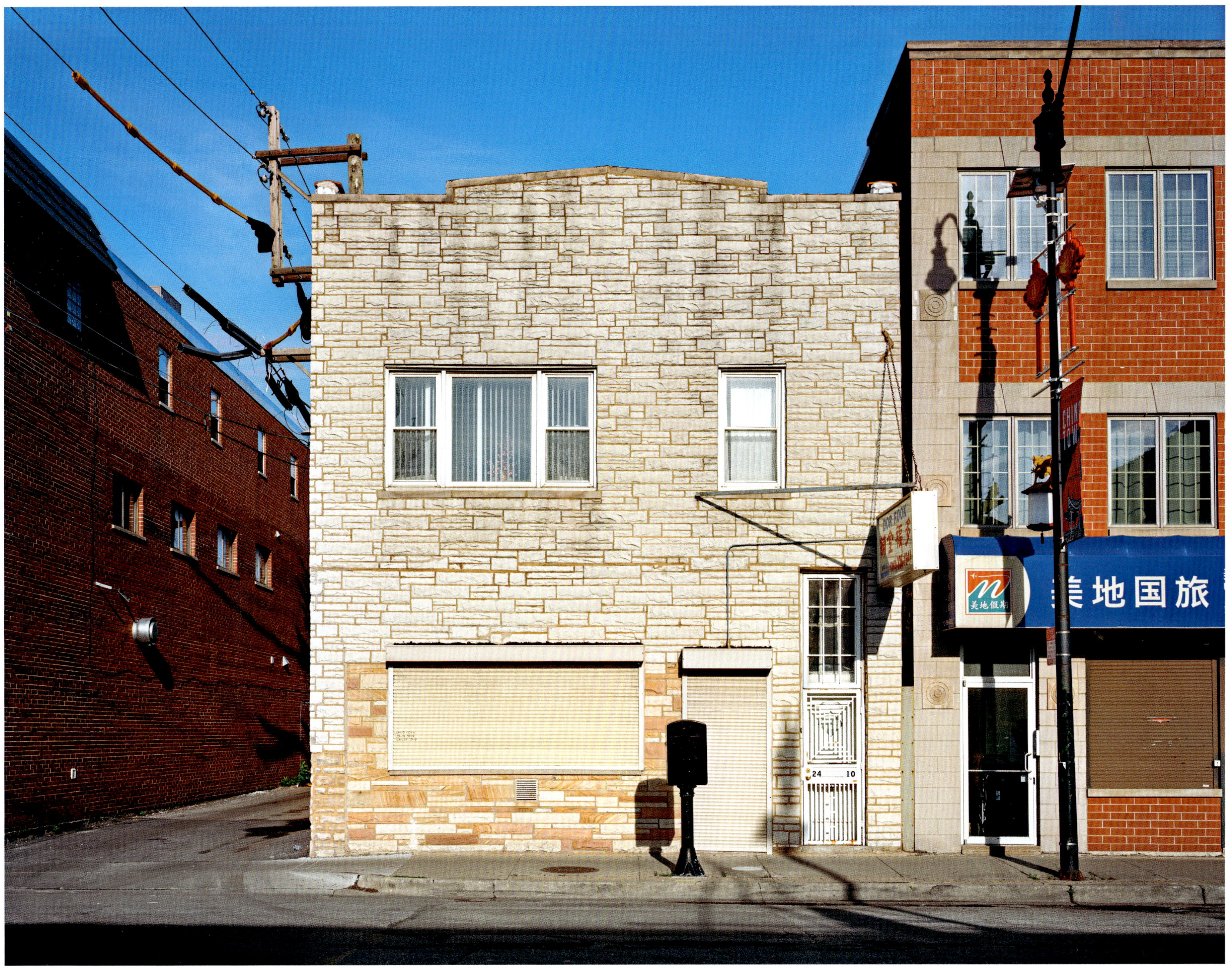

Dor Fook, Chicago, 2022

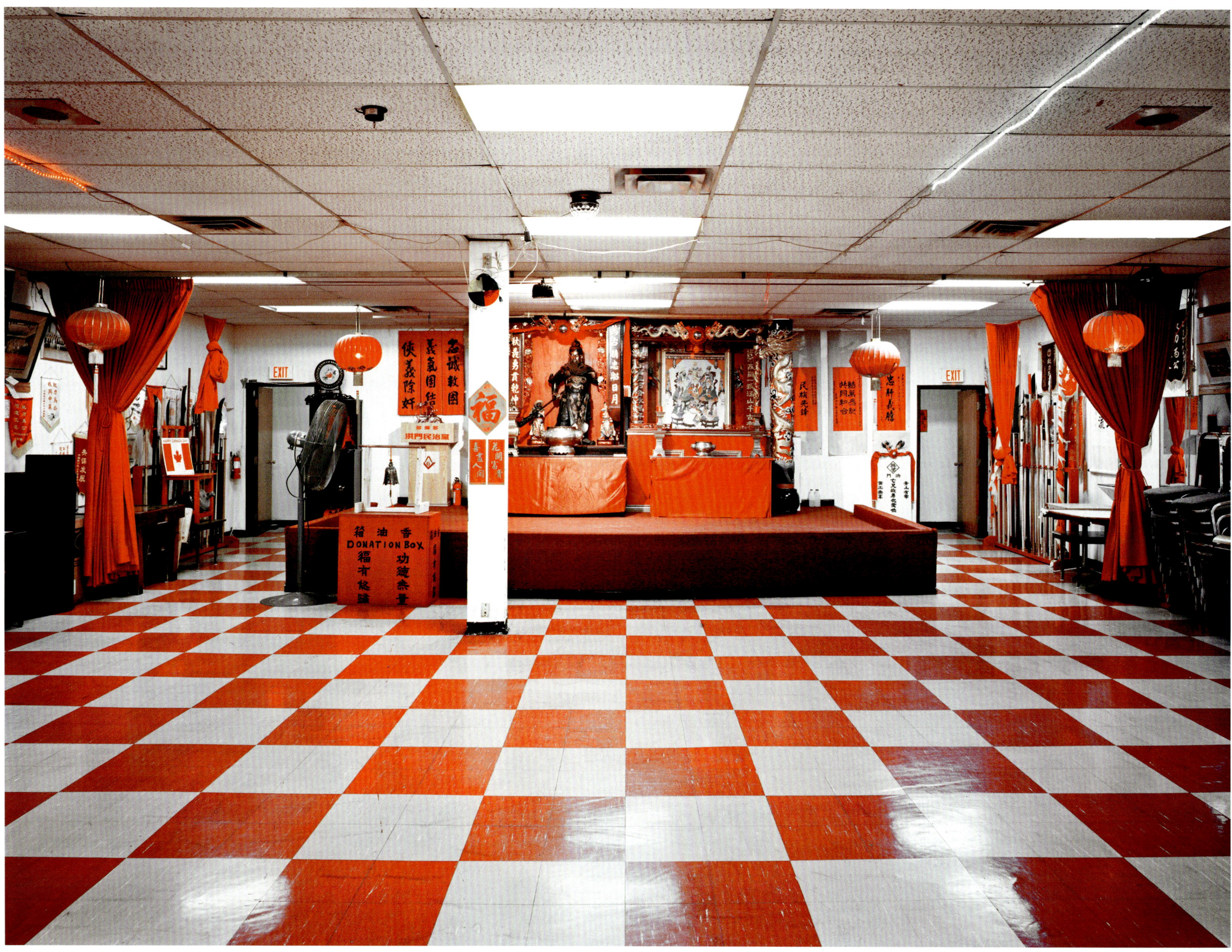

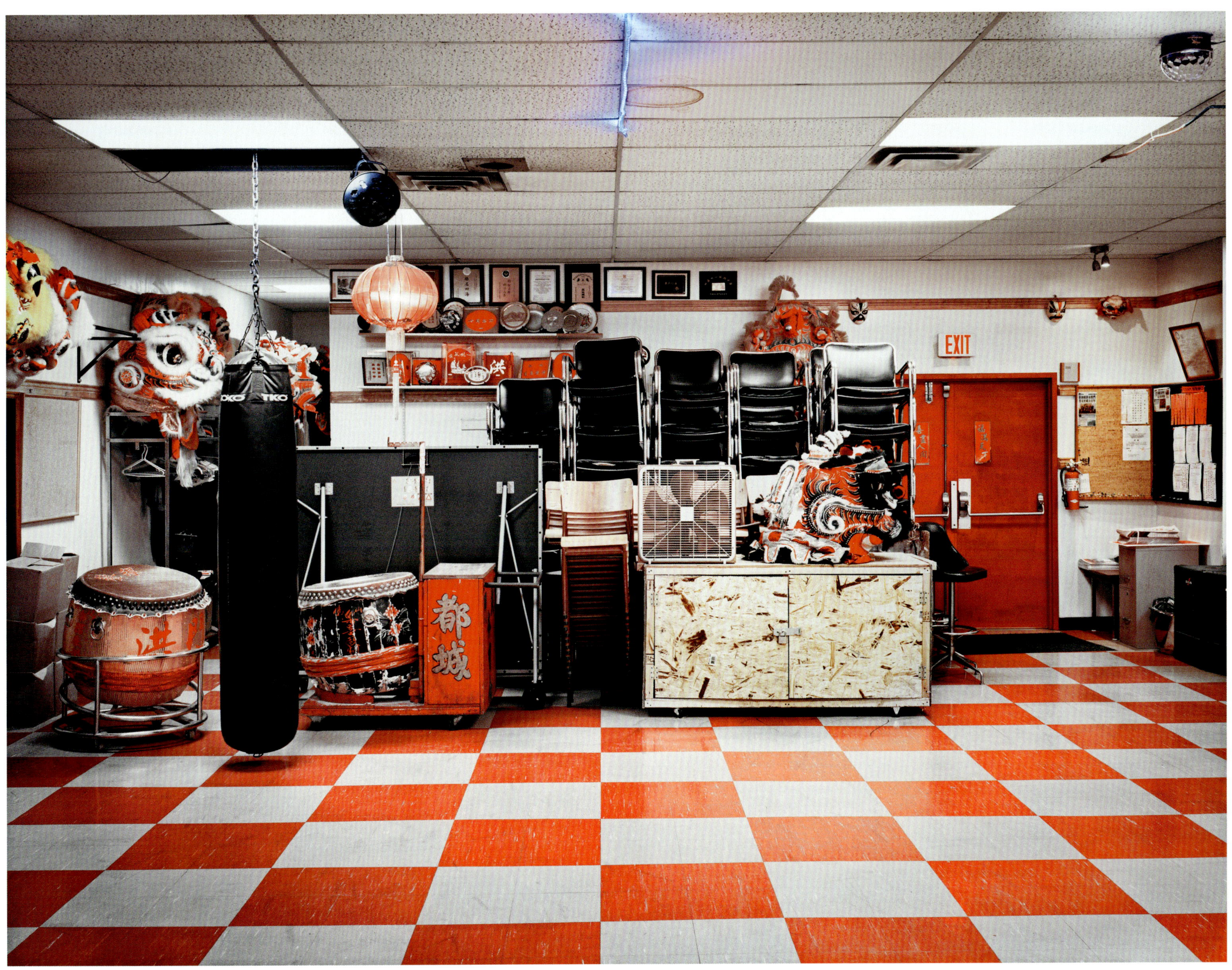

Chinese Freemason and Dart Coon Club, Toronto West Chinatown, 2017 (diptych)

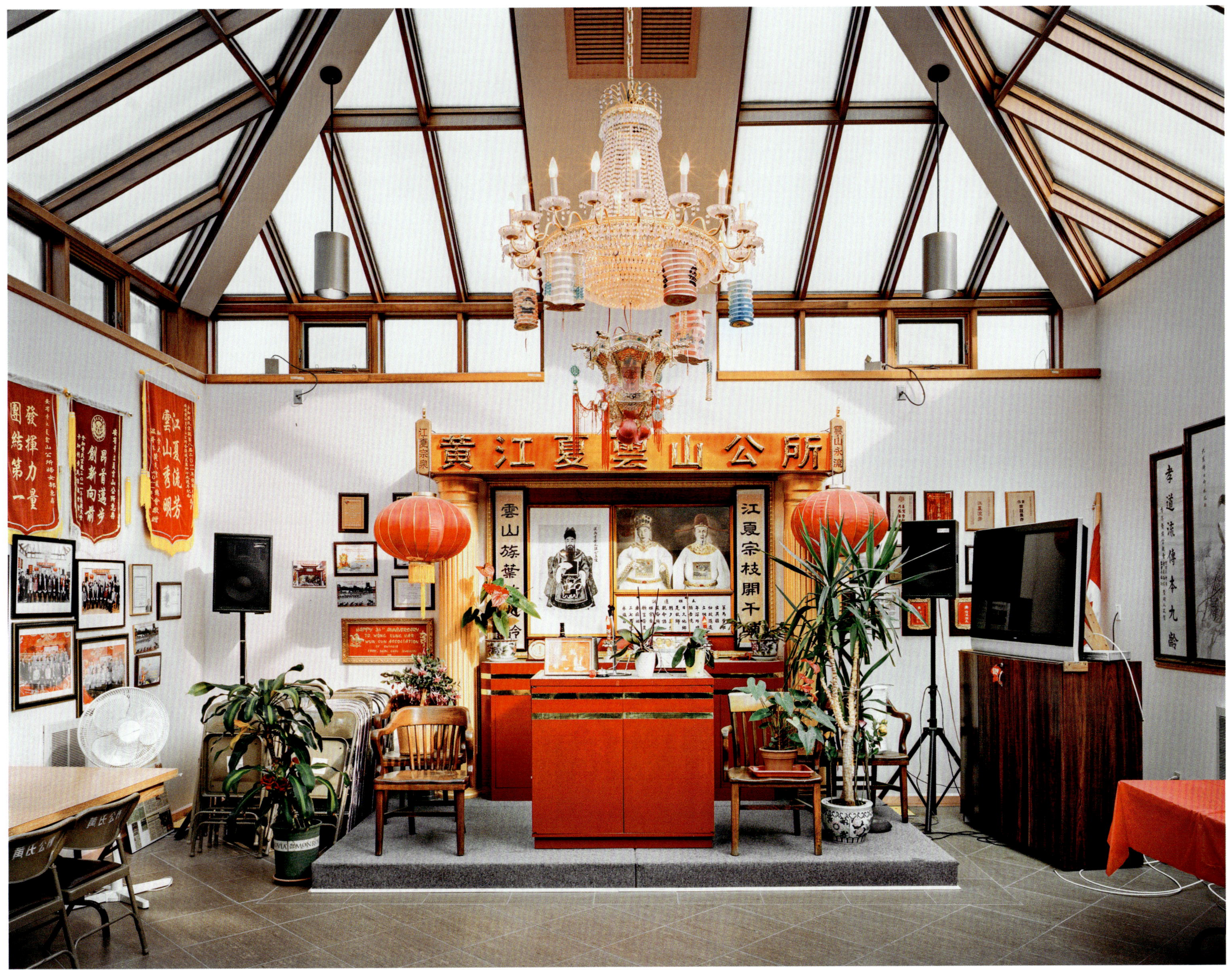

Wong Kung Har Wun Sun Association, Toronto West Chinatown, 2016

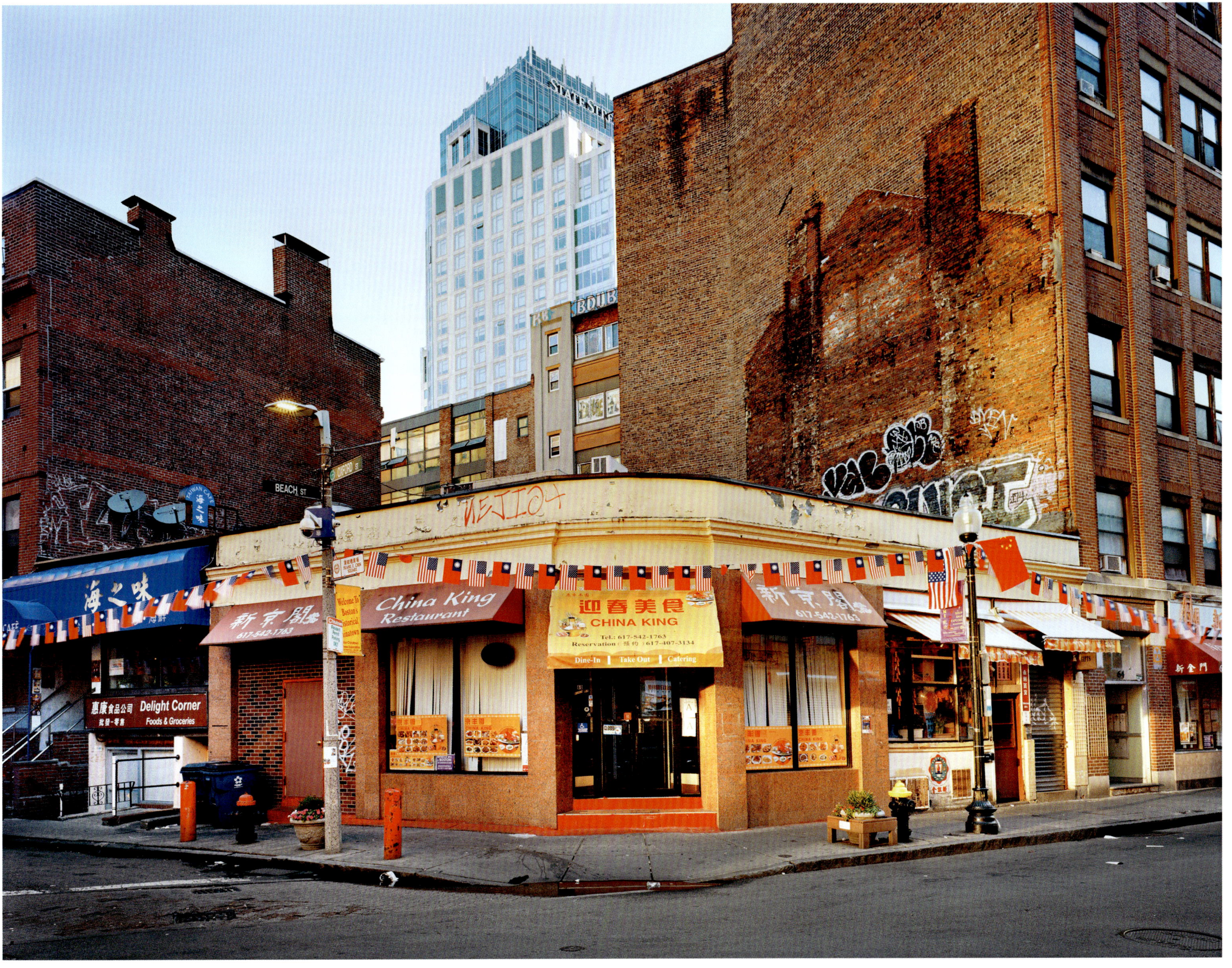

China King Restaurant, Boston, 2019

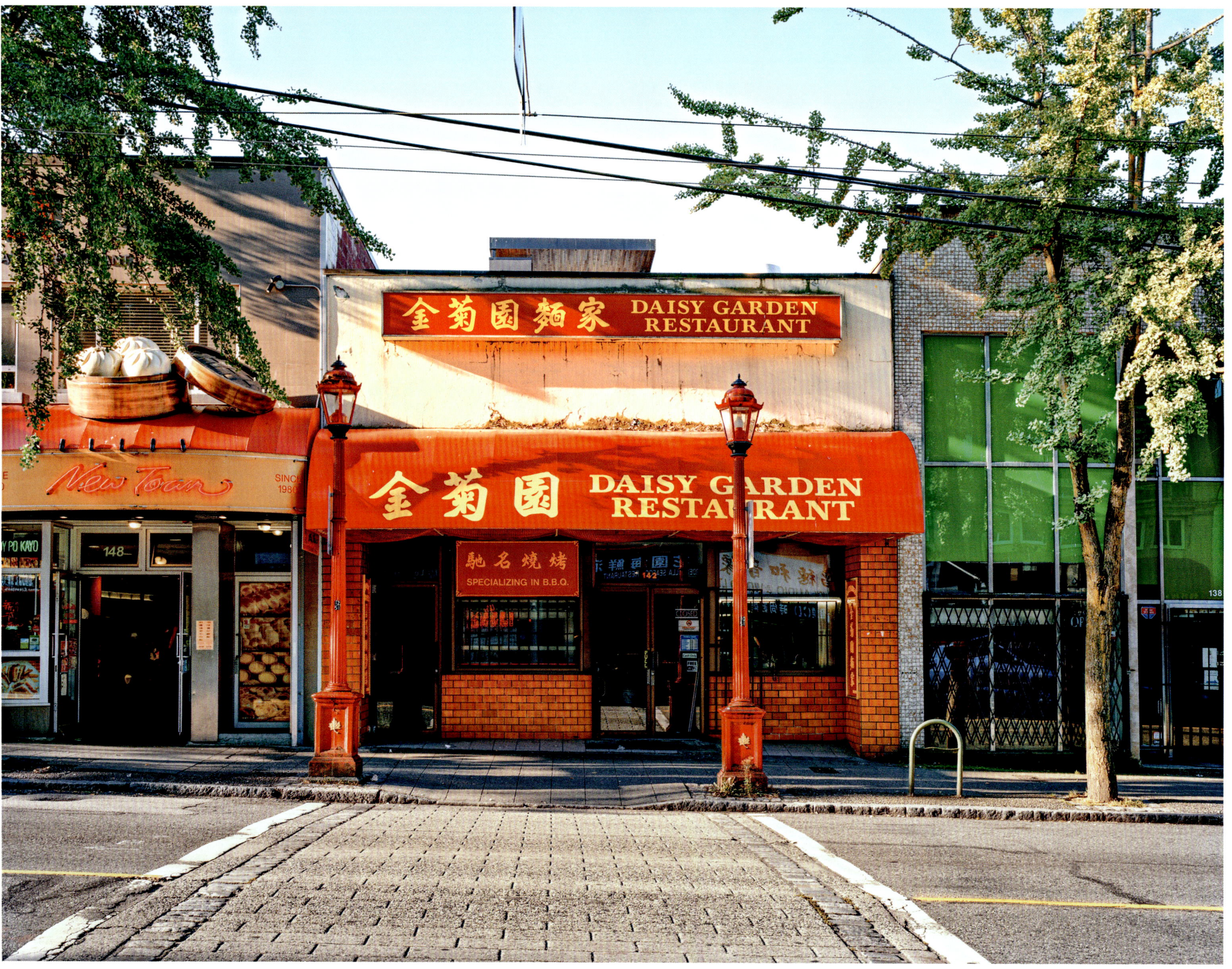

Daisy Garden Restaurant, Vancouver, 2014, 2015, 2023 (triptych)

Journey to the East Mural, Toronto West Chinatown, 2014 (painted by Allan Bender, John Nobrega, Ariel Massett; commissioned by Toronto Chinatown BIA)

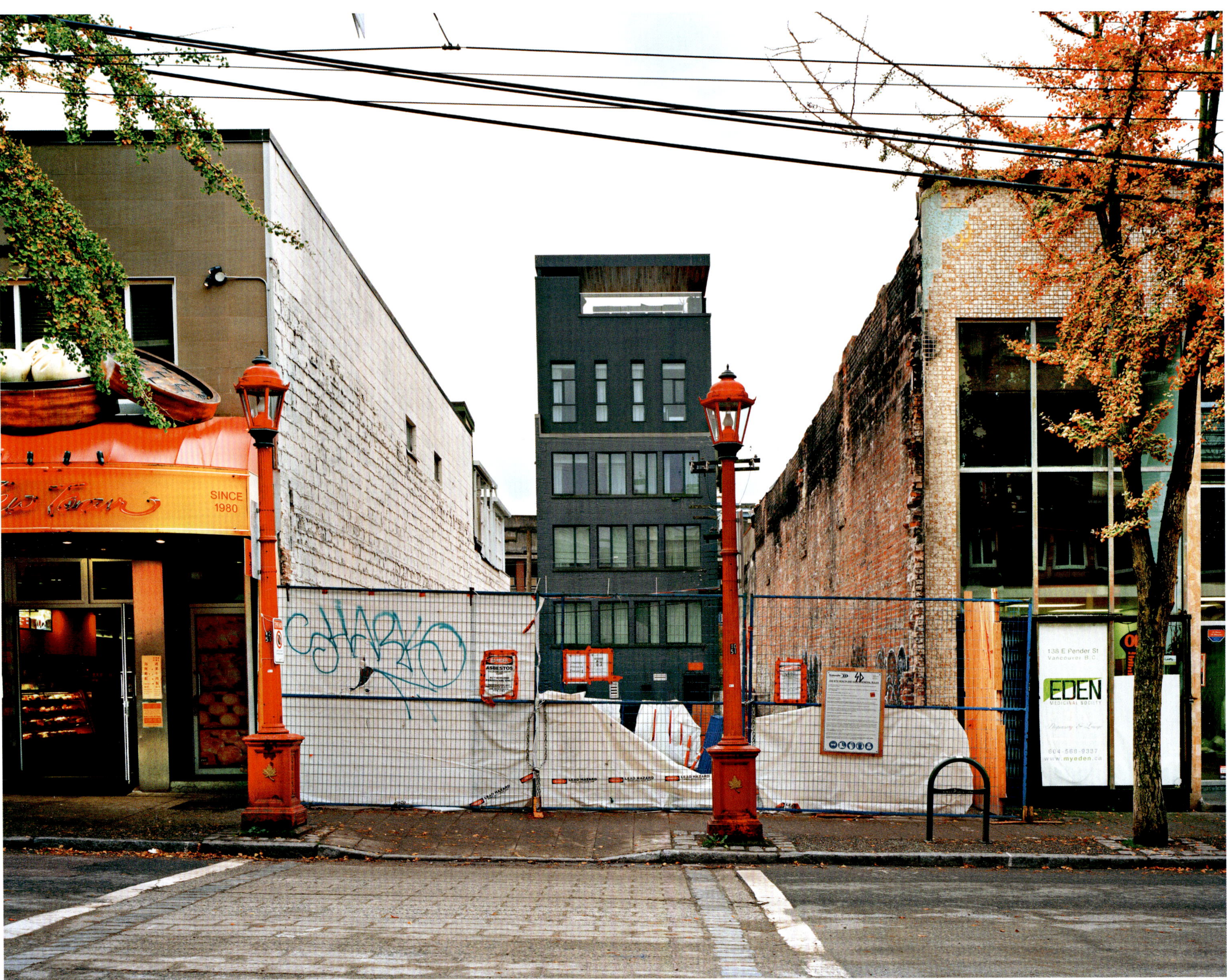

SINCE
1980
ASBESTOS
EDEN
MEDICINAL SOCIETY
138 E Pender St
Vancouver, B.C.
604-568-9337
www.myeden.ca

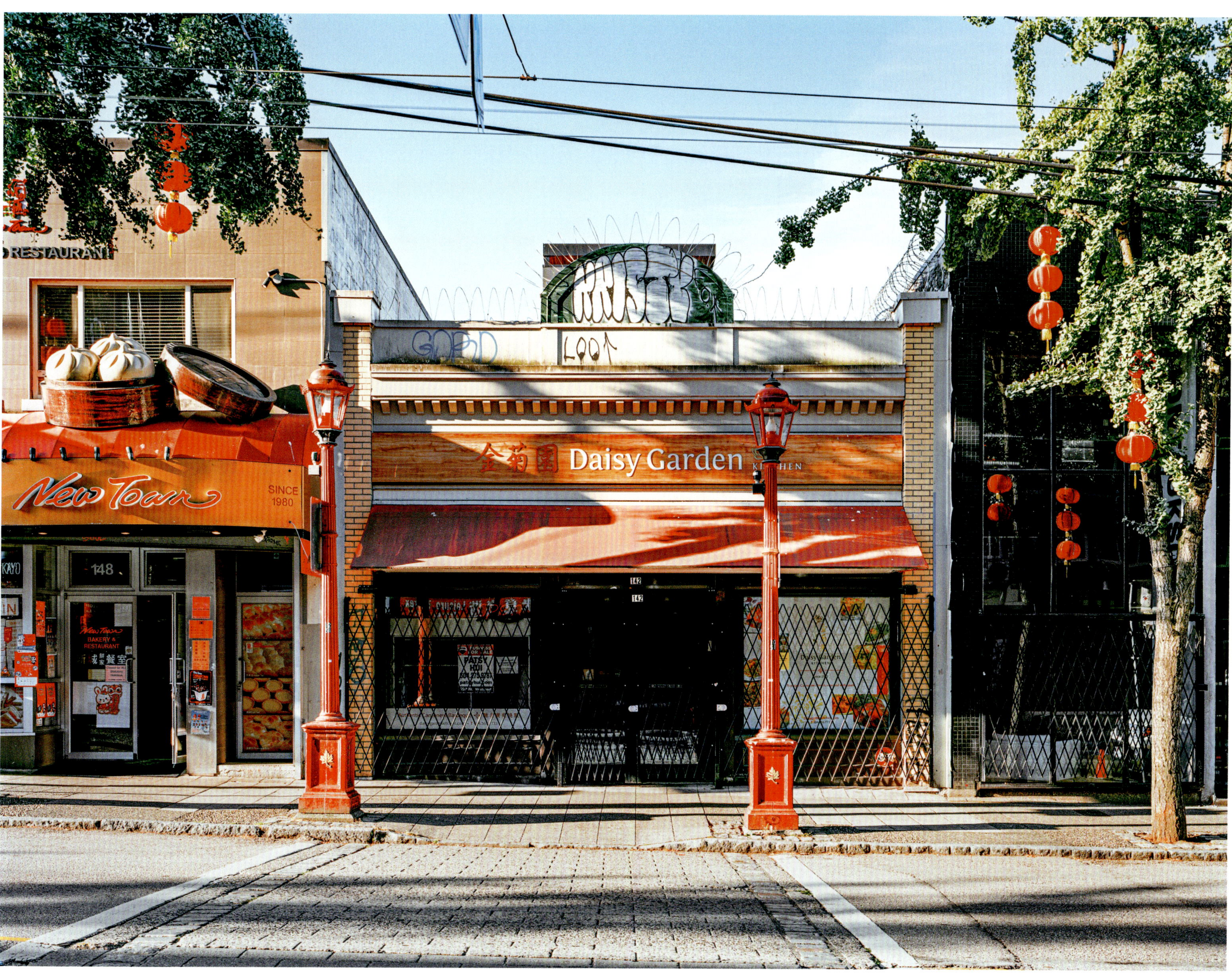
RESTAURANT
New Town
SINCE 1980
148
New Town
BAKERY &
RESTAURANT
全菊園 Daisy Garden KITCHEN
142

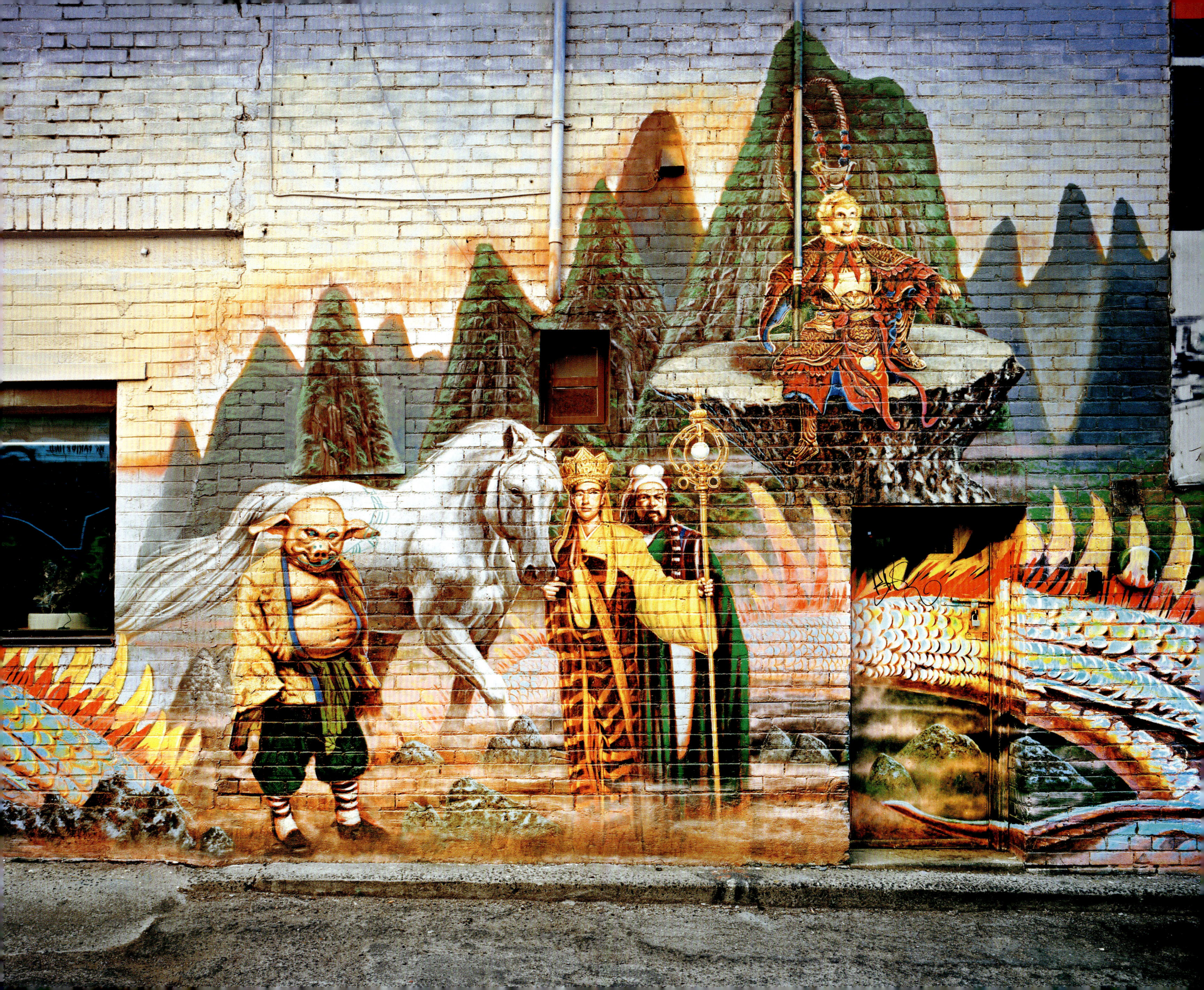

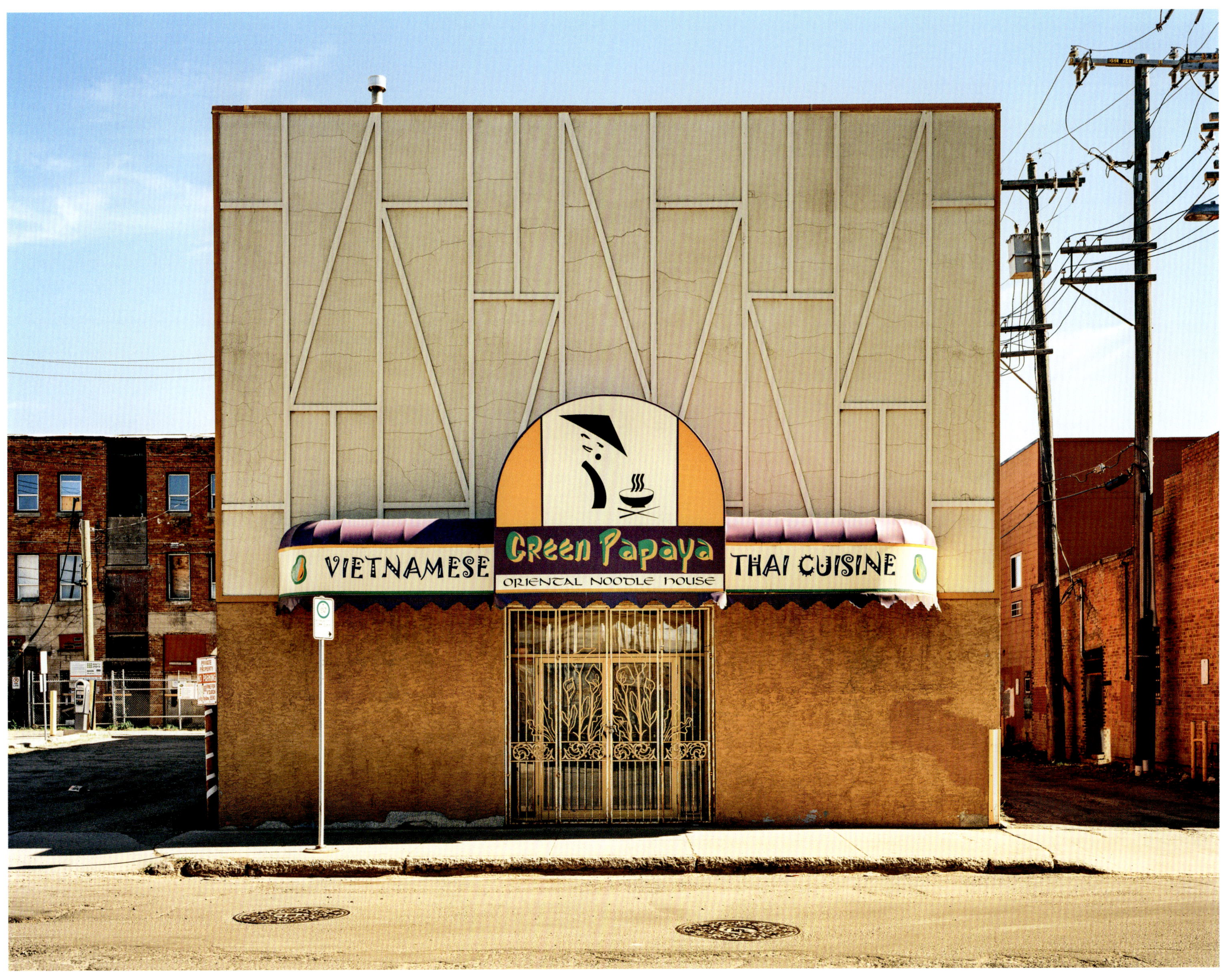

Green Papaya Oriental Noodle House, Edmonton, 2018

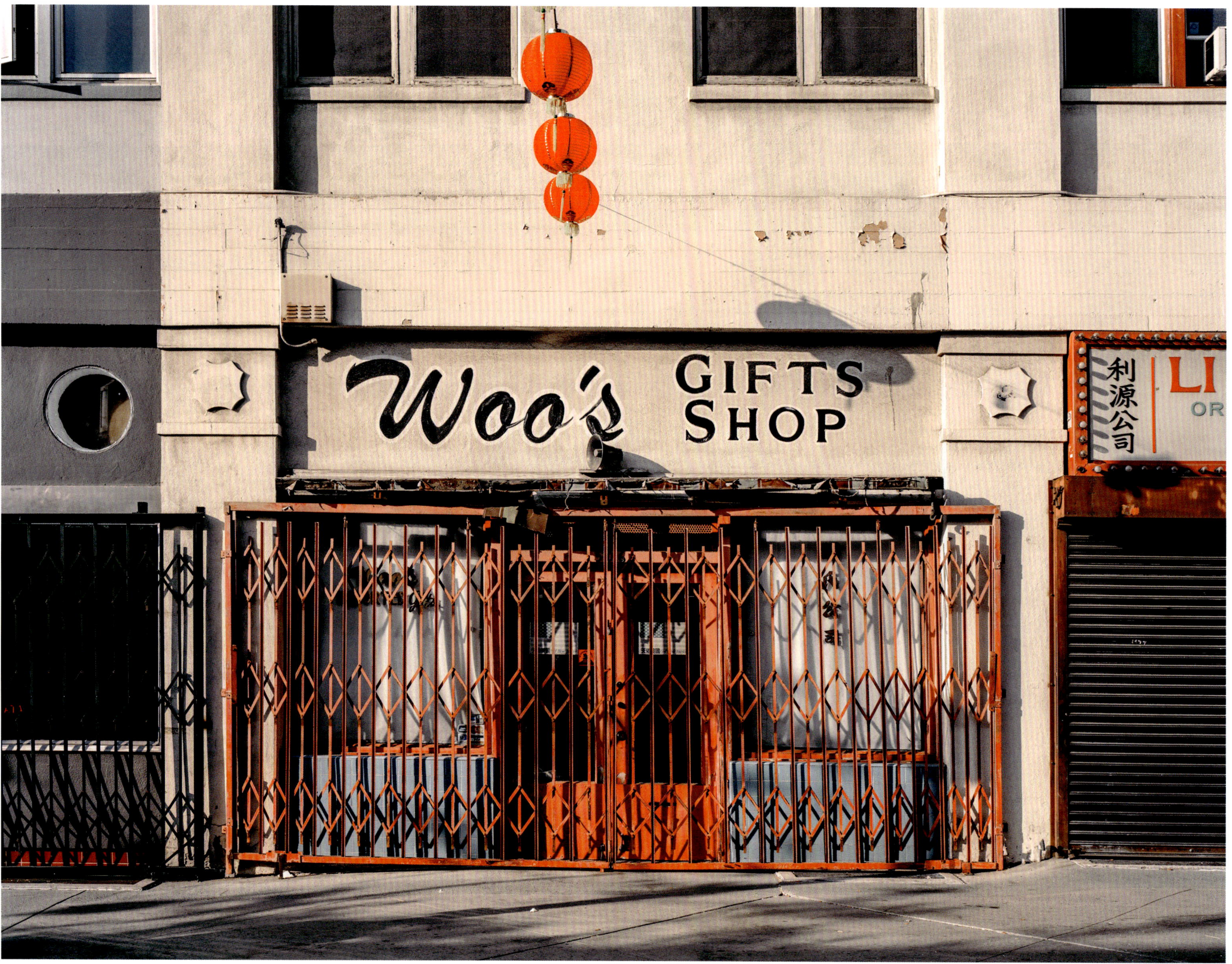

Woo's Gifts Shop, Los Angeles, 2018

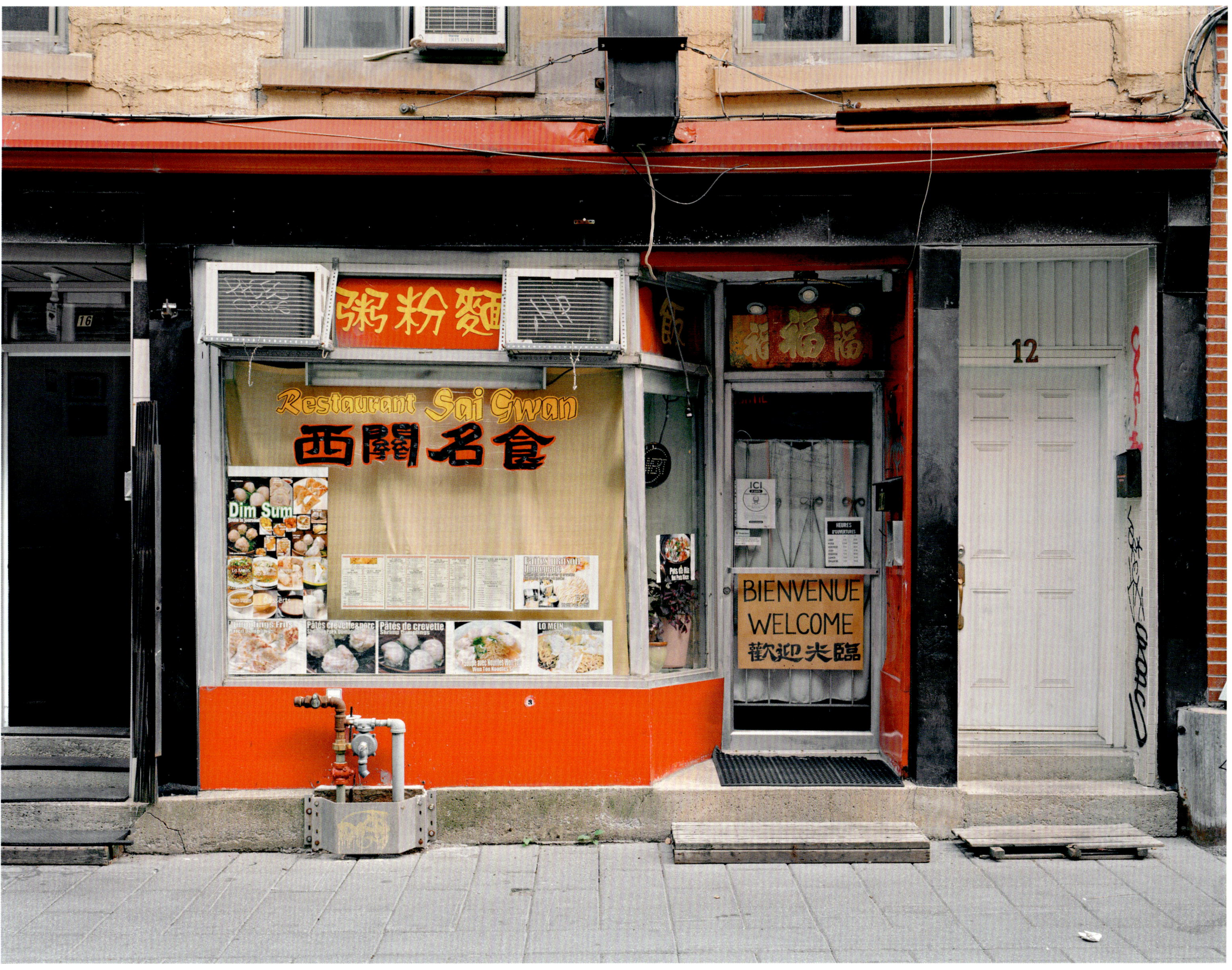

Restaurant Sai Gwan, Montreal, 2021

L.A. Chinatown Public Parking, Los Angeles, 2024

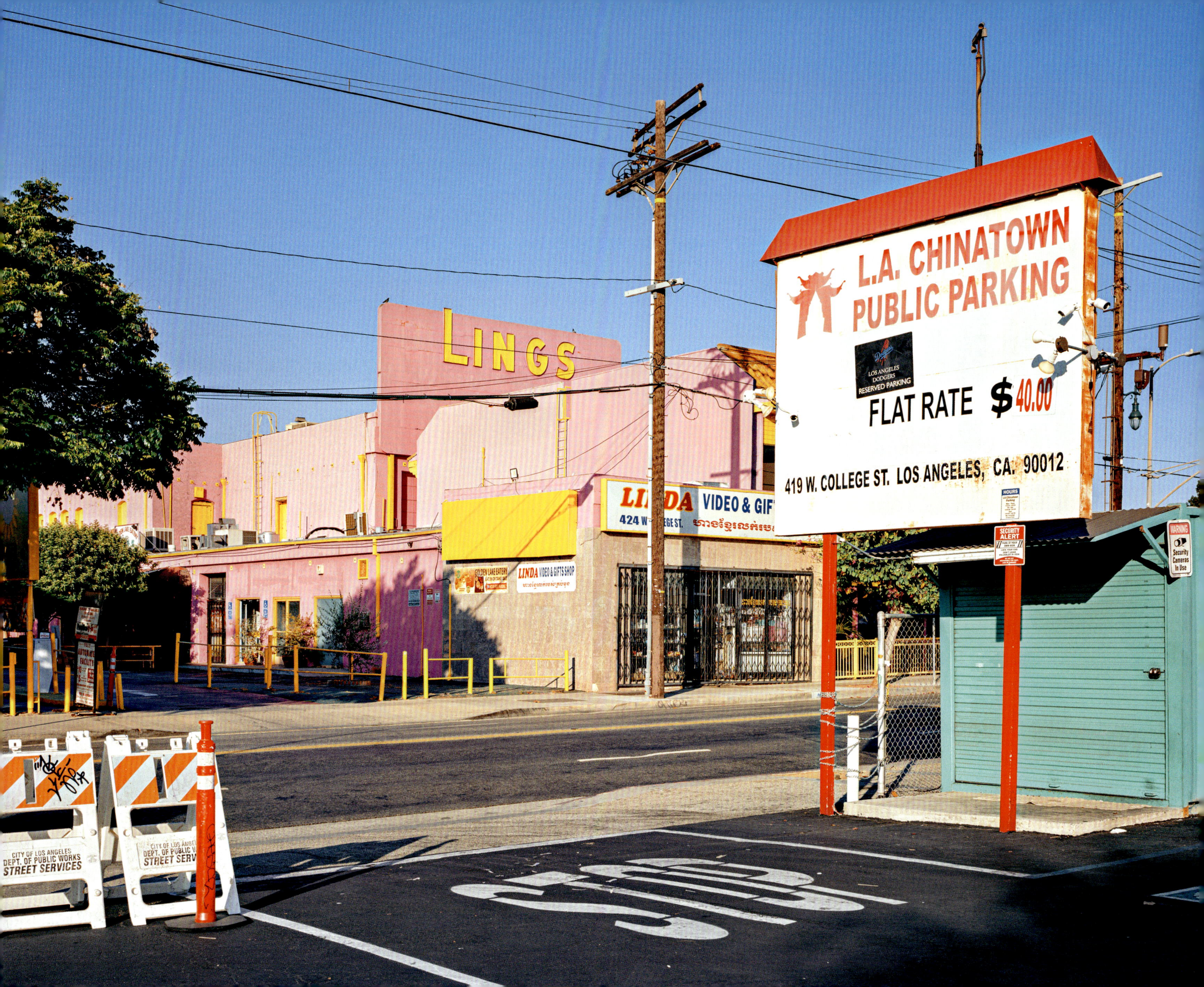

LINGS
LINDA VIDEO & GIFT
424 W. COLLEGE ST.
GOLDEN LAKE EATERY
LINDA VIDEO & GIFT SHOP
L.A. CHINATOWN PUBLIC PARKING
LOS ANGELES DODGERS RESERVED PARKING
FLAT RATE $40.00
419 W. COLLEGE ST. LOS ANGELES, CA. 90012
SECURITY ALERT
WARNING
Security Cameras In Use
HOURS
CITY OF LOS ANGELES
DEPT. OF PUBLIC WORKS
STREET SERVICES
CITY OF LOS ANGELES
DEPT. OF PUBLIC WORKS
STREET SERVICES
STOP

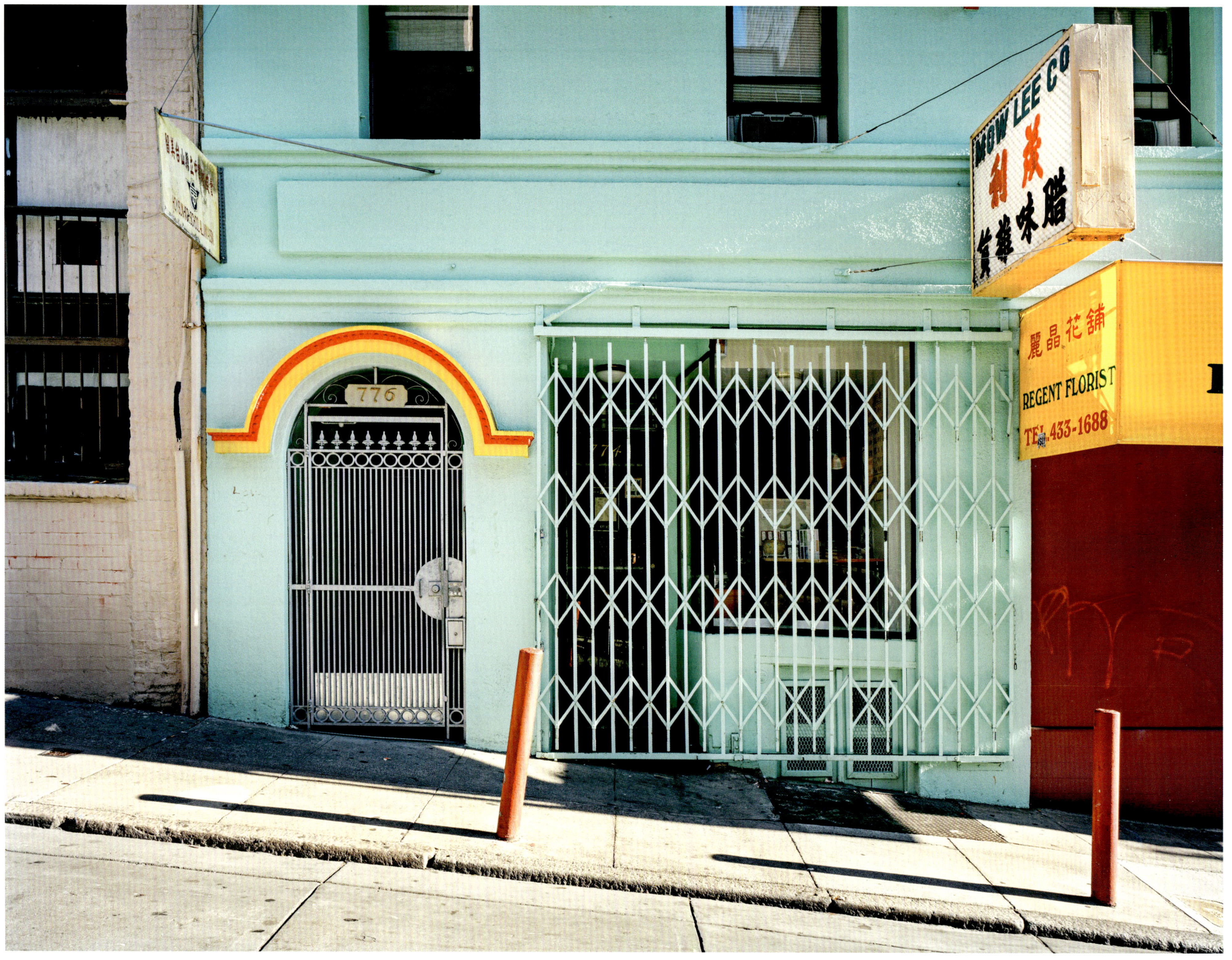

Mow Lee Co, San Francisco, 2017

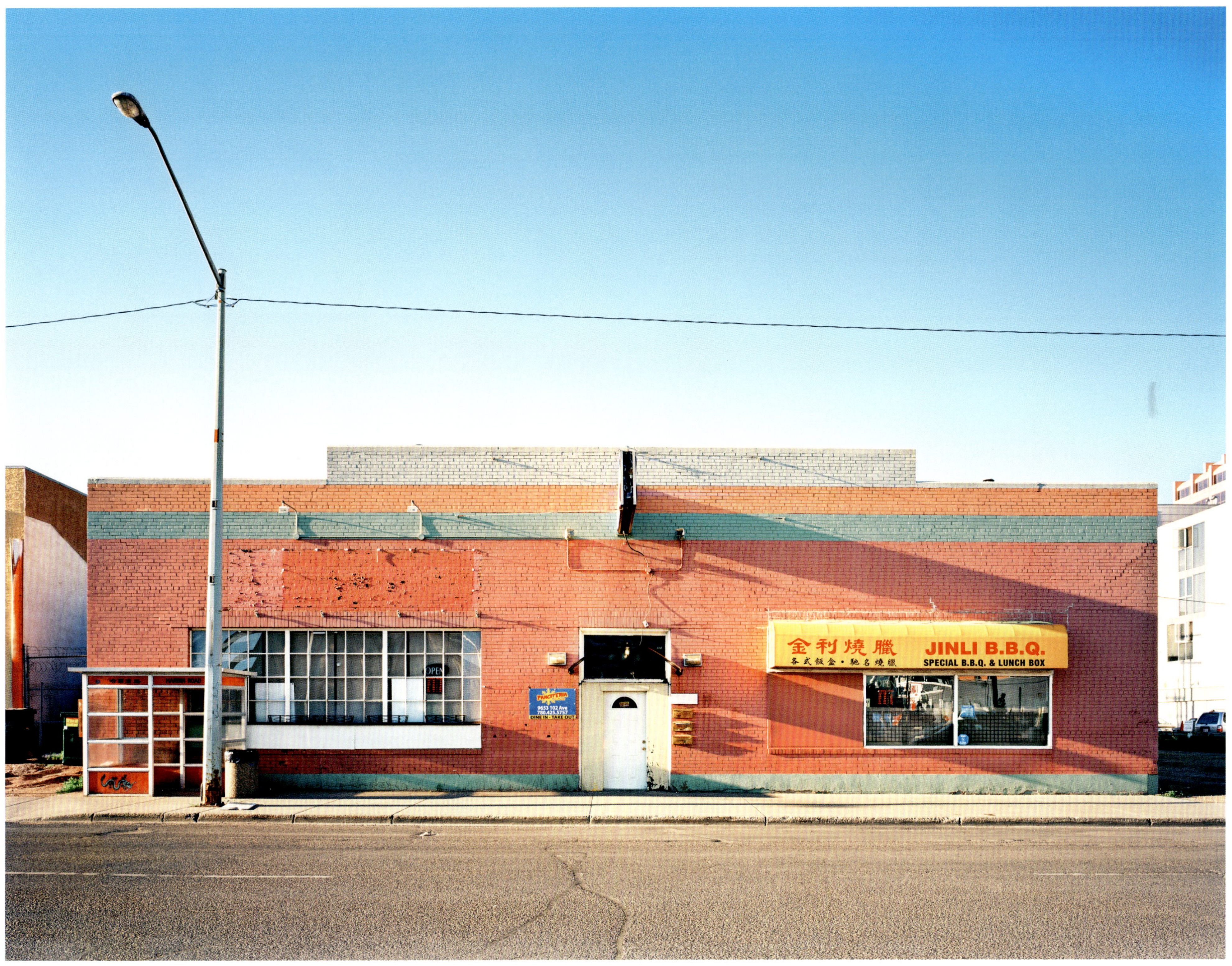

Jinli B.B.Q., Edmonton, 2015

Courtyard Between East Pender Street, Market Alley, Carrall Street, Columbia Street (West View, Staircase), Vancouver, 2013

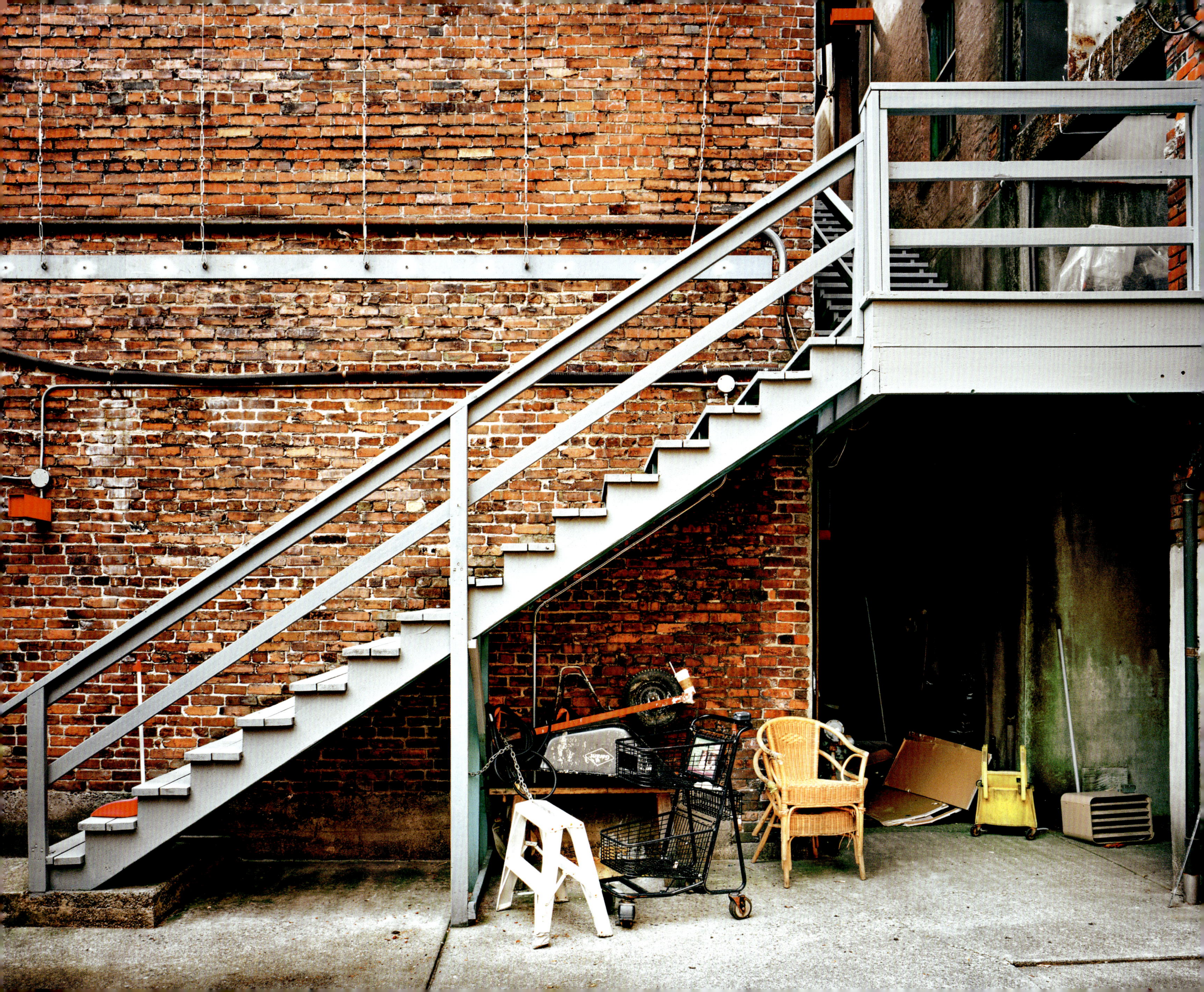

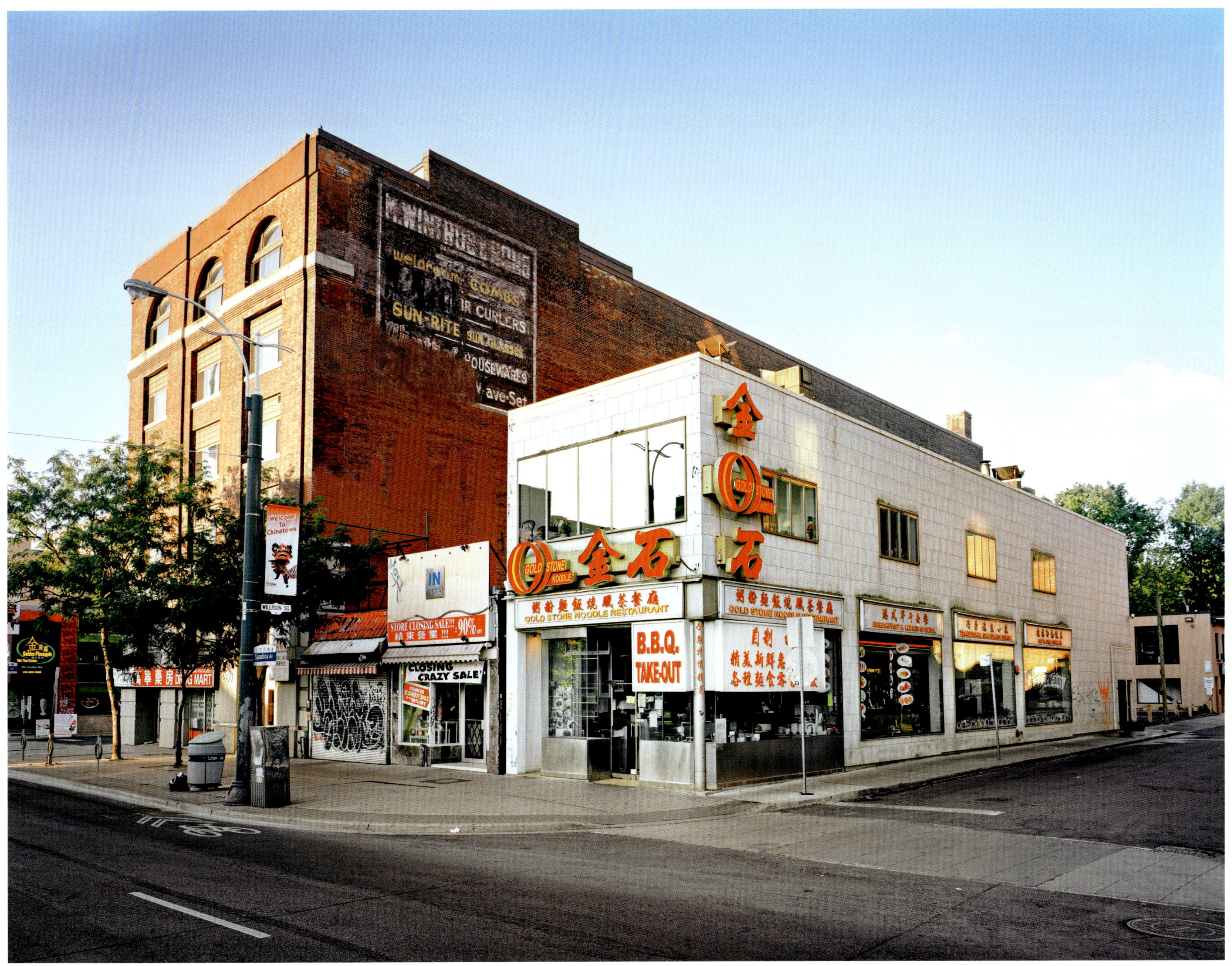

Gold Stone Noodle Restaurant, Toronto West Chinatown, 2012

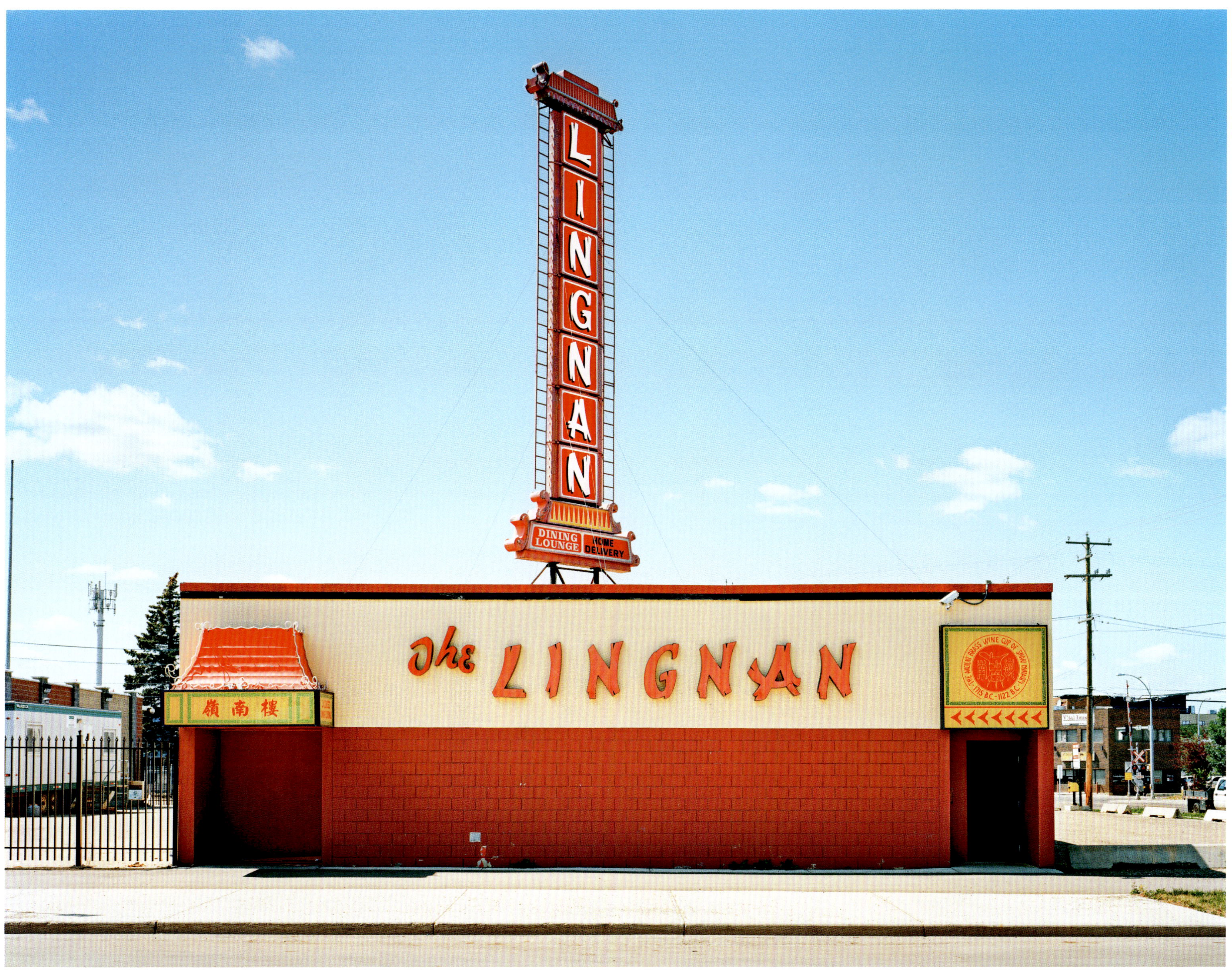

The Lingnan, Edmonton, 2015

Lim Family Benevolent Society (Altar Space), San Francisco, 2017

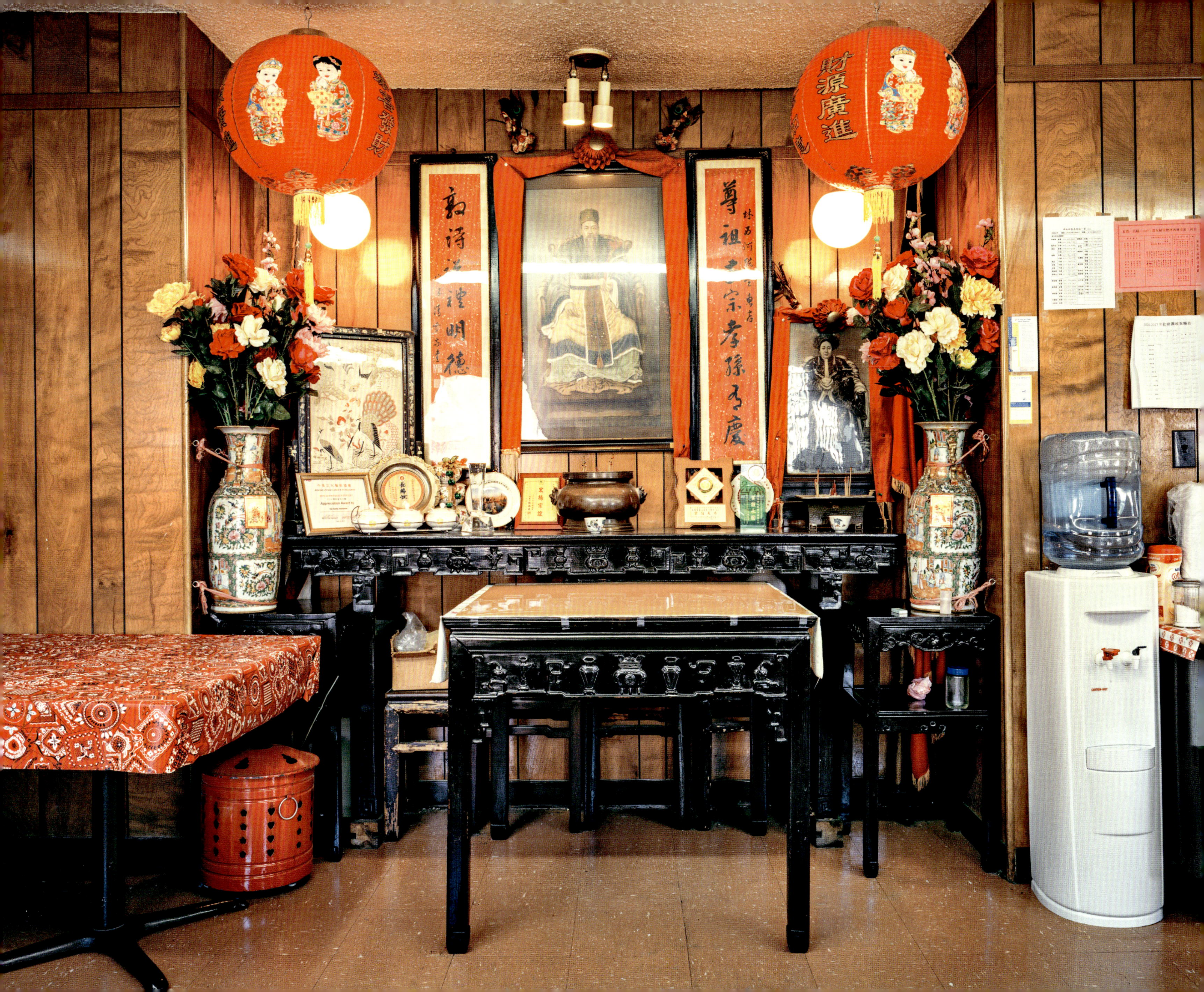

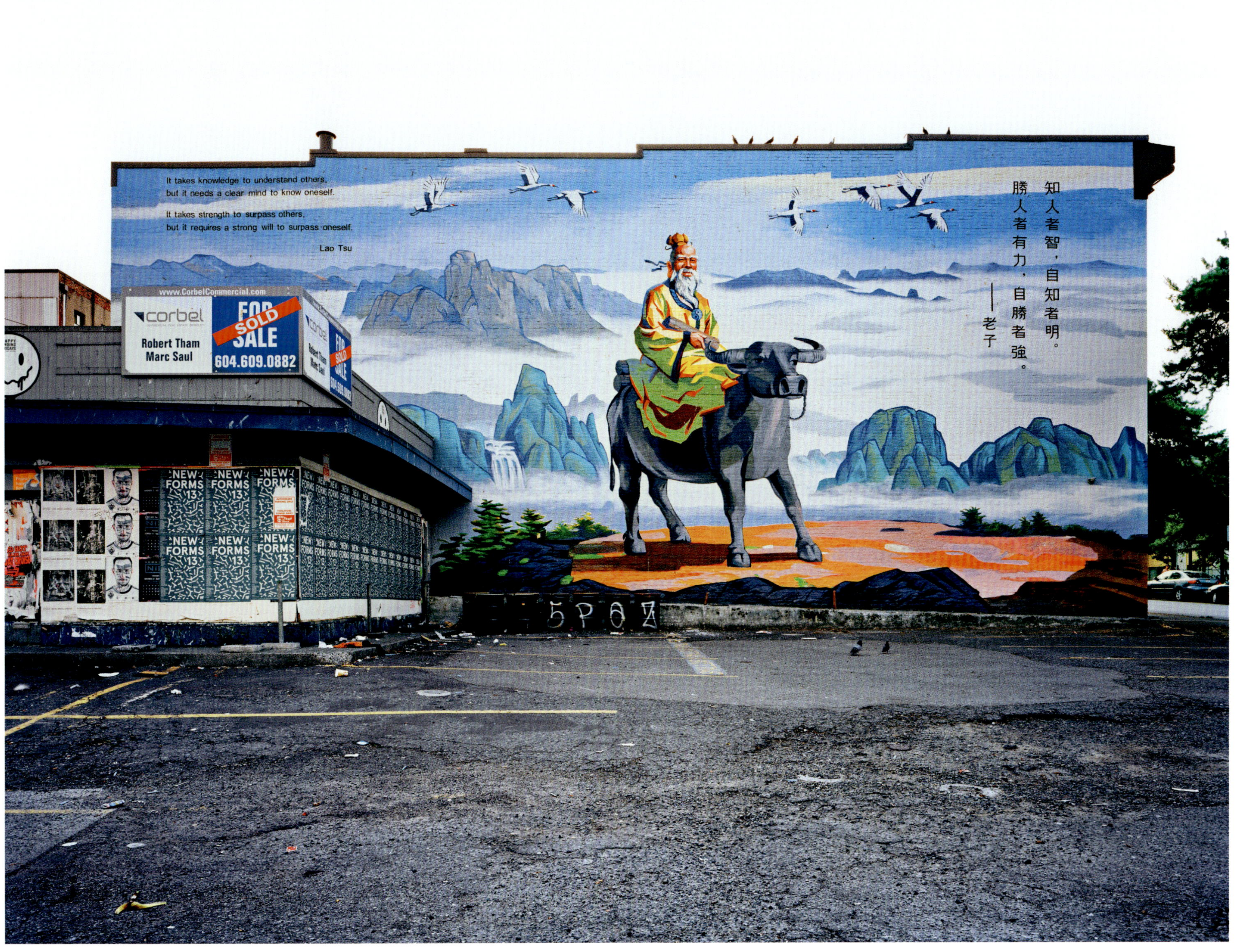

Lao Tsu Mural, Vancouver, 2013 (designed by Kenson Seto, painted by Alex Li and Falk)

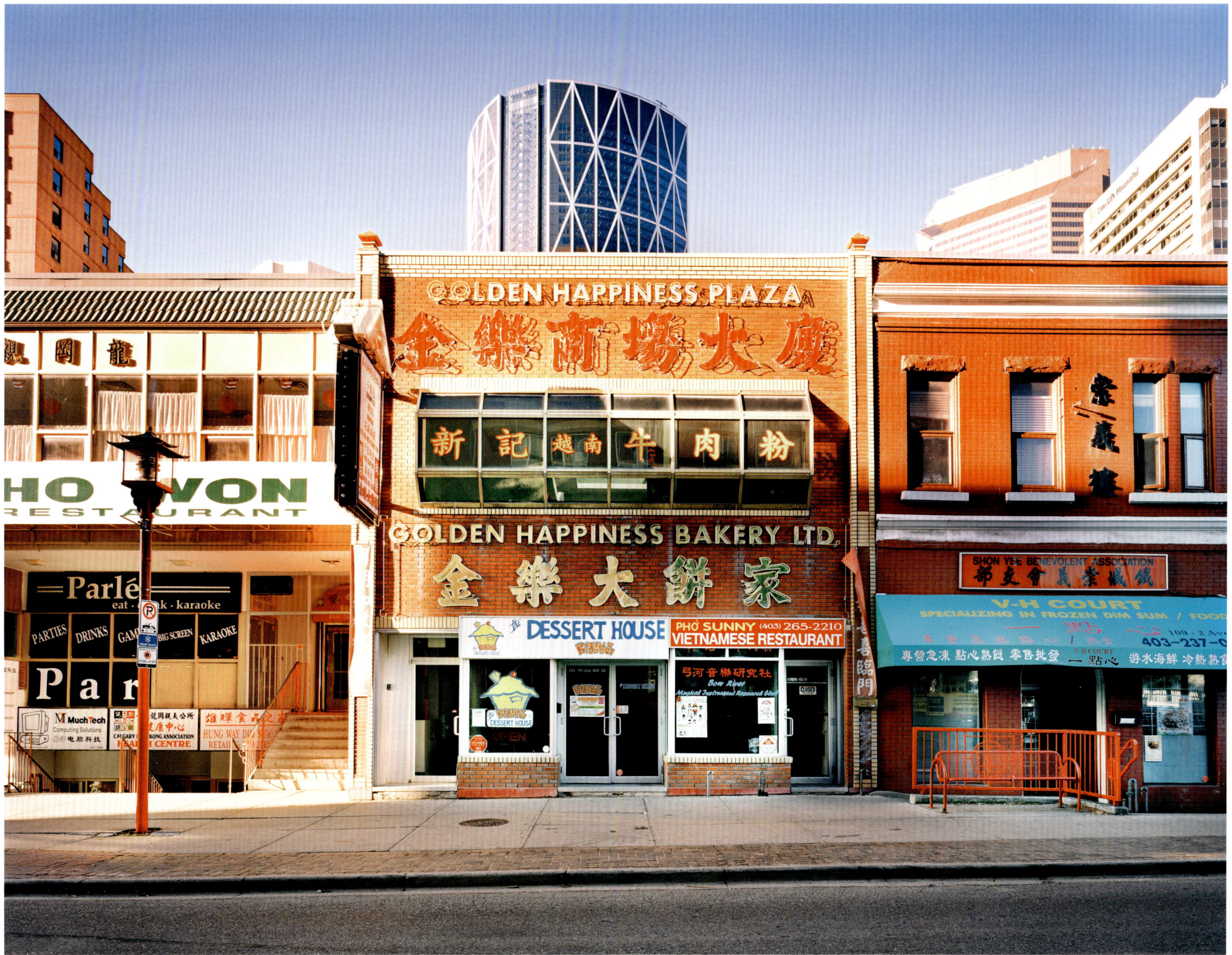

Golden Happiness Plaza, Calgary, 2015

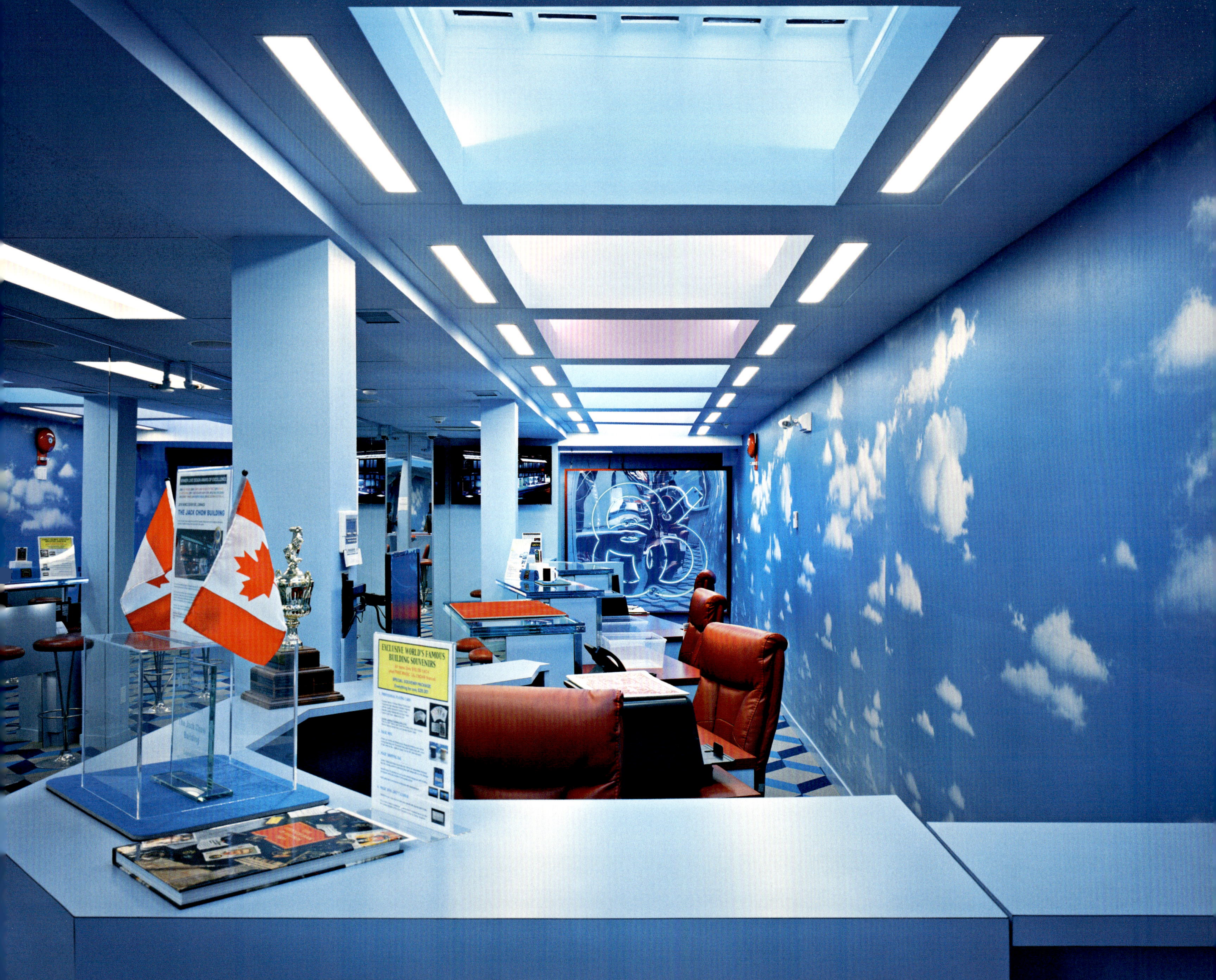
EXCLUSIVE WORLD'S FAMOUS
BUILDING SOUVENIRS

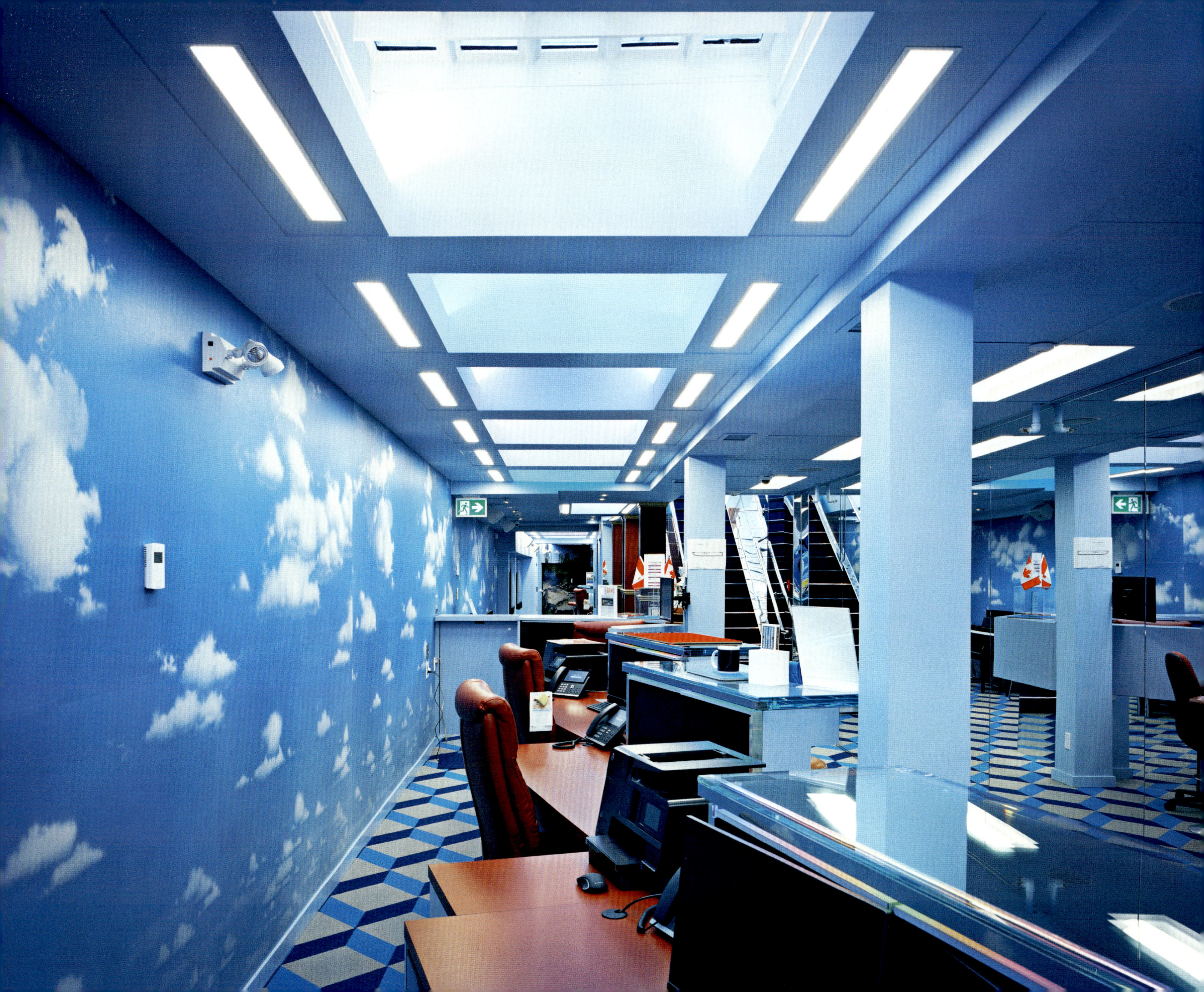

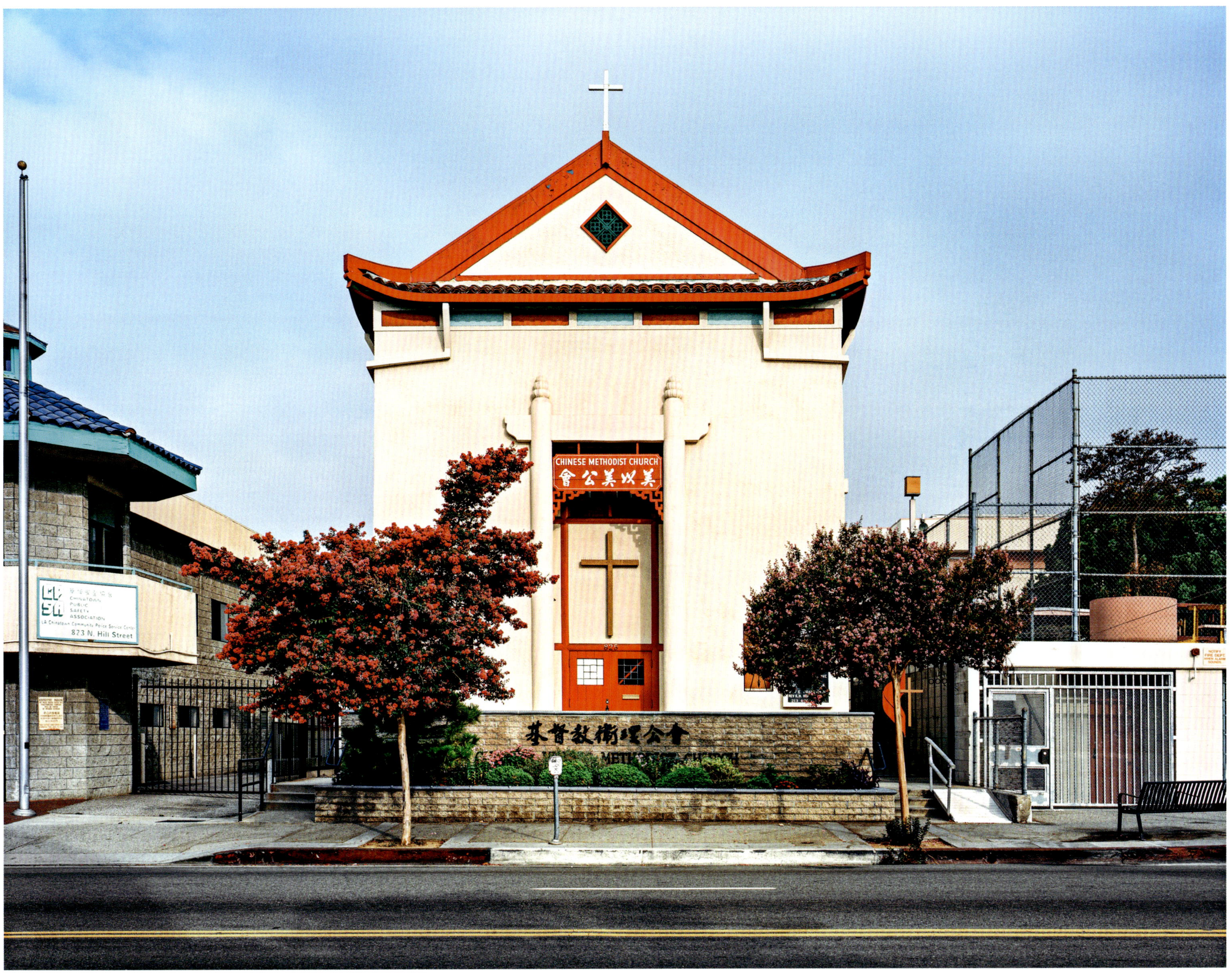

Chinese Methodist Church, Los Angeles, 2018

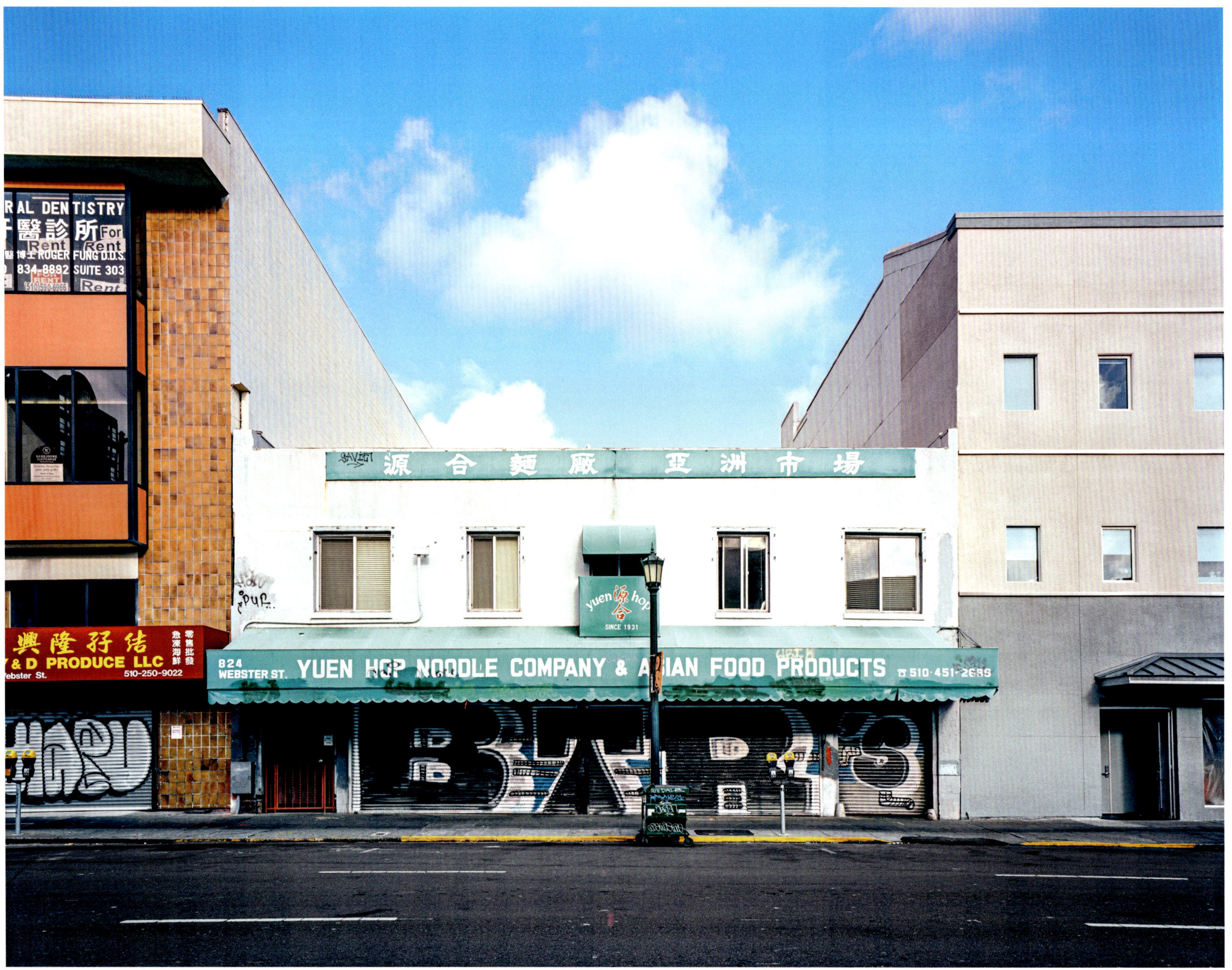

Yuen Hop Noodle Company & Asian Food Products, Oakland, 2023

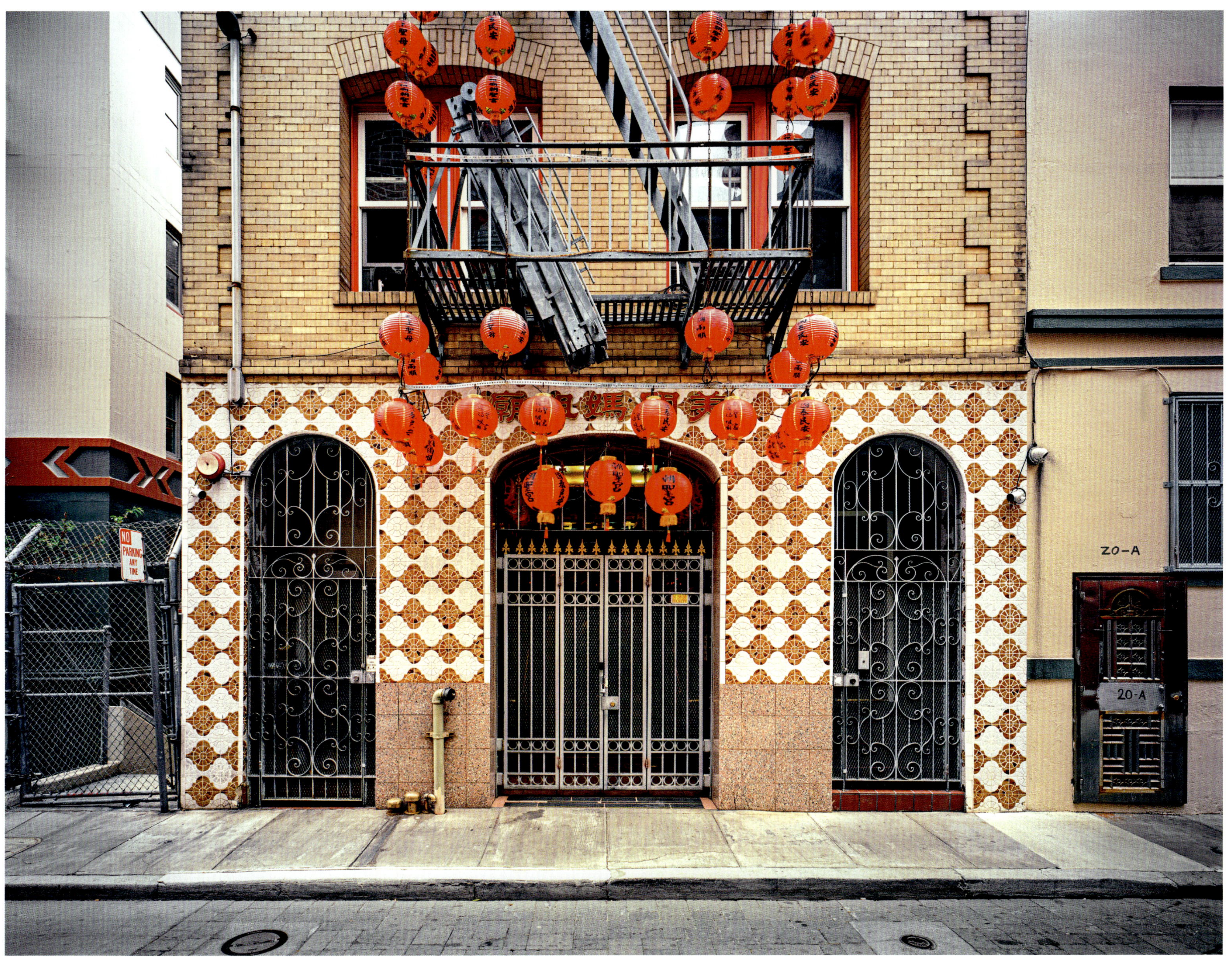

Ma Tsu Temple of USA, San Francisco, 2023

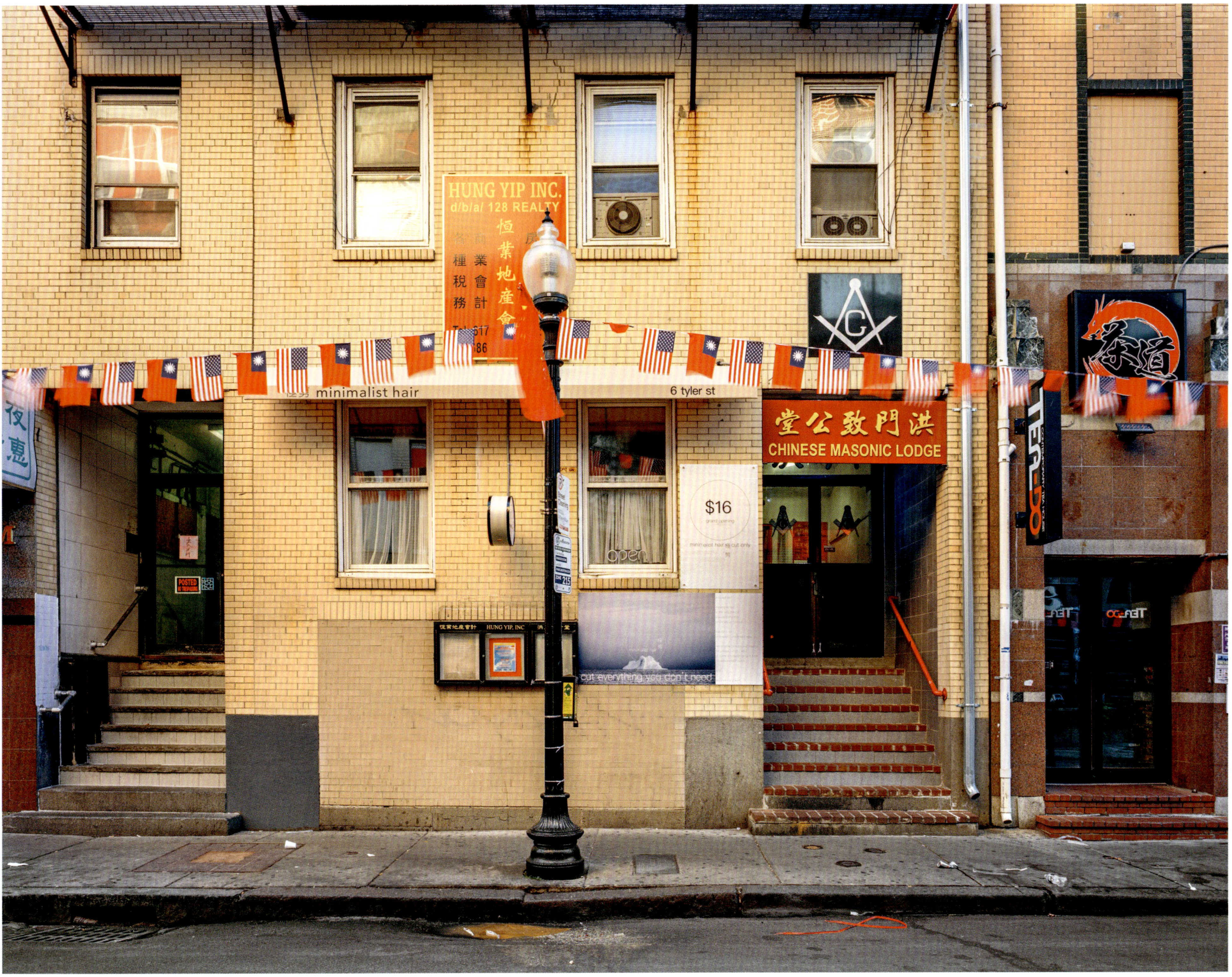

Chinese Masonic Lodge, Boston, 2019

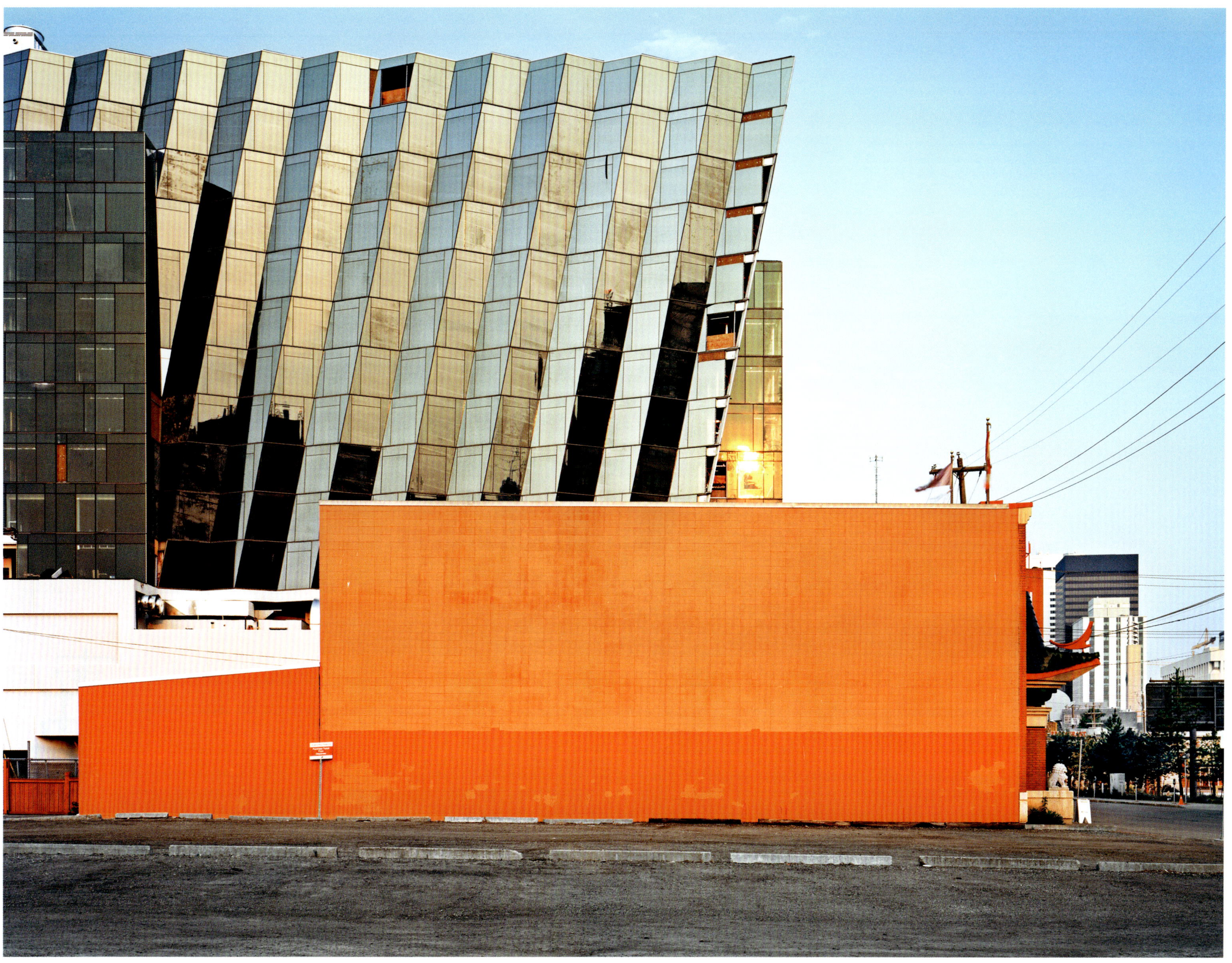

Alberta Kaiping District Association/Hyatt Place Hotel, Edmonton, 2015

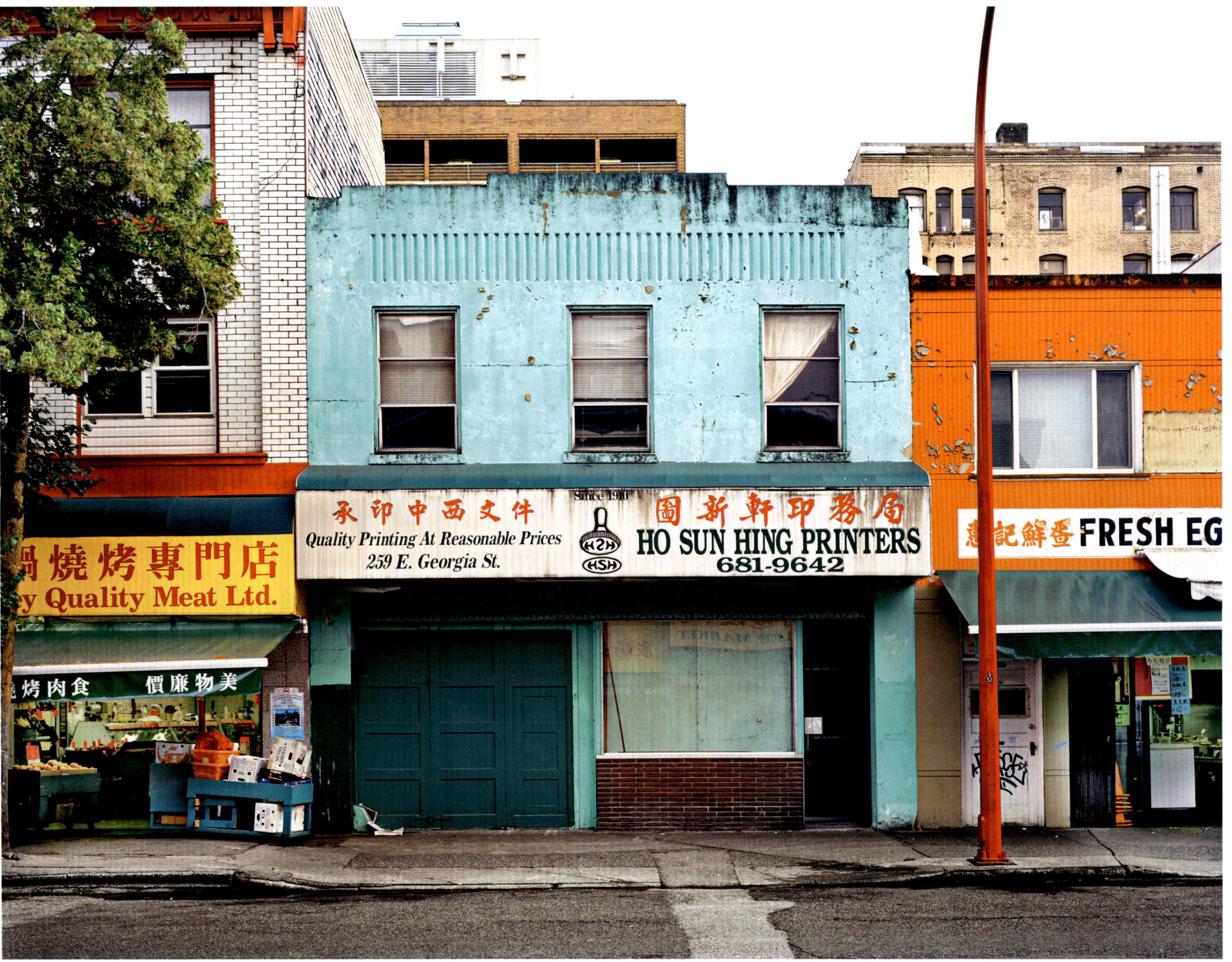
燒烤專門店
y Quality Meat Ltd.
烧烤肉食　價廉物美
承印中西文件
Quality Printing At Reasonable Prices
259 E. Georgia St.
Since 1910
圖新軒印務局
HO SUN HING PRINTERS
681-9642
HSH
意記鮮蛋 FRESH EG

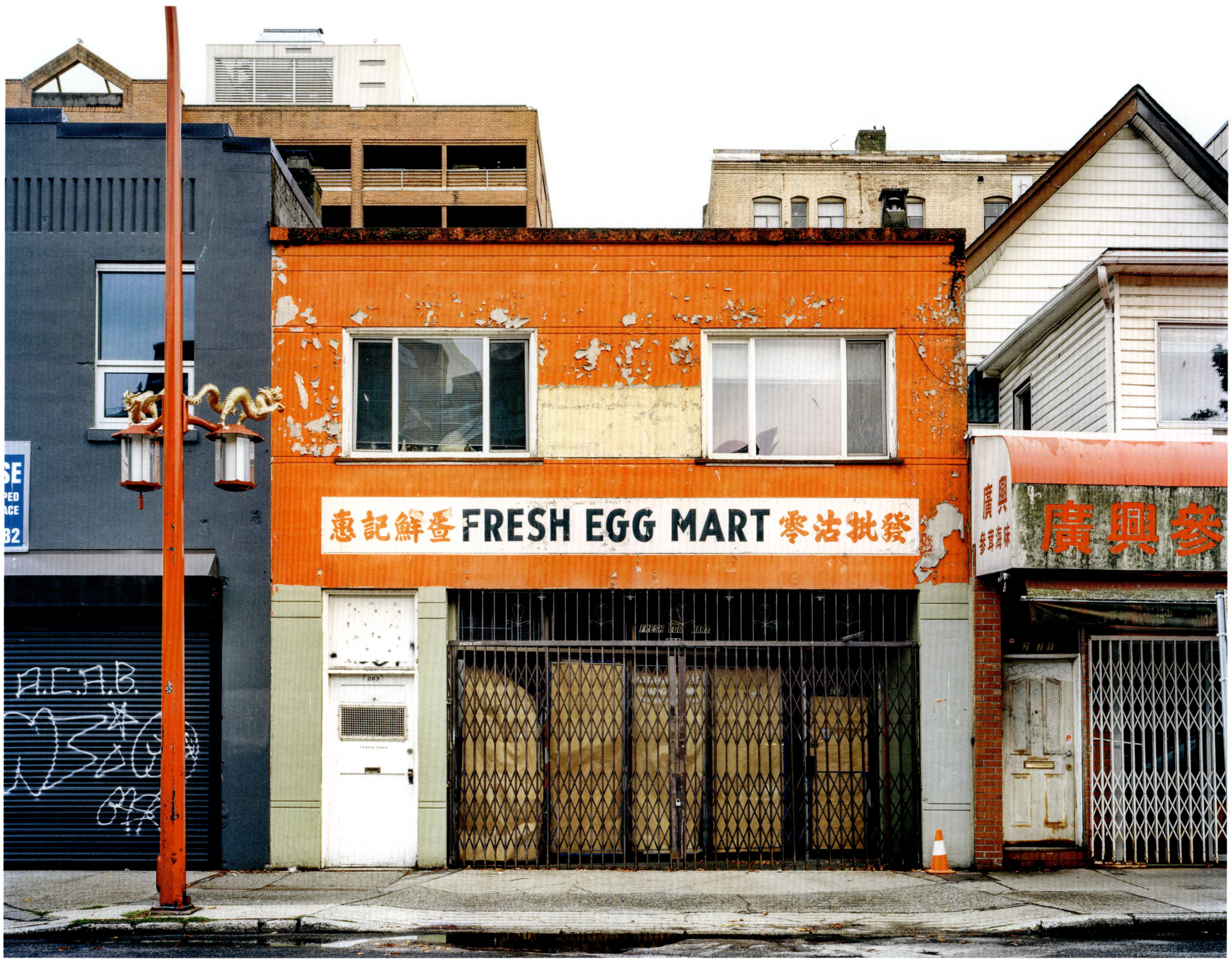

Fresh Egg Mart, Vancouver, 2017

Chinese Consolidated Benevolent Association of America (a.k.a. the Six Companies), San Francisco, 2023

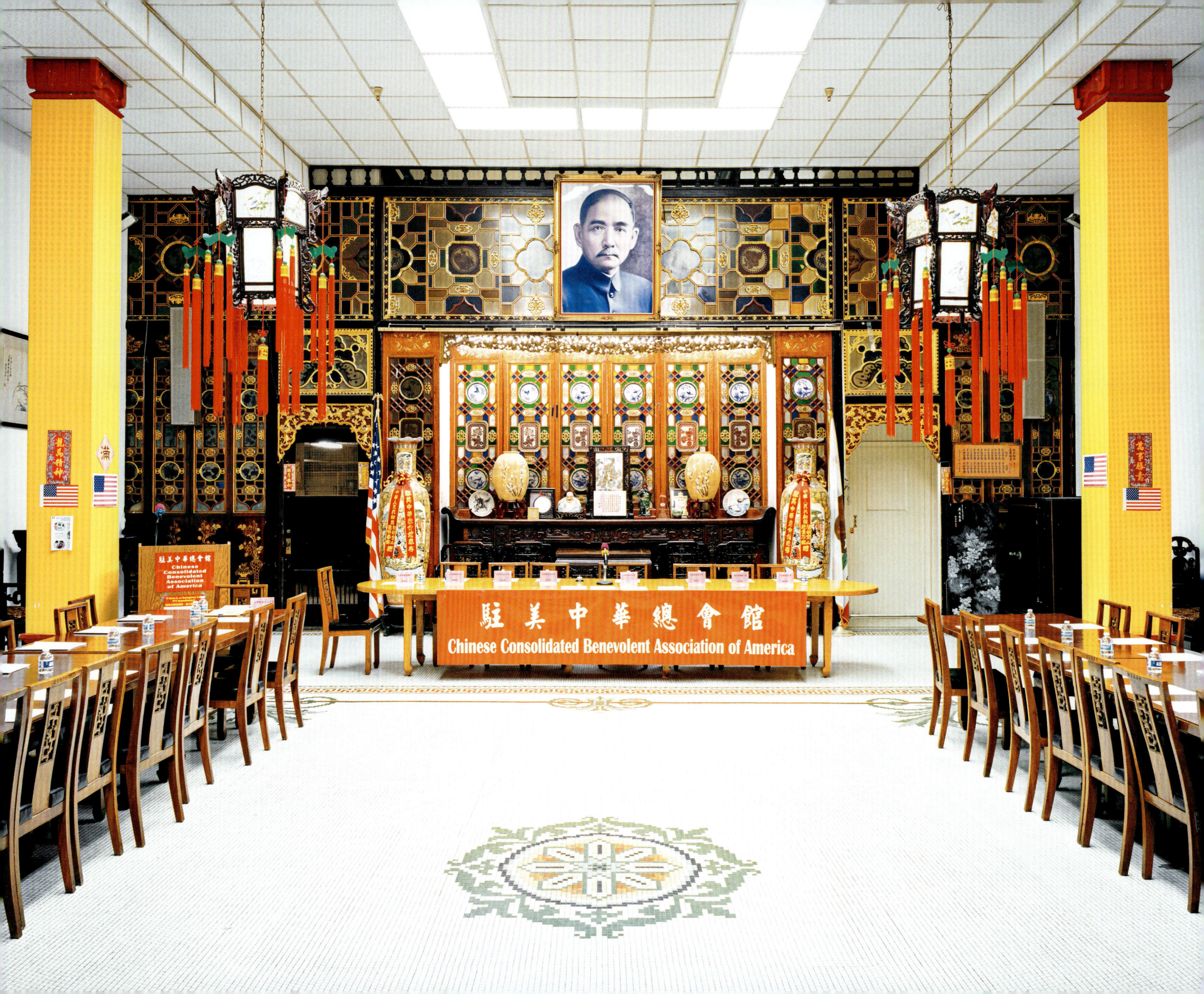

駐美中華總會館
Chinese Consolidated Benevolent Association of America

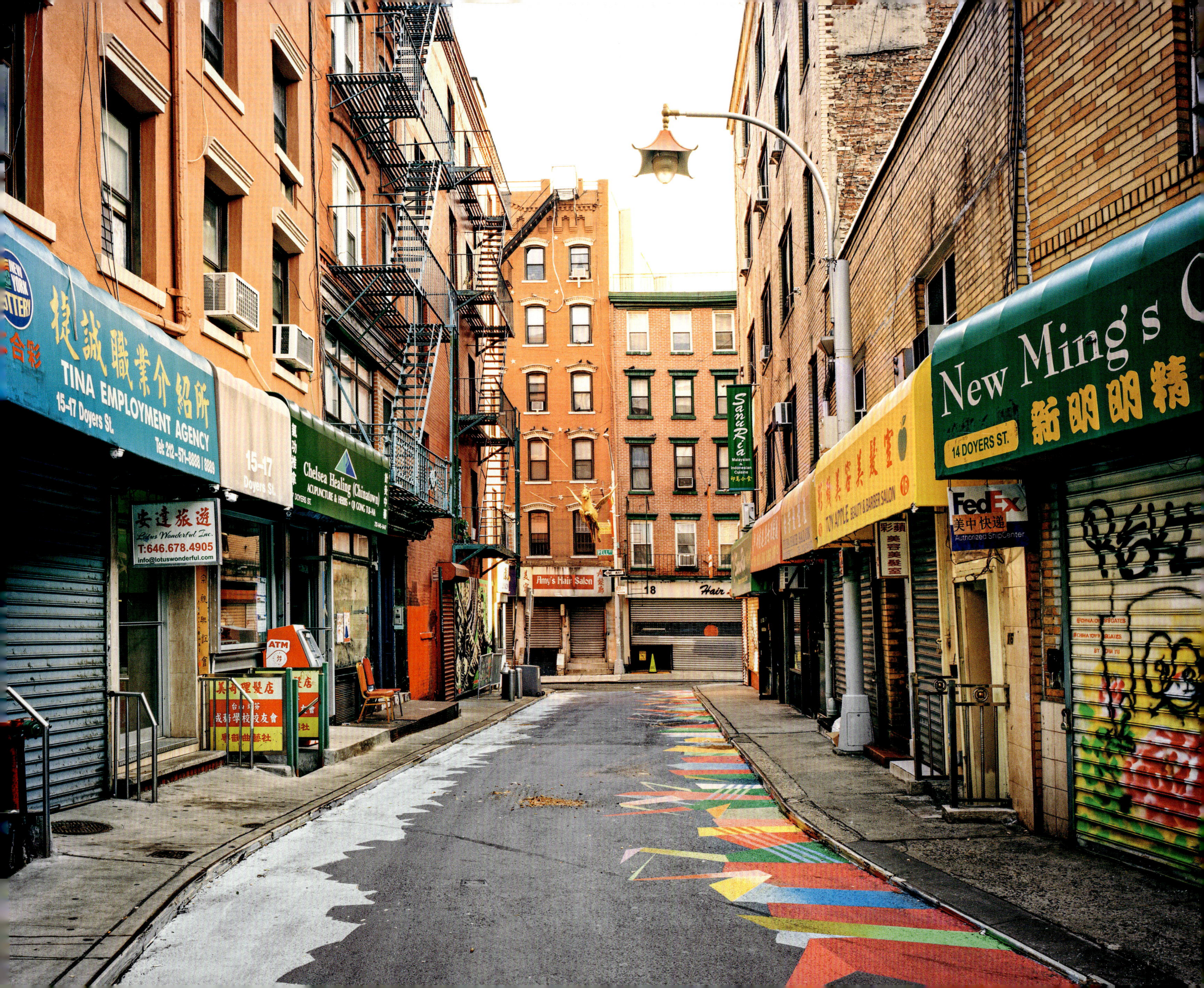

NEW YORK LOTTERY
捷 誠 職 業 介 紹 所
TINA EMPLOYMENT AGENCY
15-47 Doyers St.
Tel: 212-571-6888 | 8888
15-17 Doyers St.
安達旅遊
Lotus Wonderful Inc.
T: 646.678.4905
info@lotuswonderful.com
Chelsea Healing (Chinatown)
ACUPUNCTURE & HERBS
4 Q DONG TU-48
15-17 Doyers St.
ATM
美 句 理 髮 店
台山 芬
裁縫學校校友會
粵劇曲藝社
Amy's Hair Salon
18
Hair
SanuRia
Malaysian & Indonesian Cuisine
New Ming's
新明明精
14 DOYERS ST.
TON APPLE BEAUTY & BARBER SALON
彩 顏
美 容 美 髮 室
FedEx
美中快遞
Authorized ShipCenter

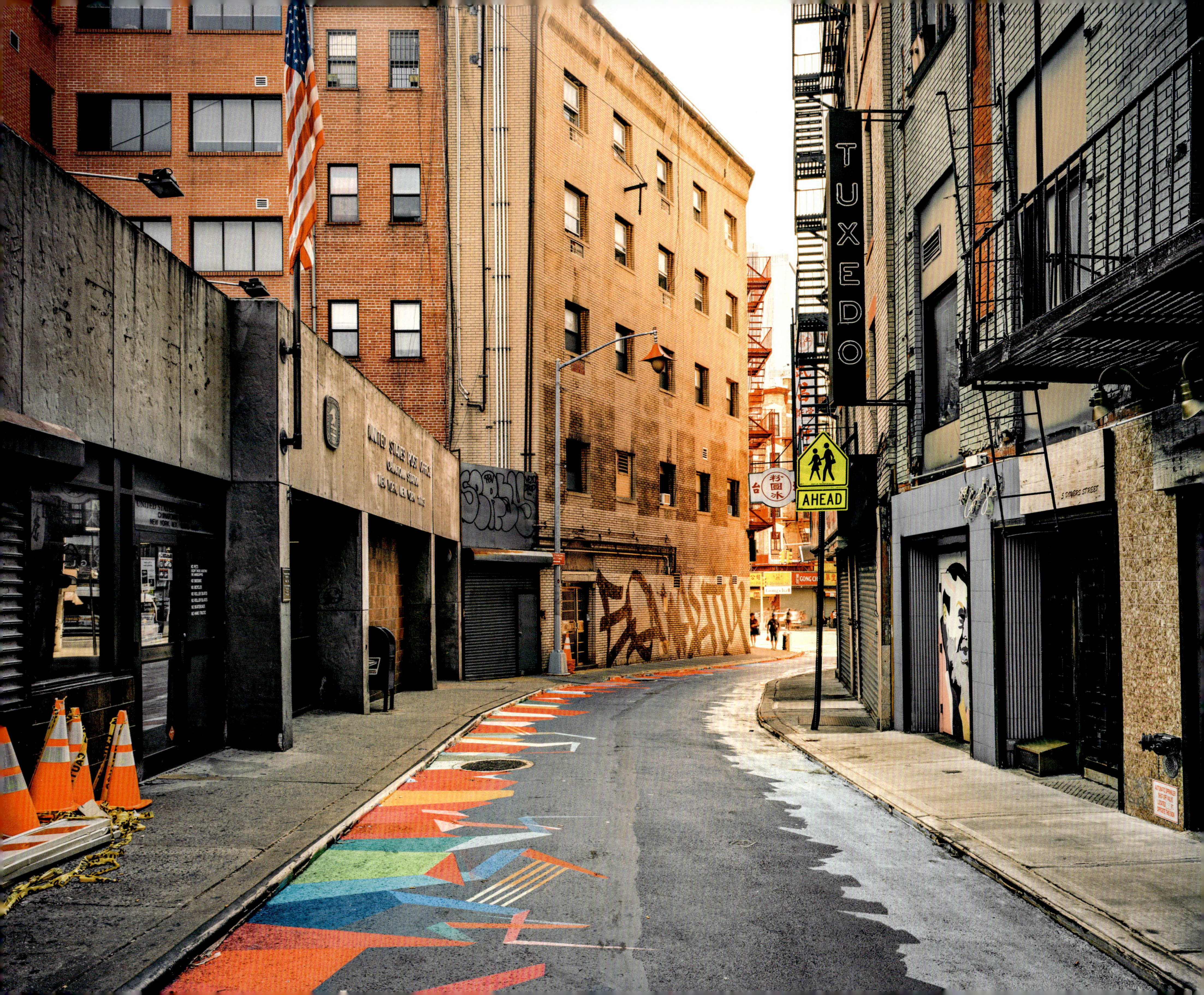
TUXEDO
AHEAD
GONG CHI
UNITED STATES POST OFFICE
5 DOYERS STREET

previous spread
Doyers Street, Manhattan, 2019 (diptych)

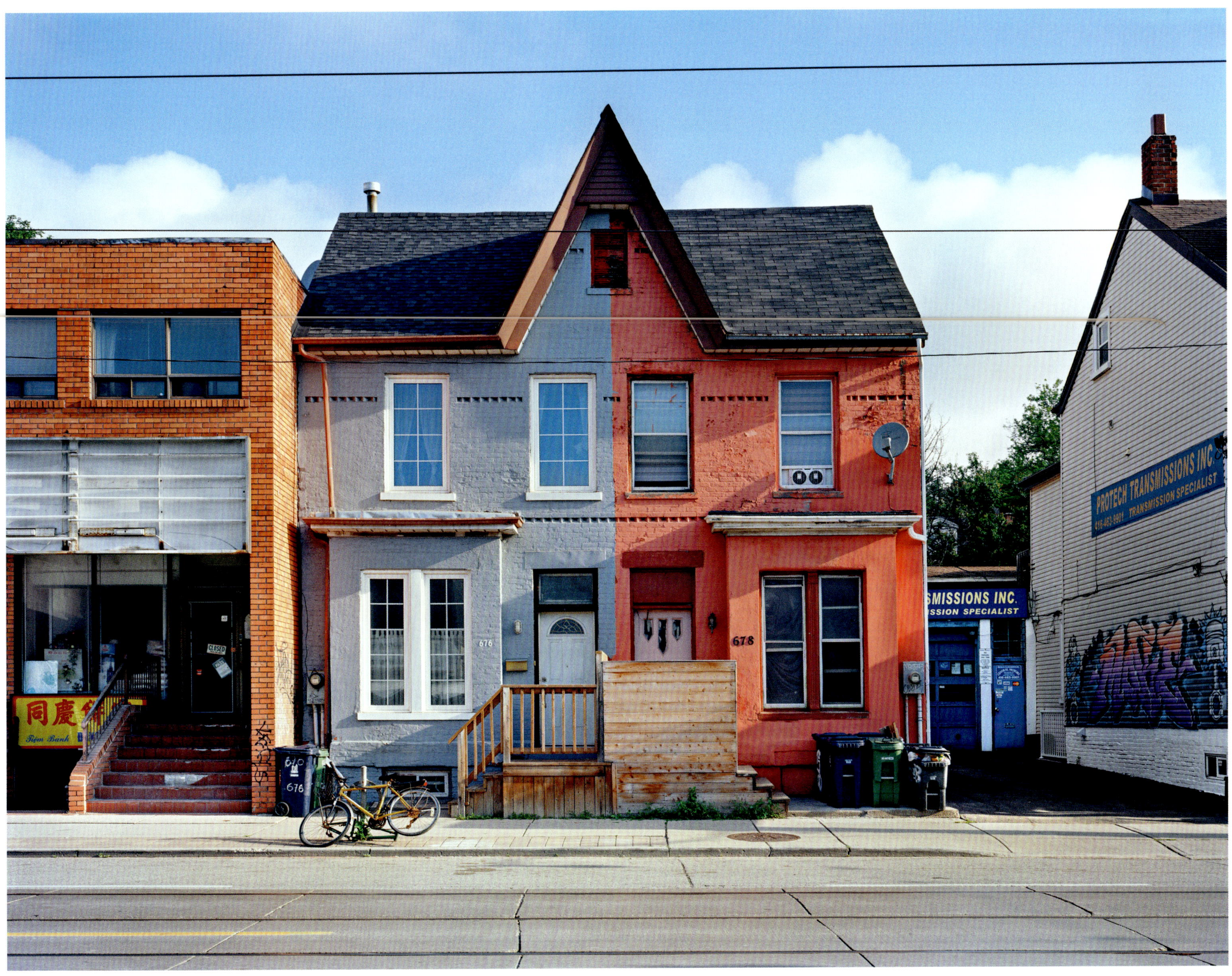
676–678 Gerrard Street, Toronto East Chinatown, 2021

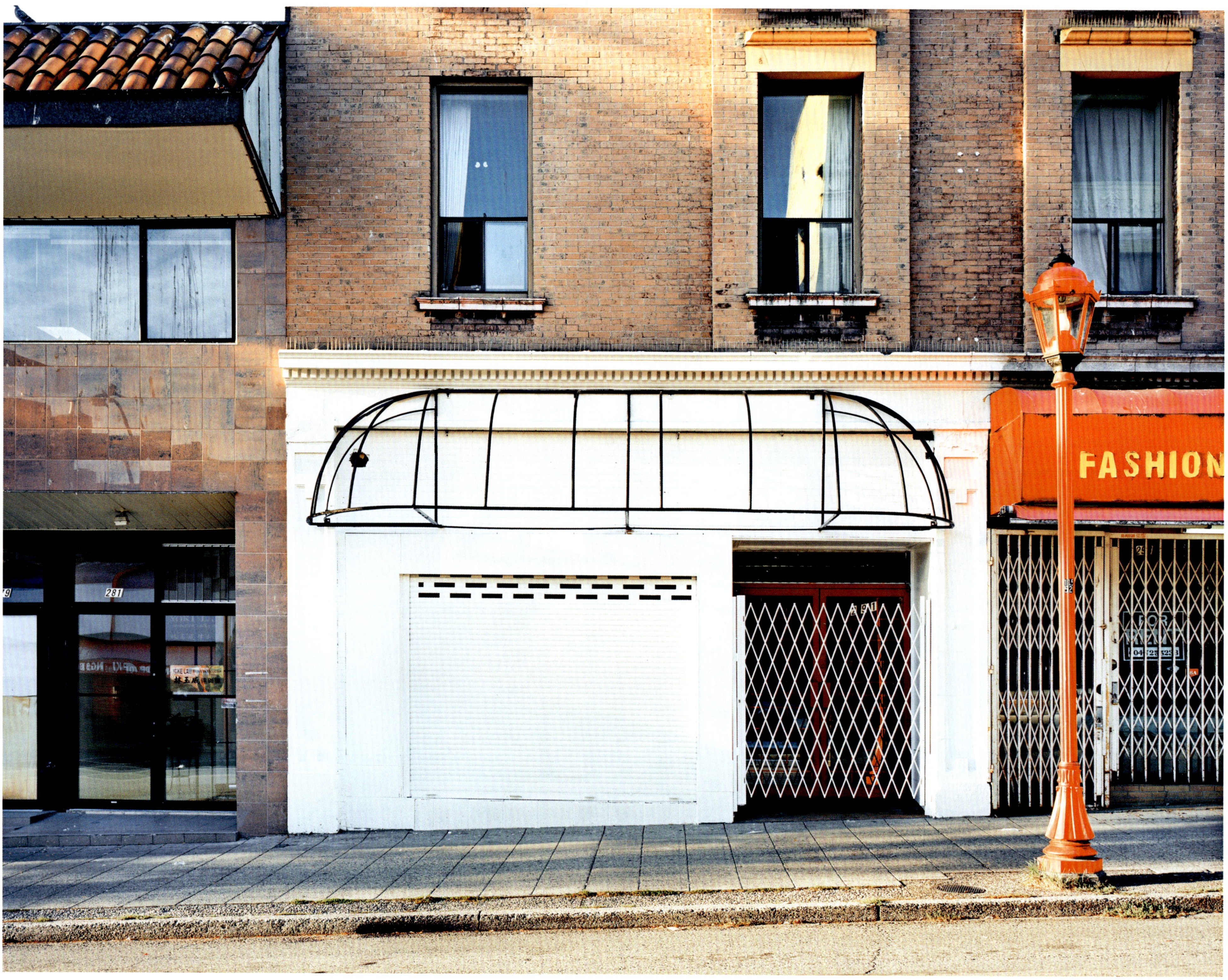

291 East Pender Street, Vancouver, 2016

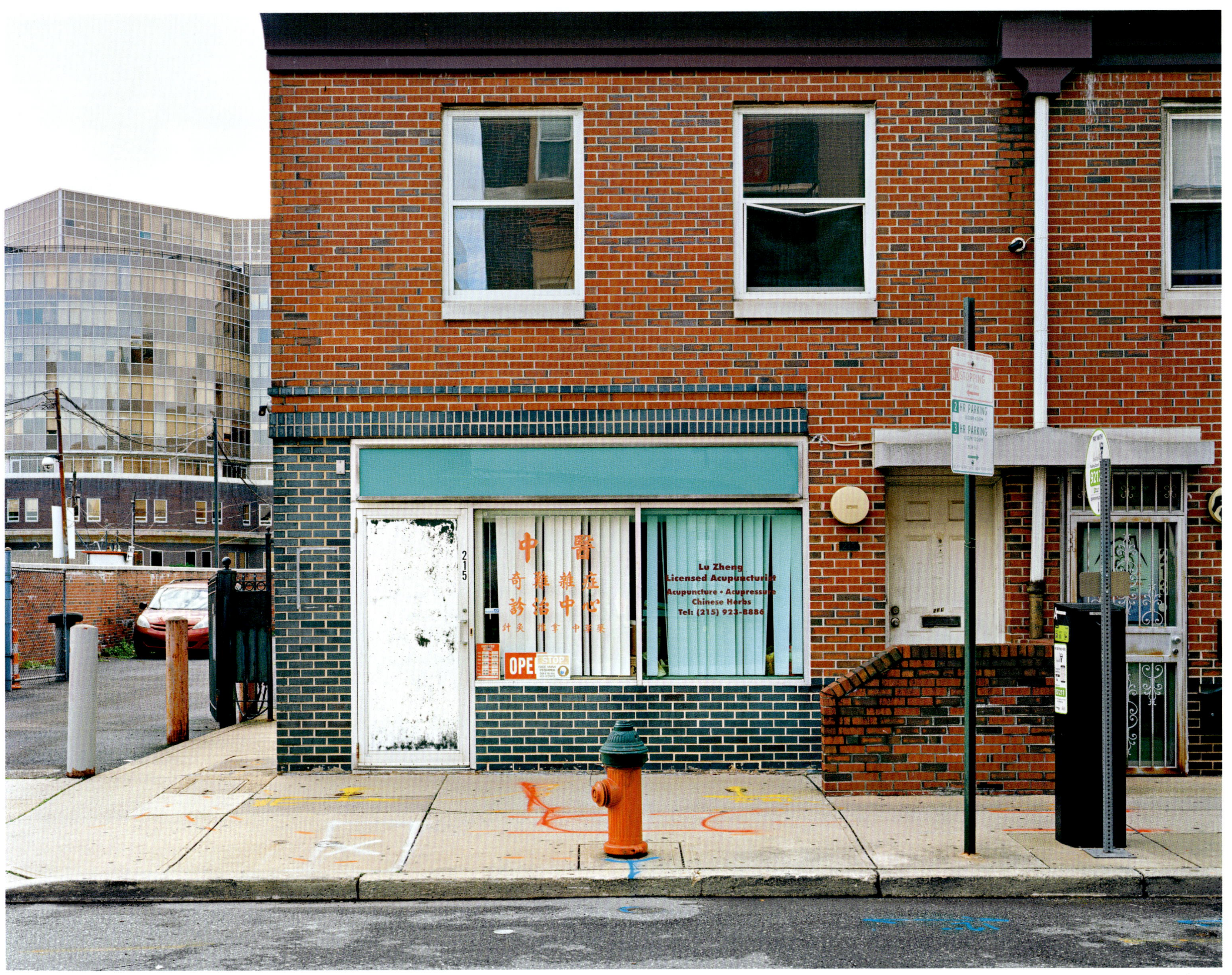

Lu Zheng Licensed Acupuncturist, Philadelphia, 2022

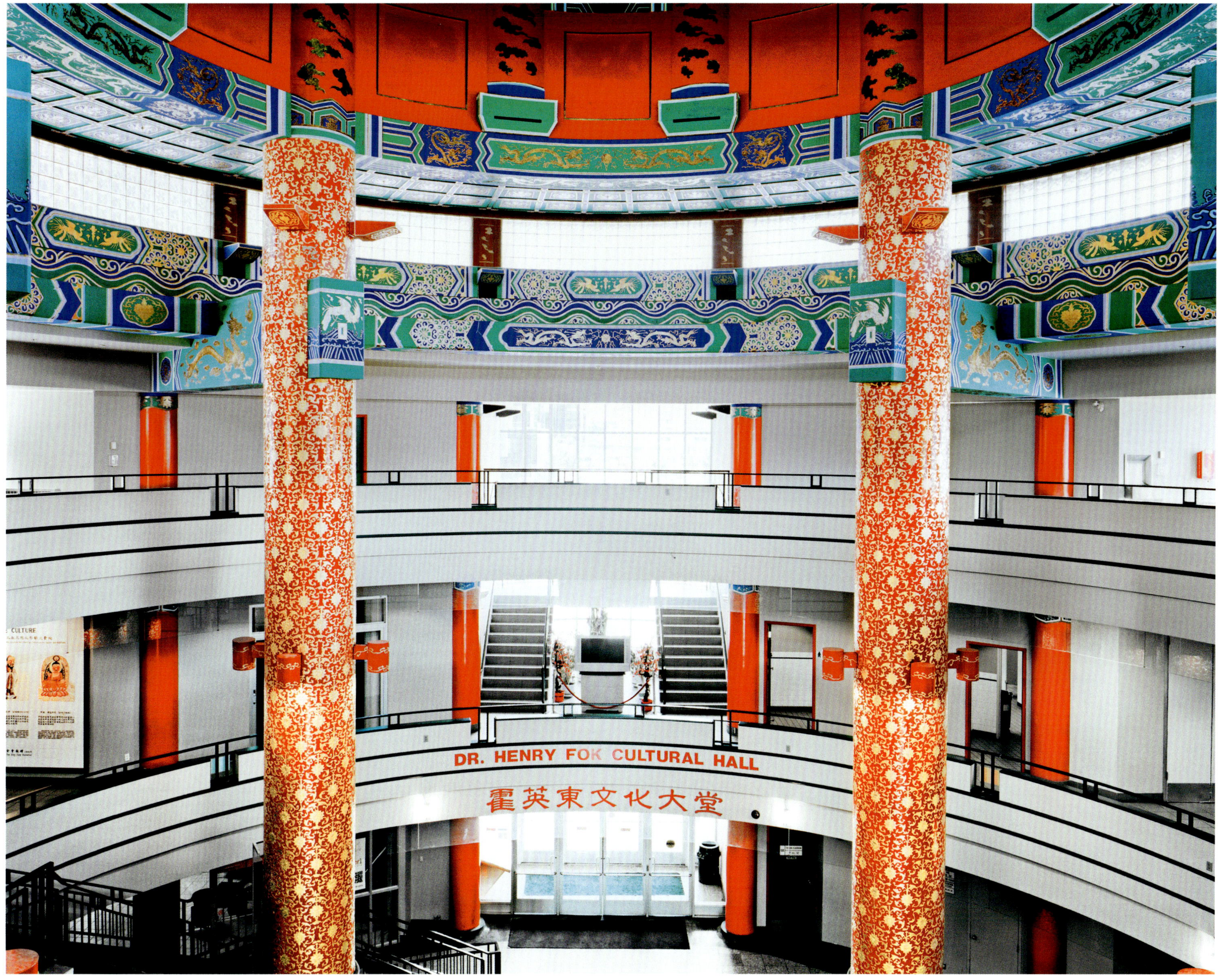

Calgary Chinese Cultural Centre, Calgary, 2015

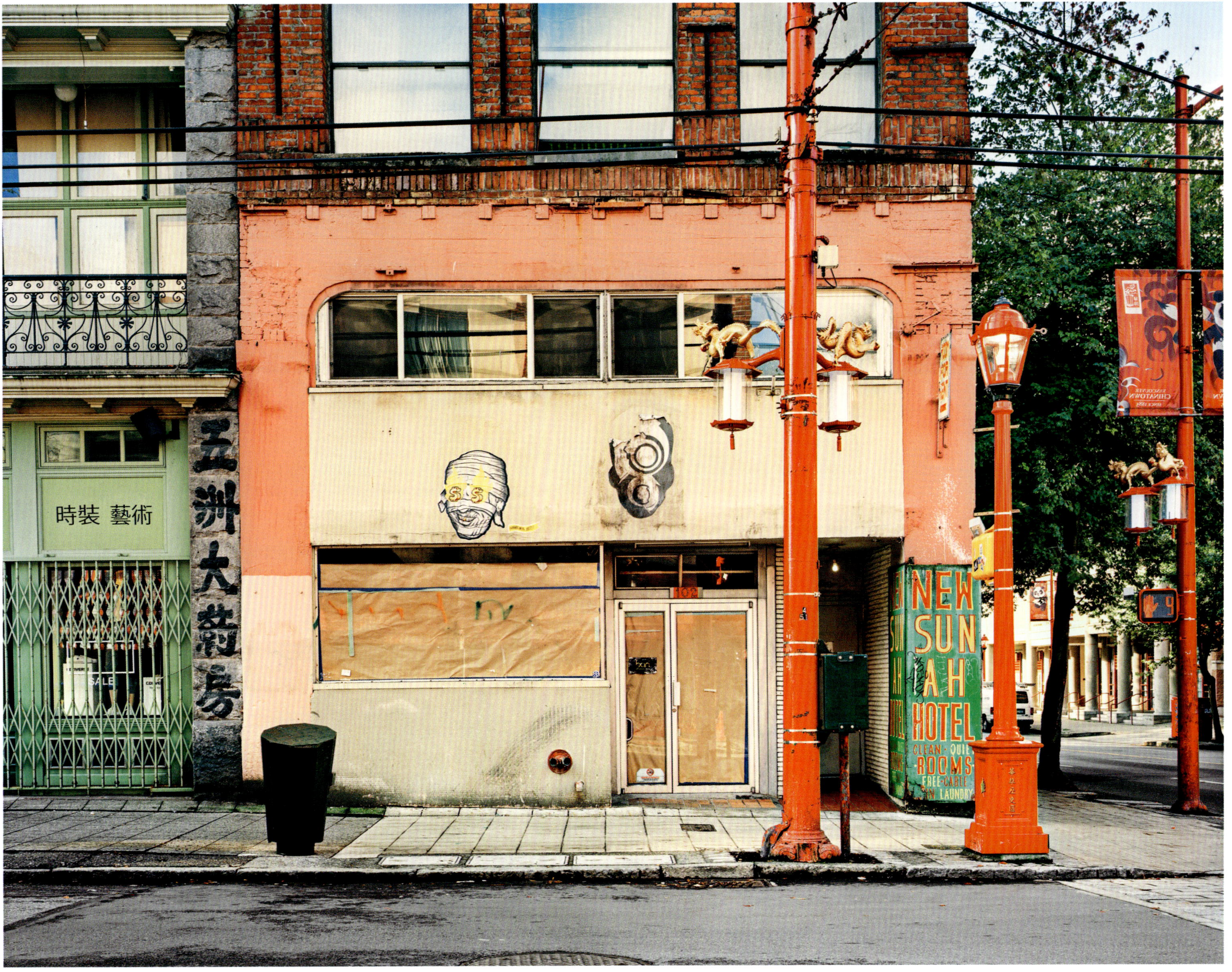

Foo's Ho Ho, Vancouver, 2017

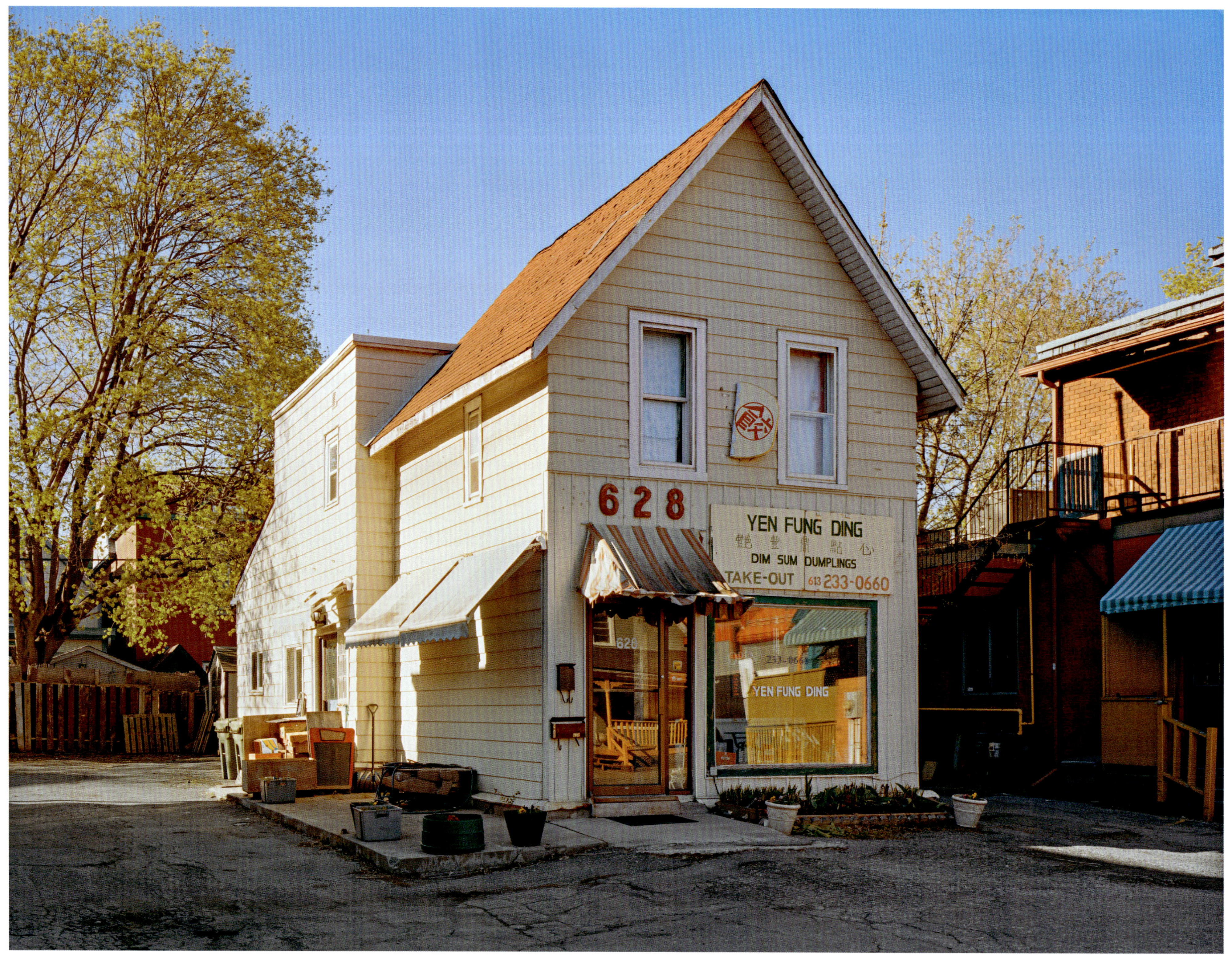

Yen Fung Ding, Ottawa, 2023

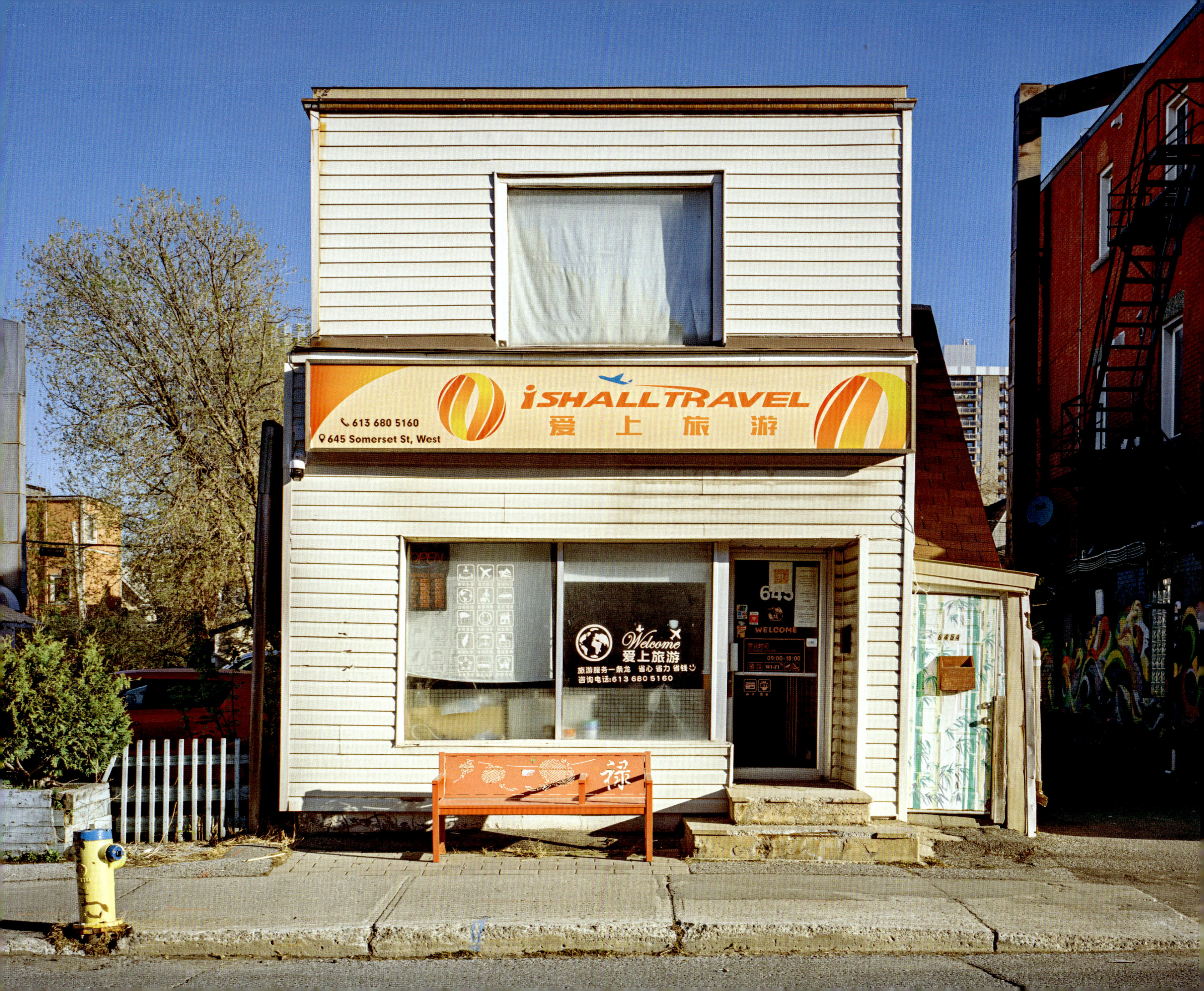
iSHALLTRAVEL
爱 上 旅 游
613 680 5160
645 Somerset St, West
OPEN
Welcome
爱上旅游
旅游服务一条龙　省心 省力 省钱
咨询电话:613 680 5160
WELCOME
09:00-18:00
645
645A
禄

previous page
iShall Travel, Ottawa, 2023

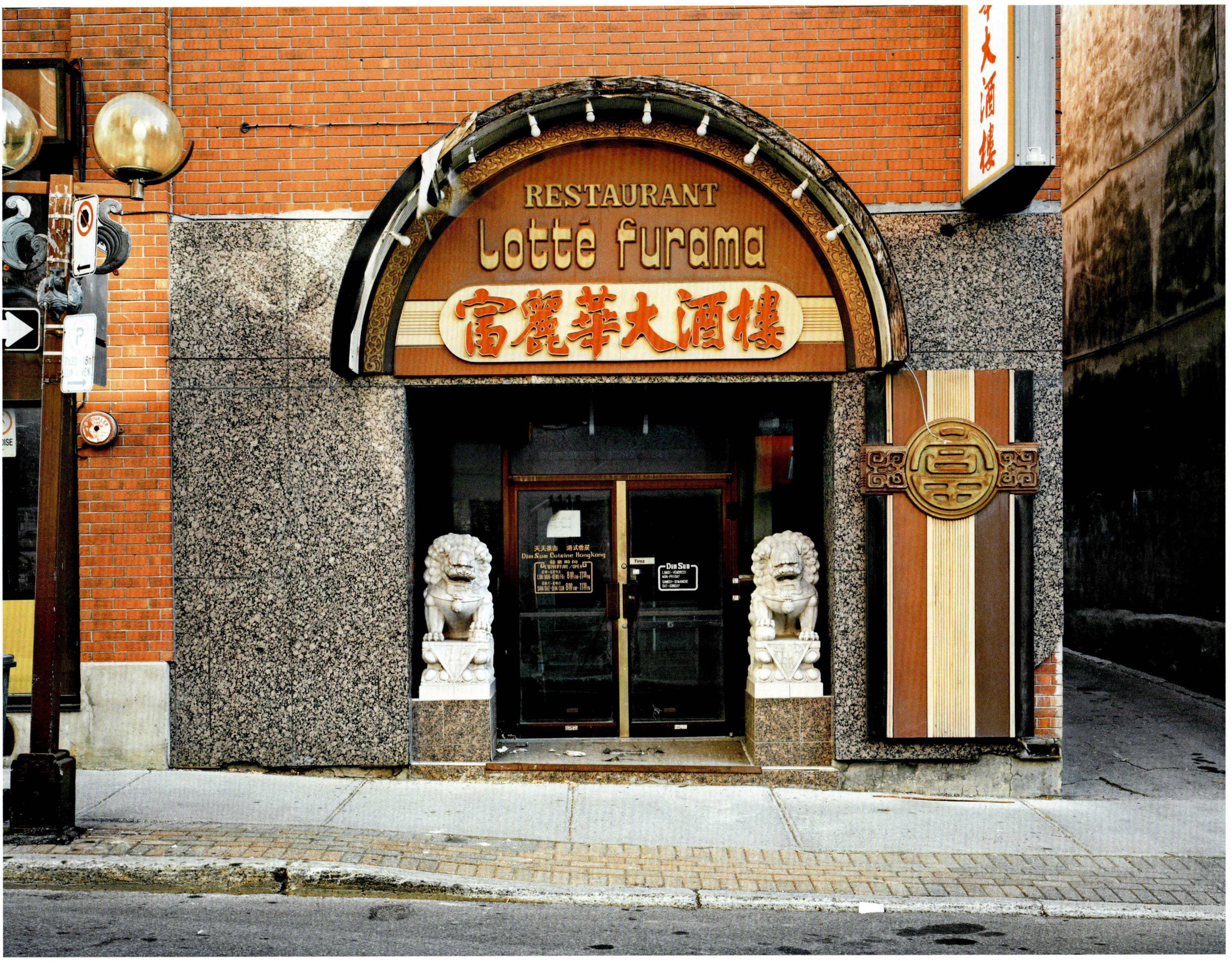

Restaurant Lotté Furama, Montreal, 2014

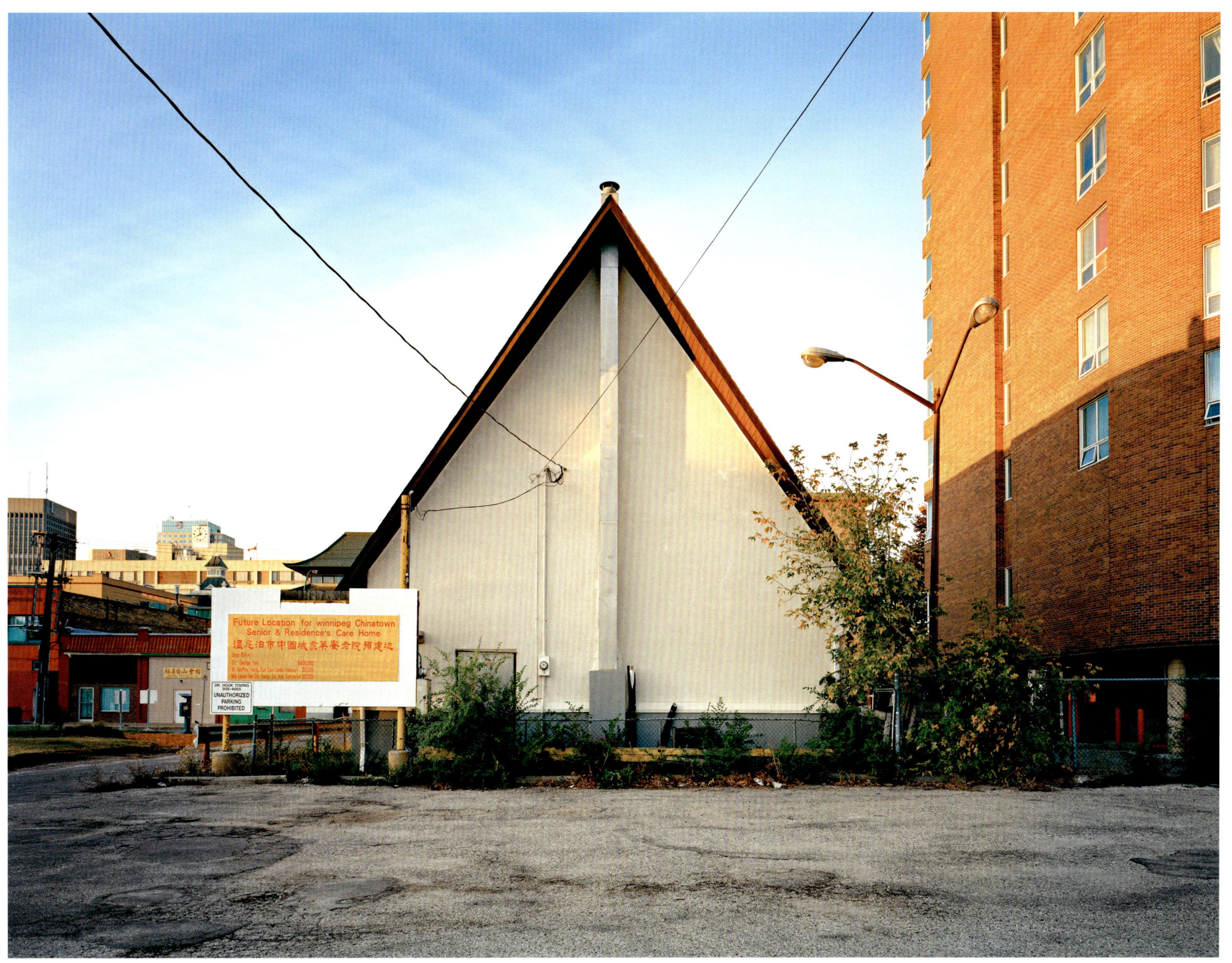

Future Location for Winnipeg Chinatown Senior & Residence's Care Home, Winnipeg, 2013

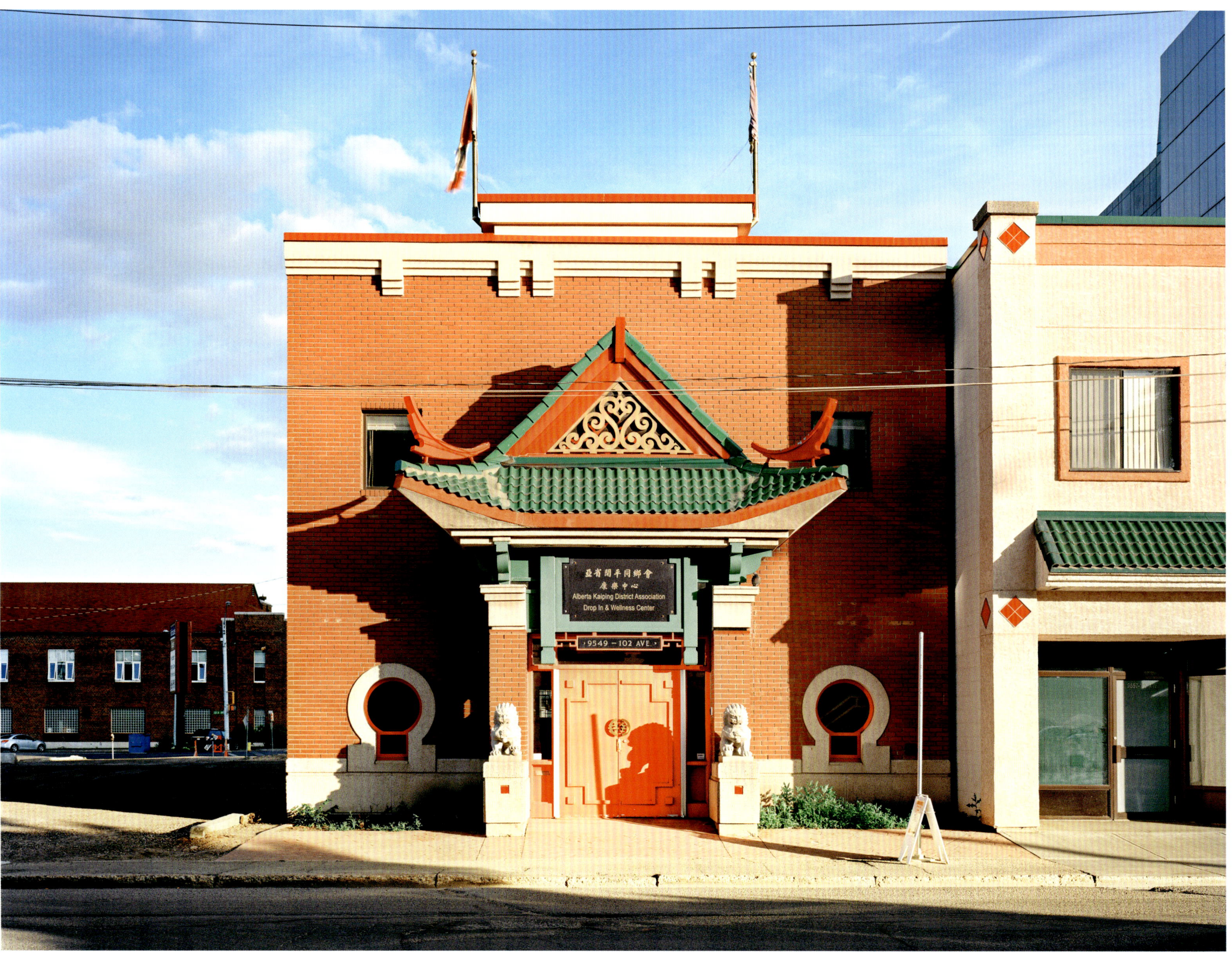

Alberta Kaiping District Association, Edmonton, 2015

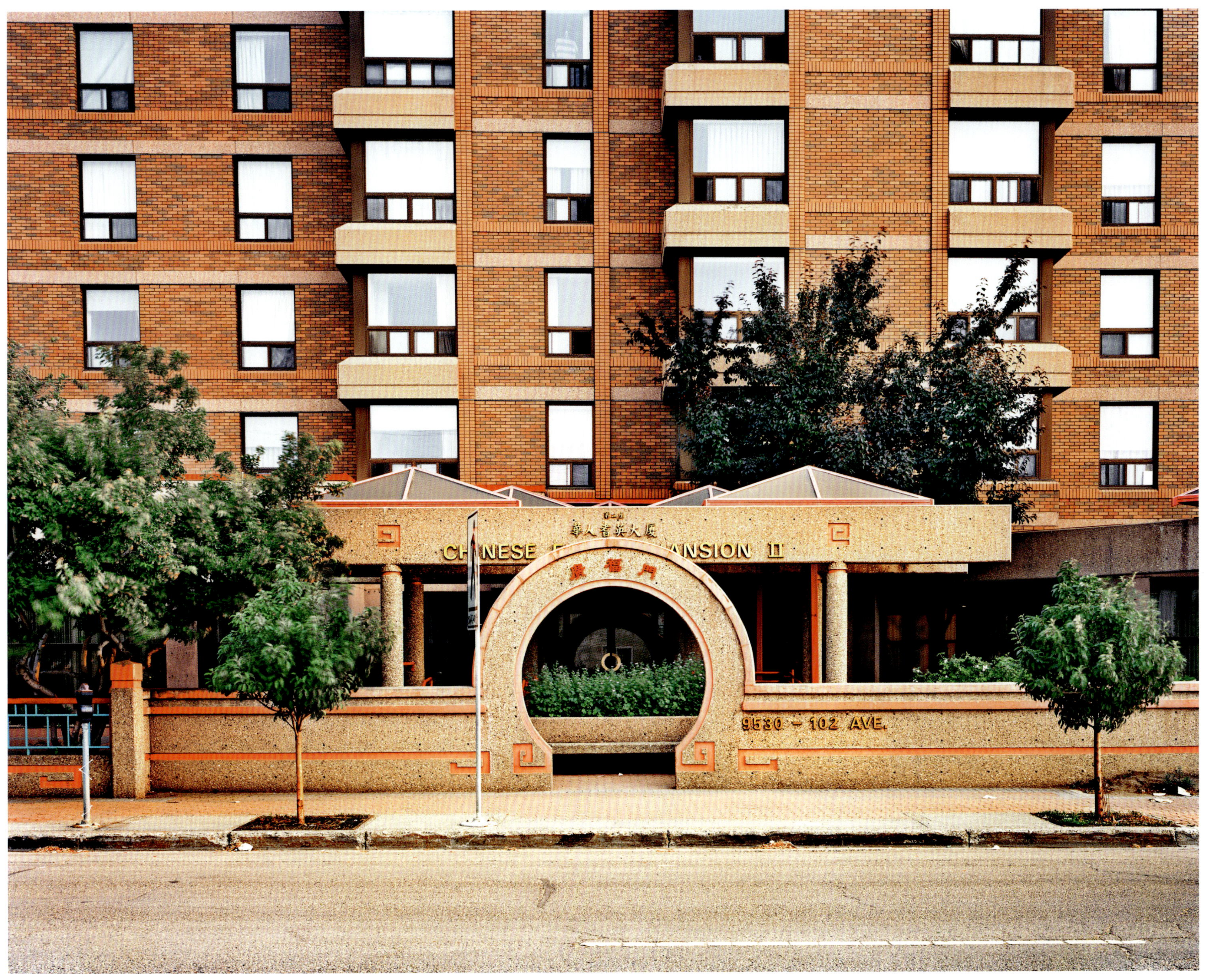

Chinese Elders Mansion II, Edmonton, 2015

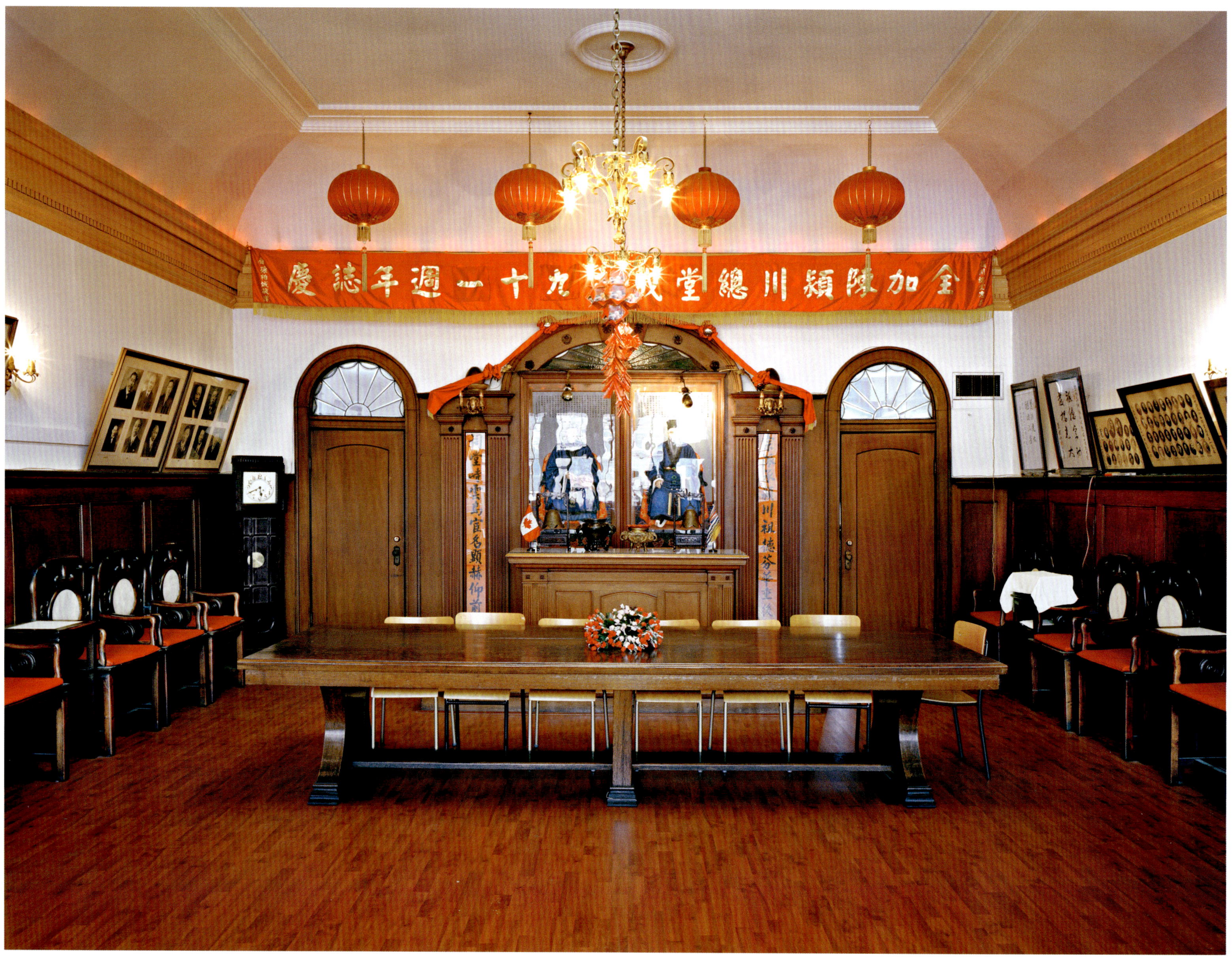
全加陳潁川總堂九十一週年誌慶

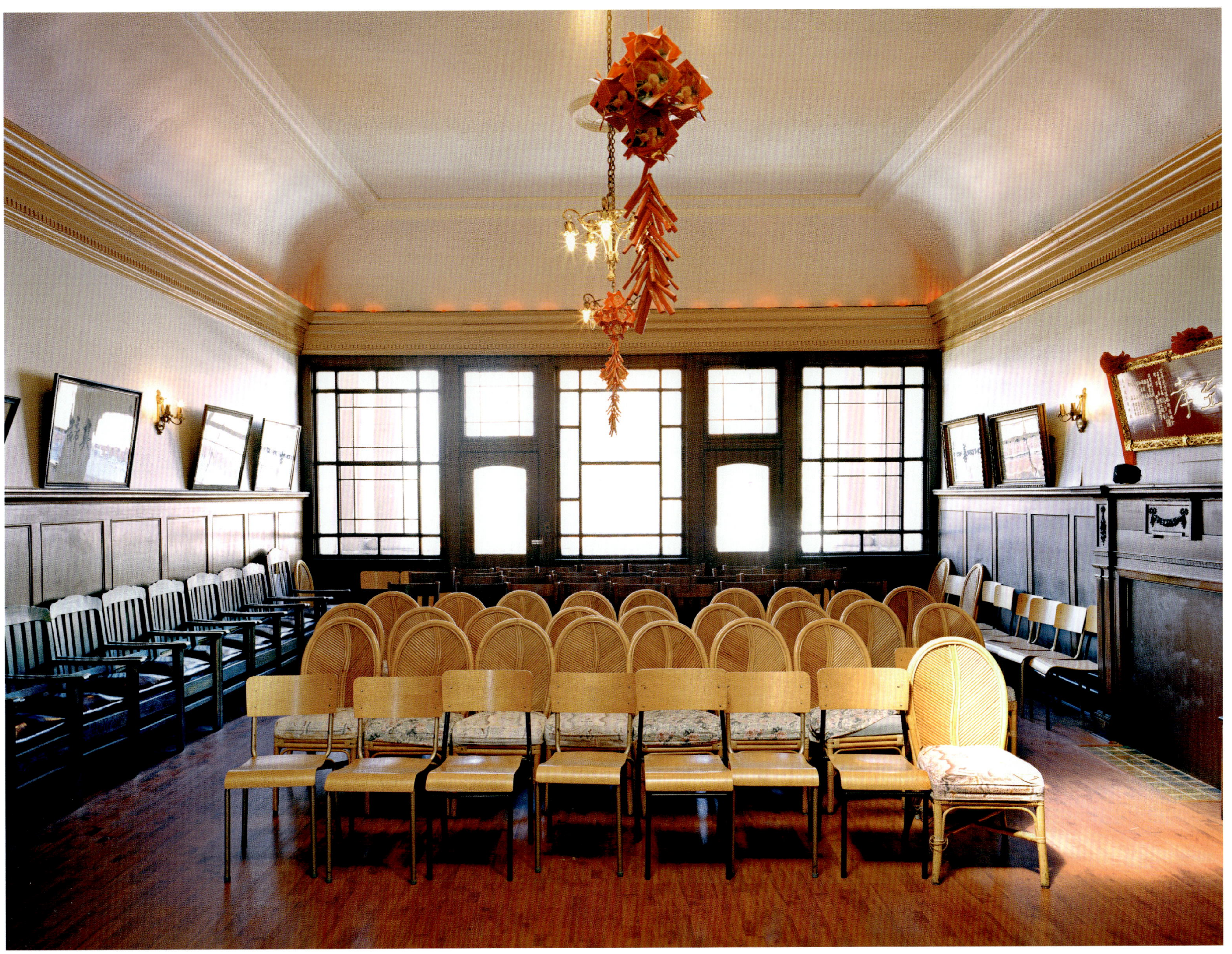

Chin Wing Chun Society, Vancouver, 2014 (diptych)

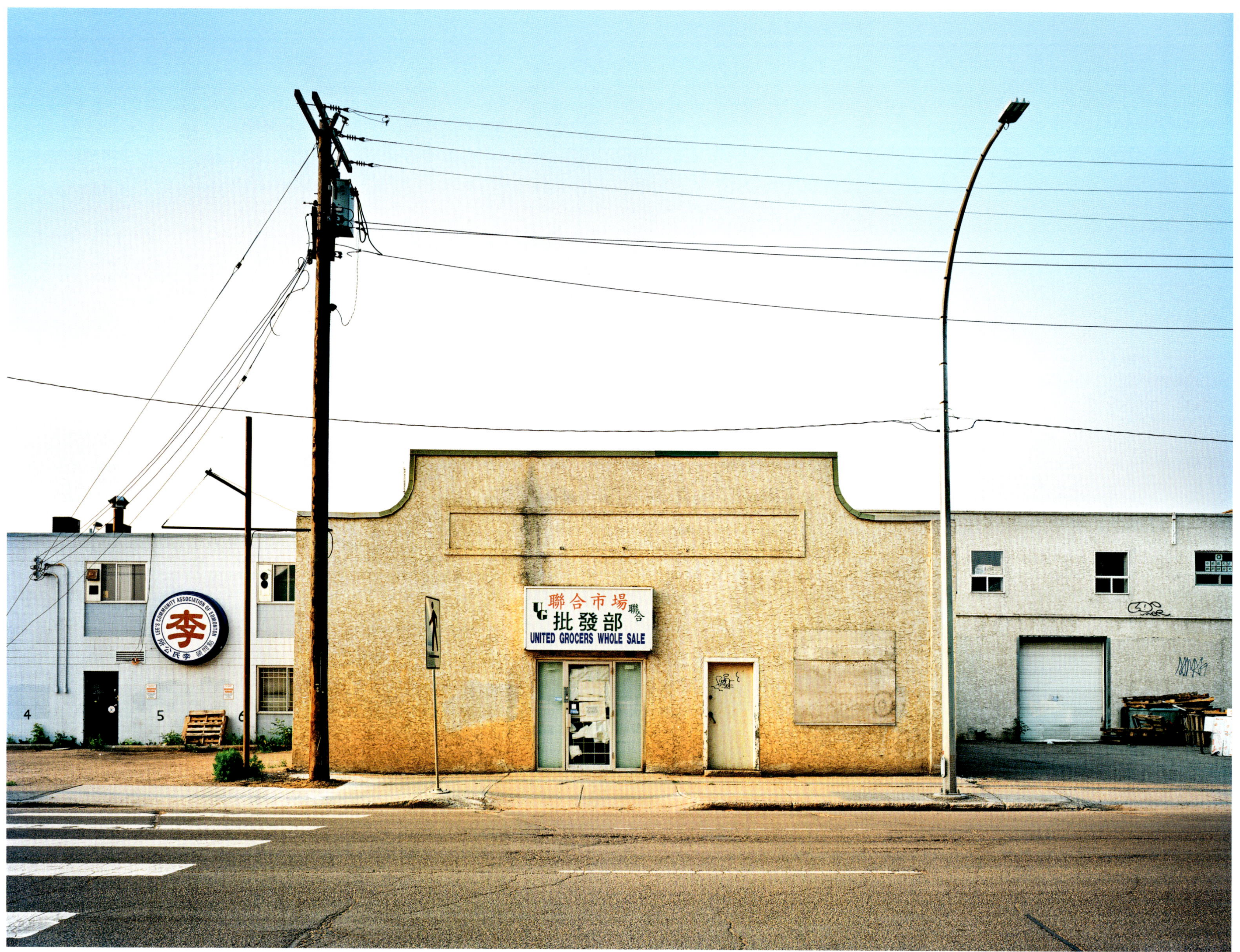

United Grocers Whole Sale, Edmonton, 2015

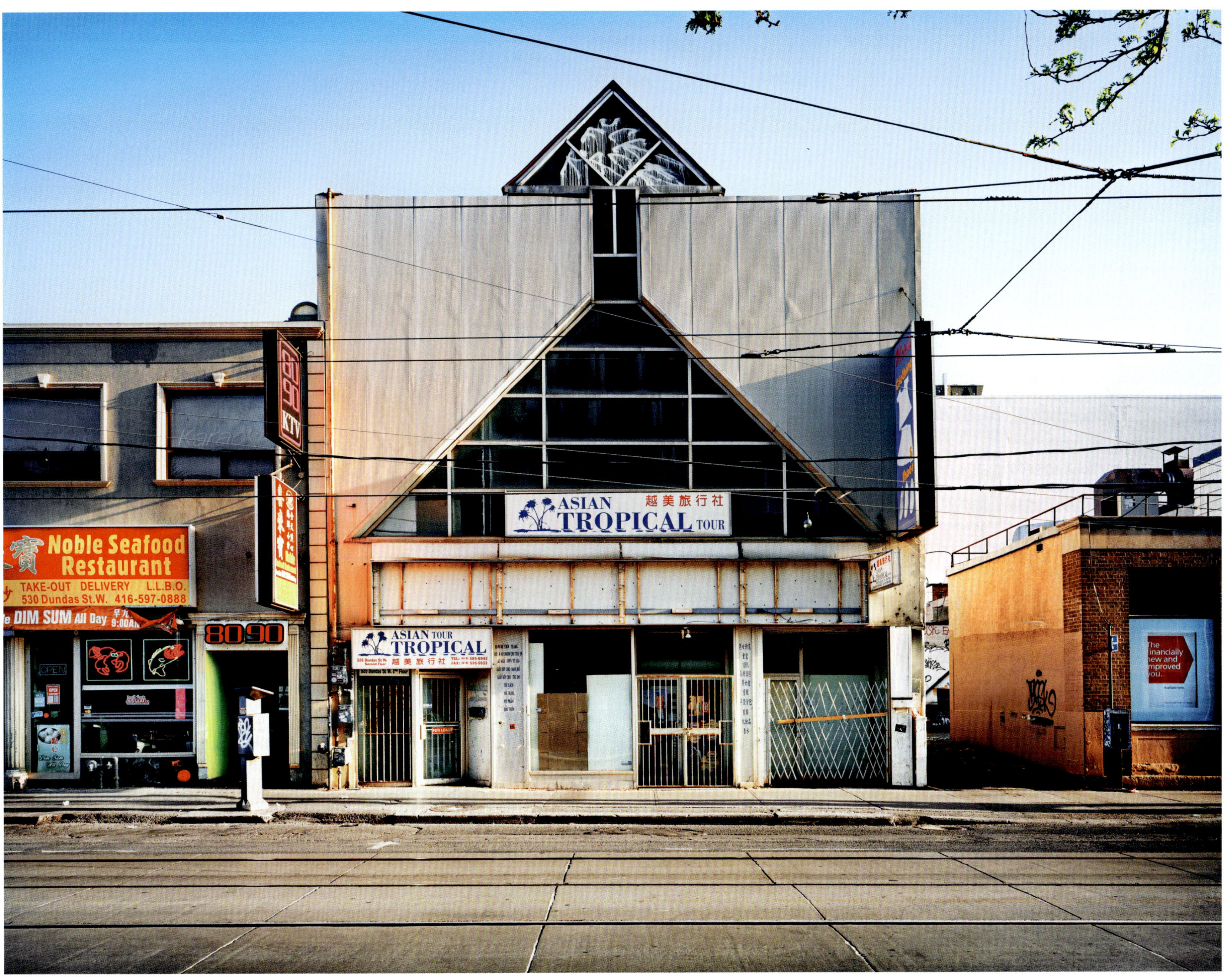

Asian Tropical Tour, Toronto West Chinatown, 2015

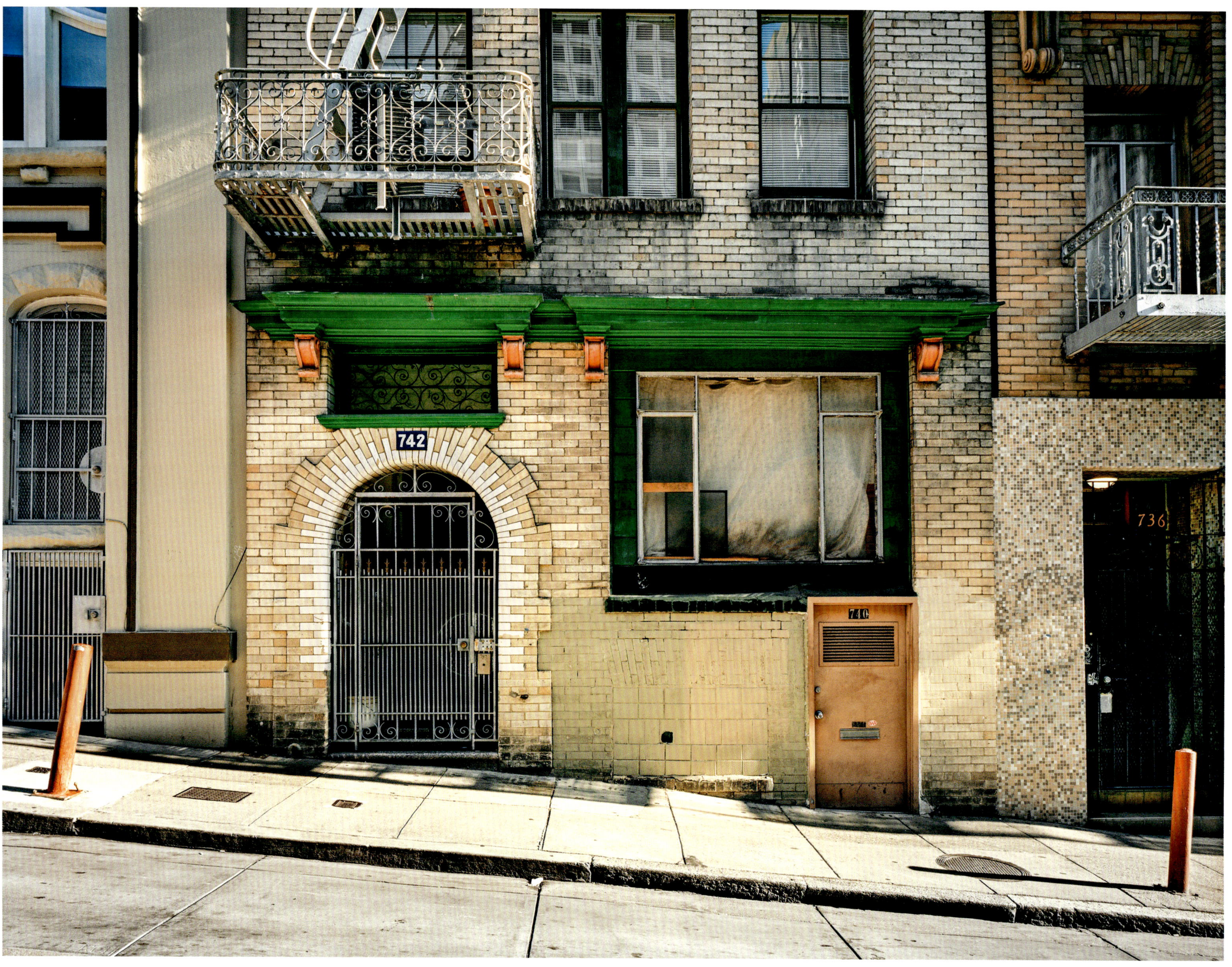

742 Commercial Street, San Francisco, 2017

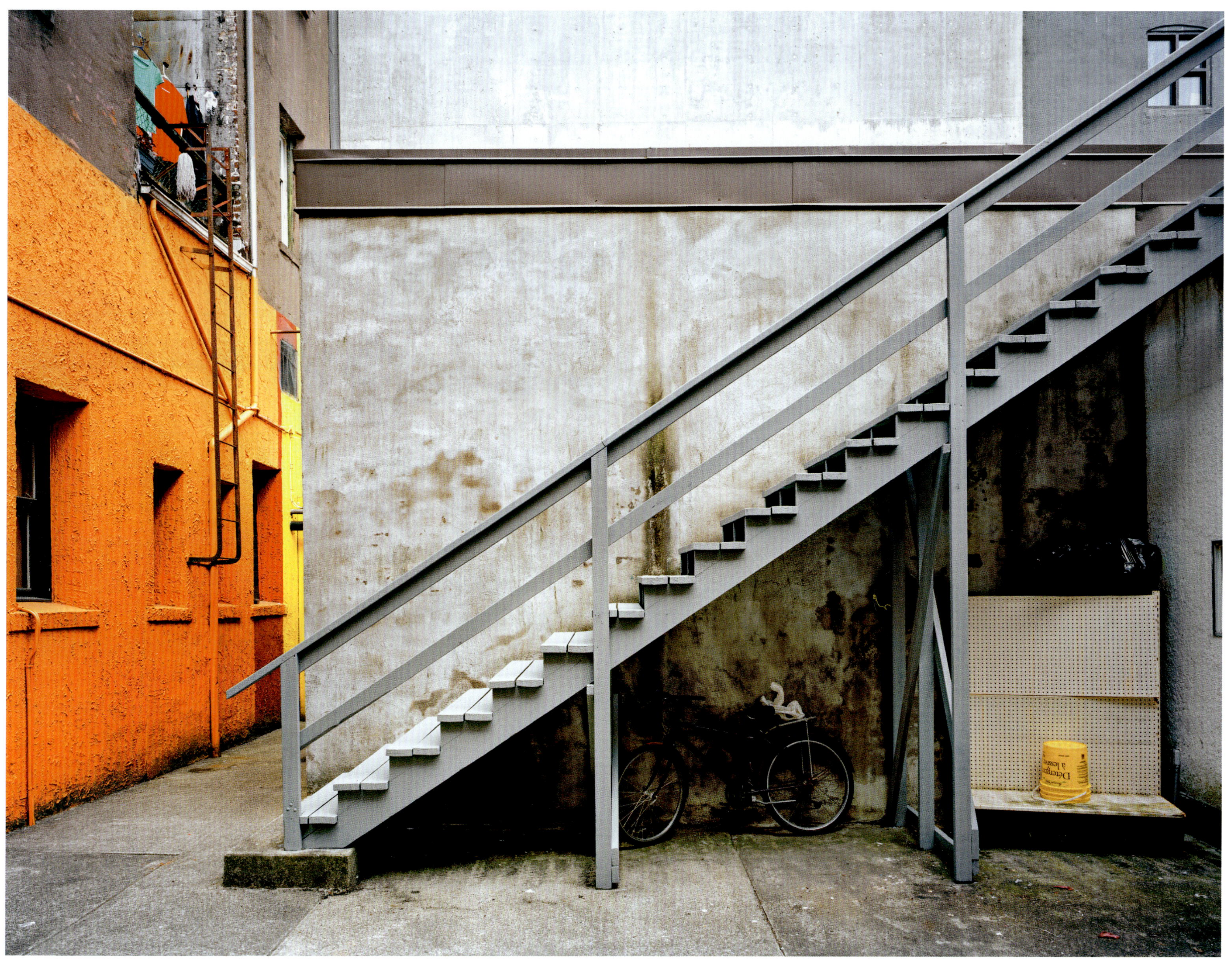

Courtyard Between East Pender Street, Market Alley, Carrall Street, Columbia Street (East View, Staircase), Vancouver, 2013

Lim Sai Hor Kow Mock Benevolent Association (Altar Space), Vancouver, 2014

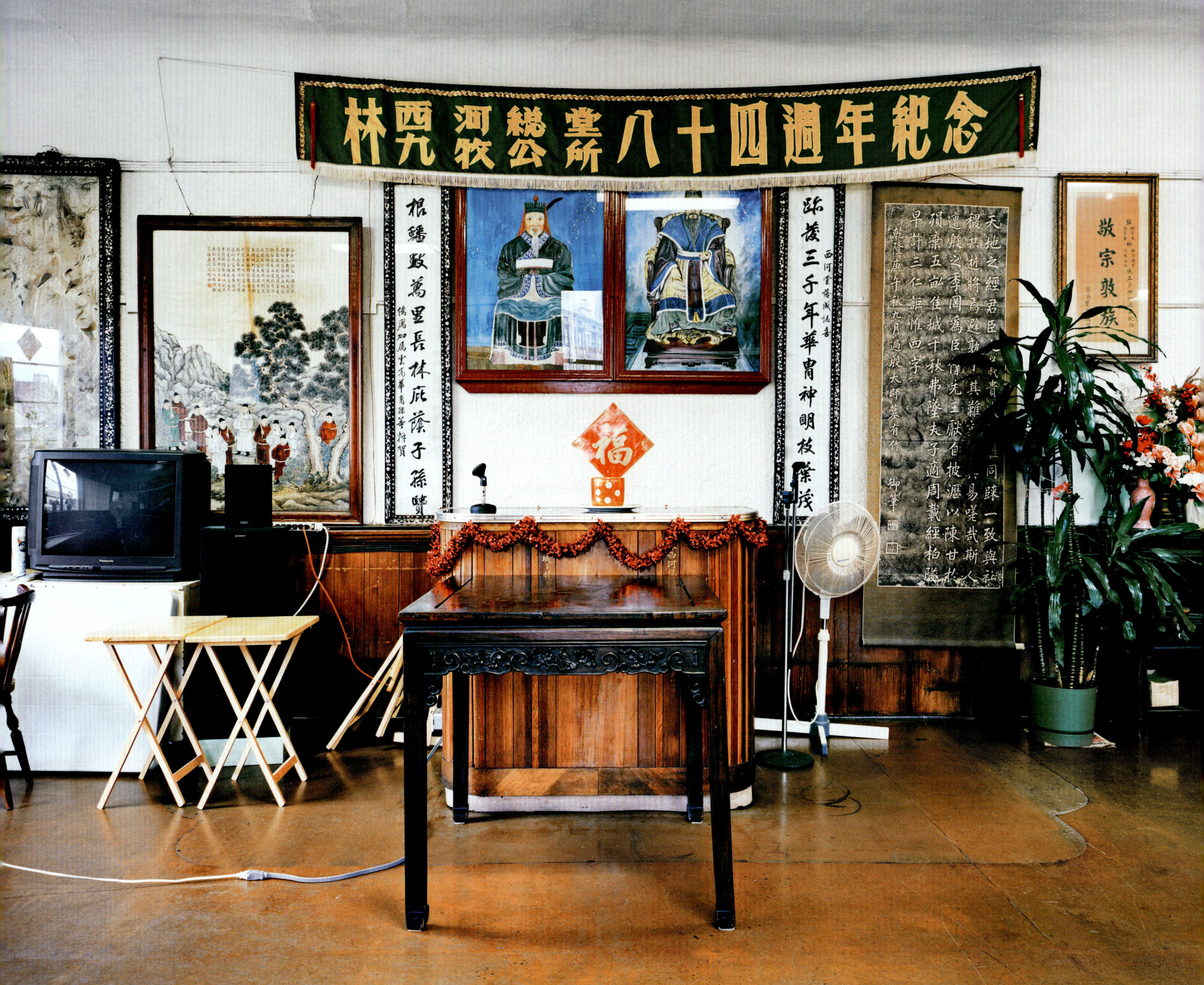

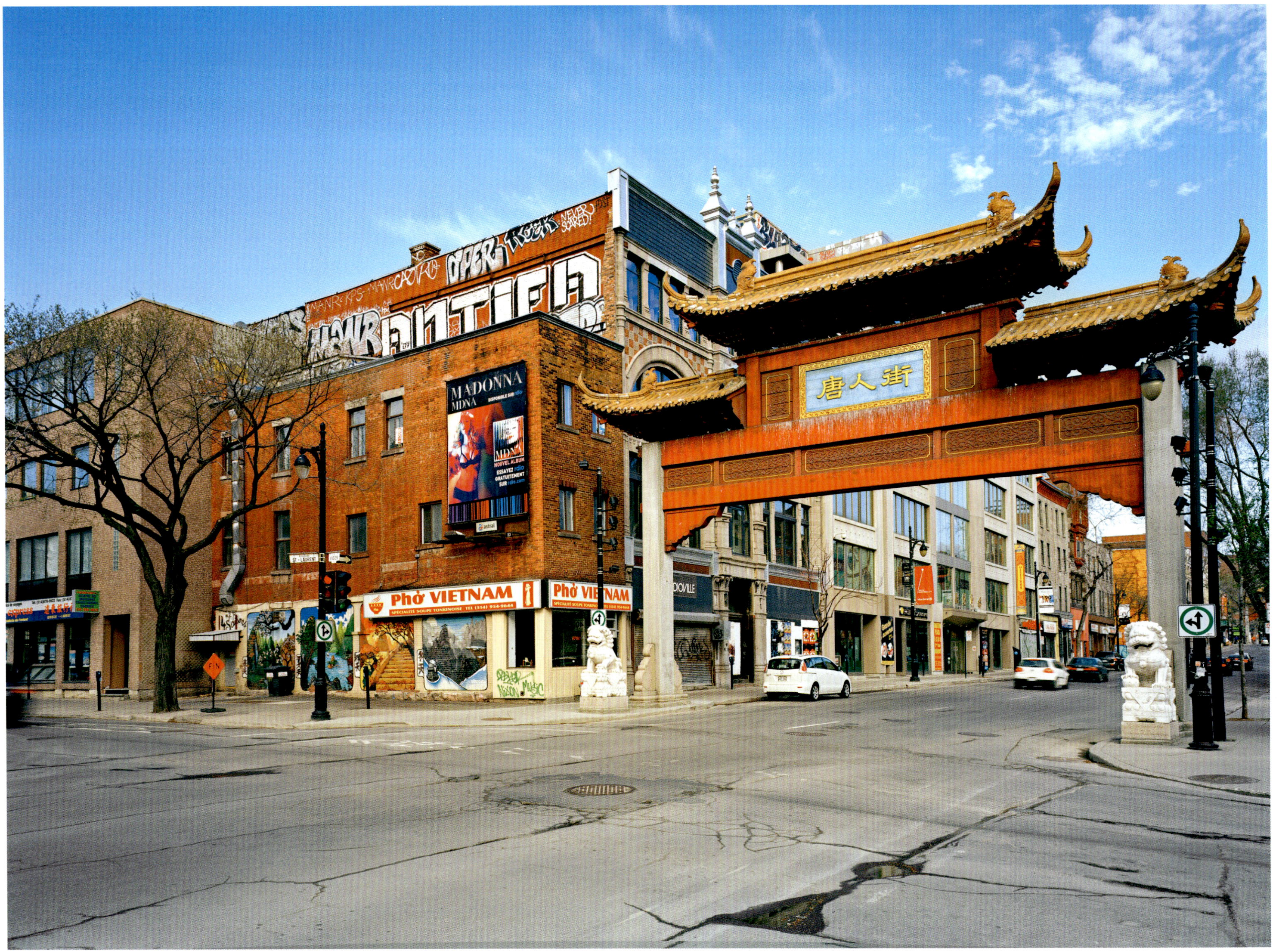

唐人街
MADONNA
MDNA
Phở VIETNAM
SPÉCIALITÉ SOUPE TONKINOISE

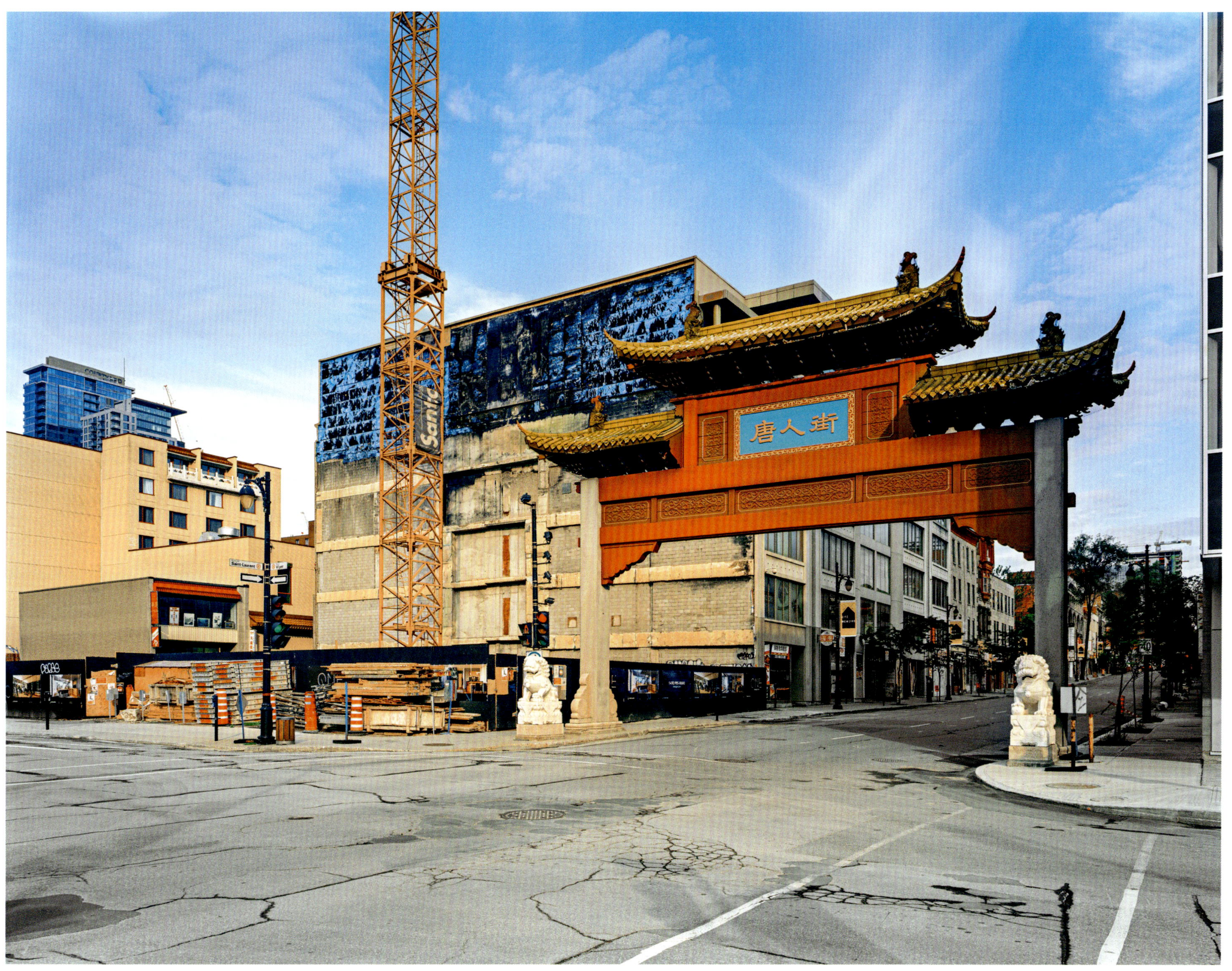

Chinatown South Paifang, Montreal, 2013, 2021 (diptych)

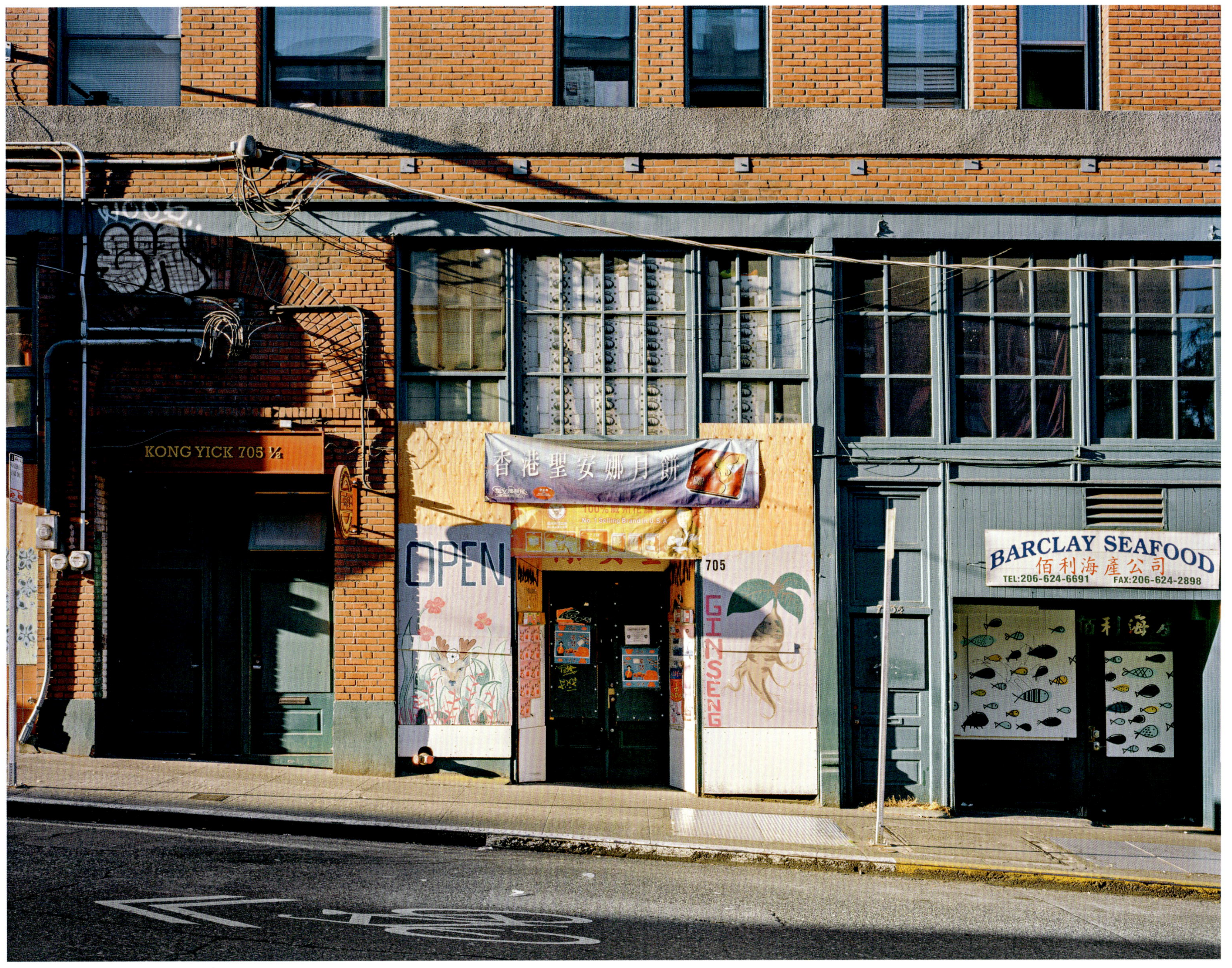

Bao An Tang Herb and Grocery Store, Seattle Chinatown–International District, 2022

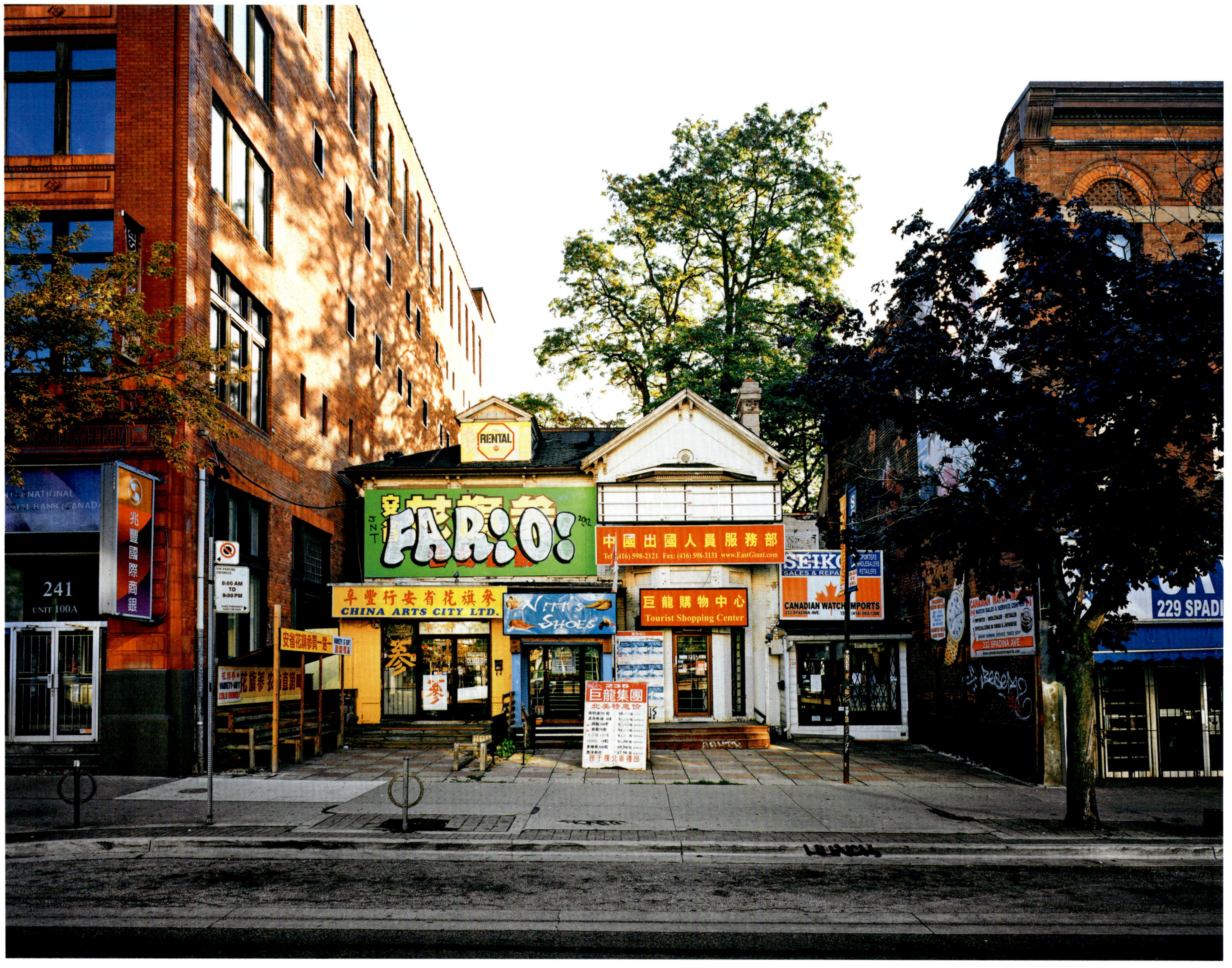

233–235 Spadina Avenue, Toronto West Chinatown, 2012, 2013, 2016 (triptych)

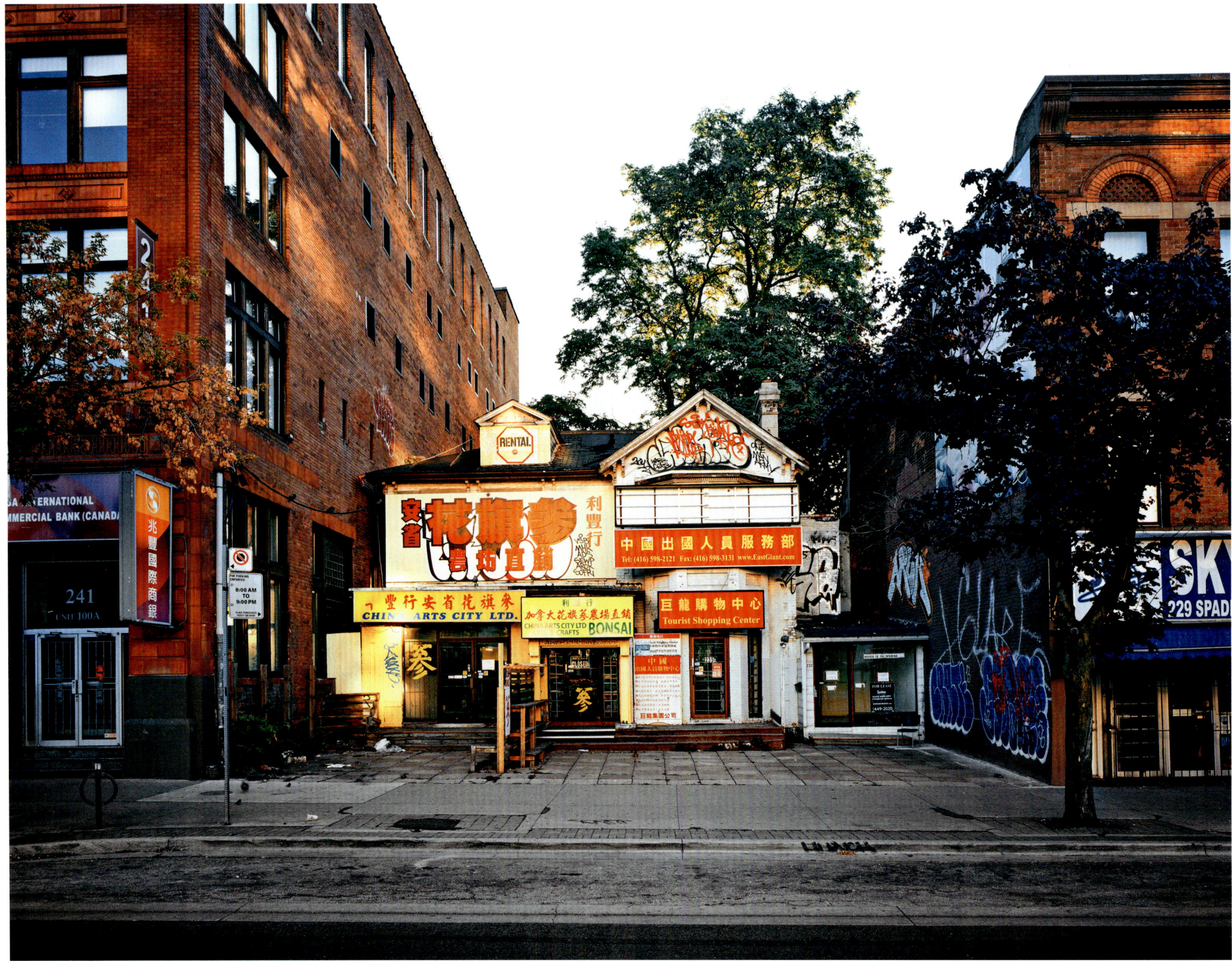
RENTAL
安省 花旗參 利豐行
豐坊直銷
中國出國人員服務部
Tel: (416) 598-2121 Fax: (416) 598-3131 www.EastGiant.com
丁 豐行安省花旗參
CHINA ARTS CITY LTD.
利豐行
加拿大花旗參農場直銷
CHINA ARTS CITY LTD
ARTS & CRAFTS BONSAI
巨龍購物中心
Tourist Shopping Center
中國
出國人員購物中心
巨龍集團公司
CLOSED
OPEN
FOR LEASE
449-2020
GA INTERNATIONAL
MMERCIAL BANK (CANADA)
兆豐國際商銀
241
UNIT 100A
NO PARKING
8:00 AM
TO
9:00 PM
SKY
229 SPAD

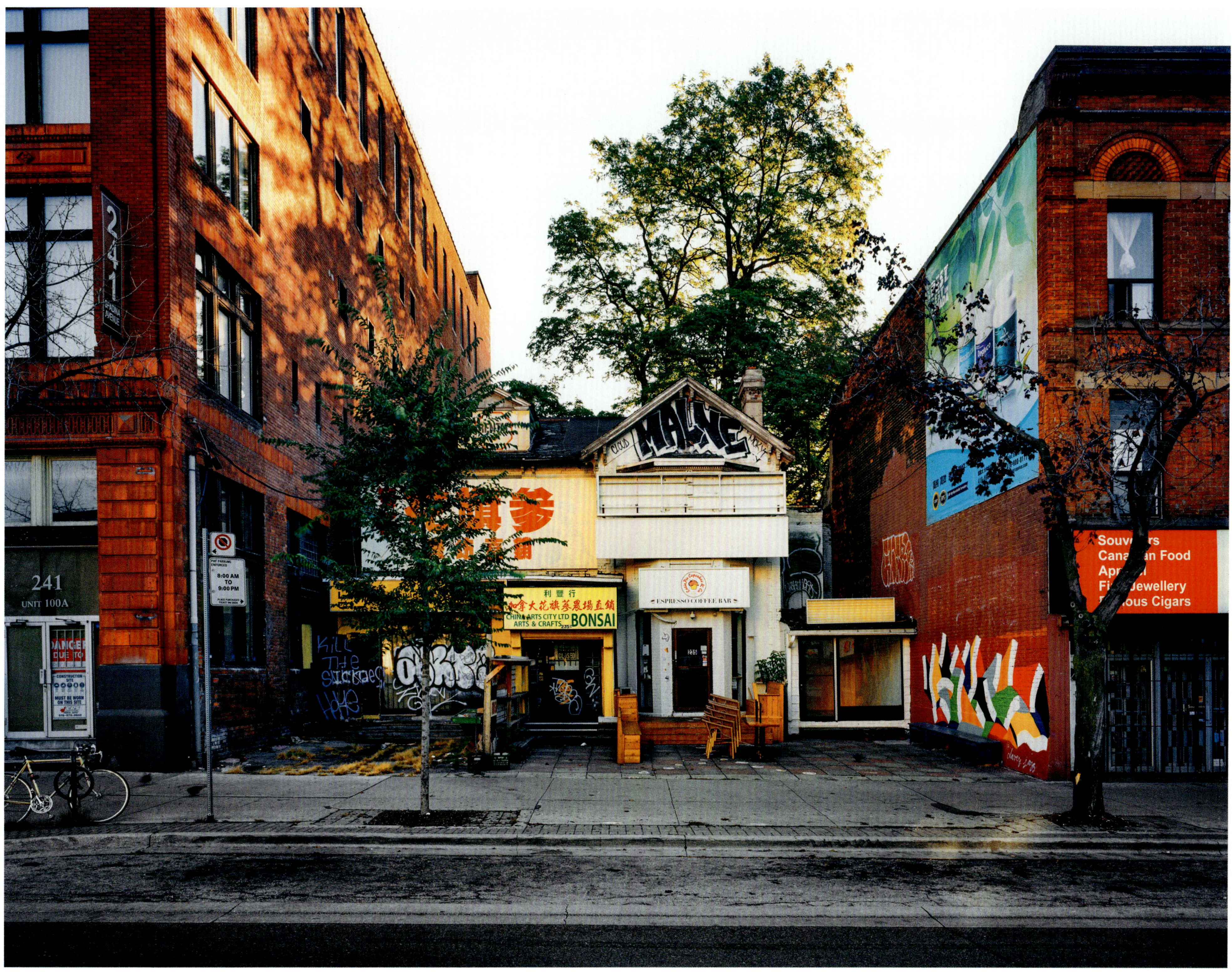
241
241
UNIT 100A
MALNE
CHINA ARTS CITY LTD
ARTS & CRAFTS
BONSAI
ESPRESSO COFFEE BAR
Souvenirs
Canadian Food
Apparel
Fine Jewellery
Famous Cigars

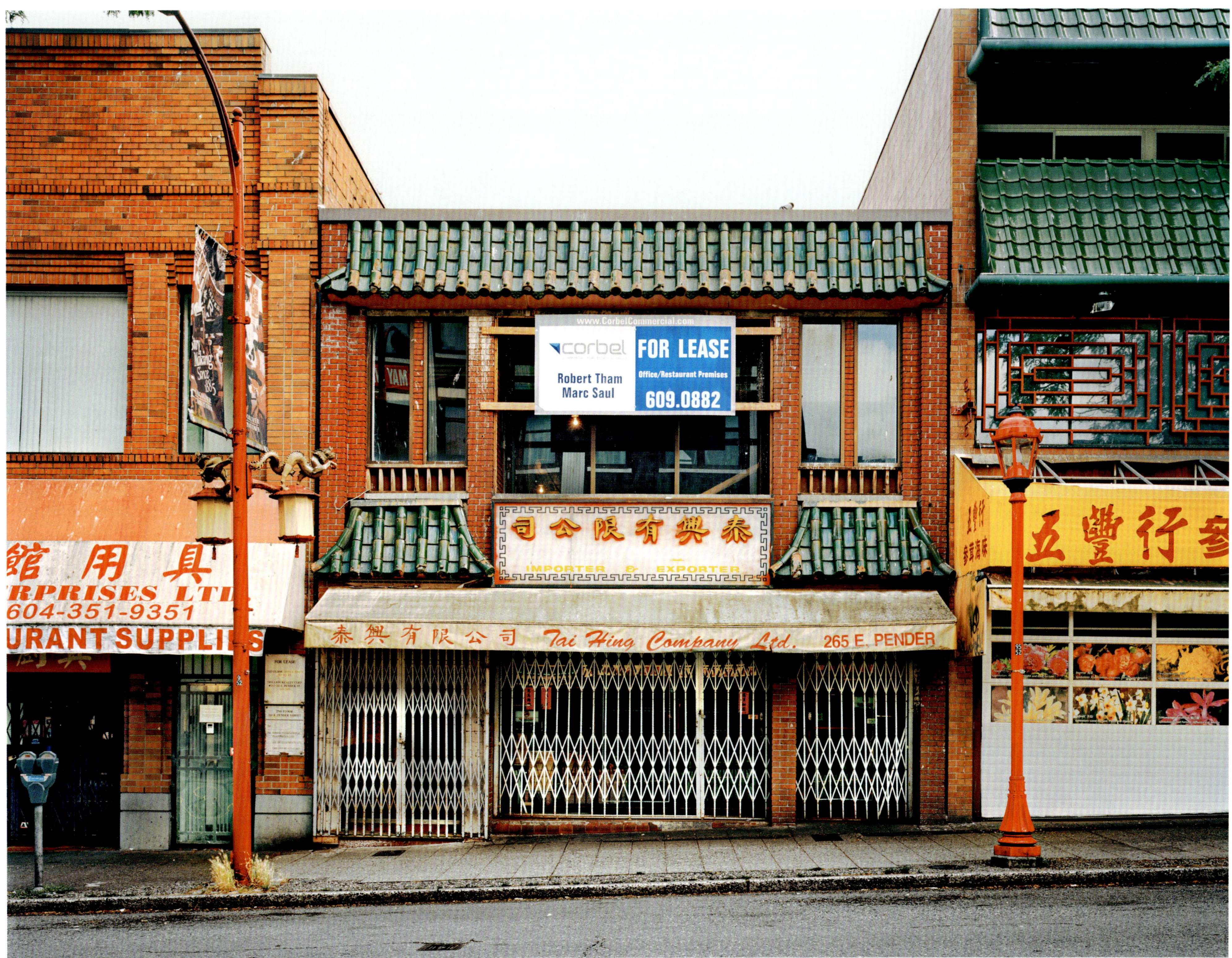

Tai Hing Company Ltd., Vancouver, 2013

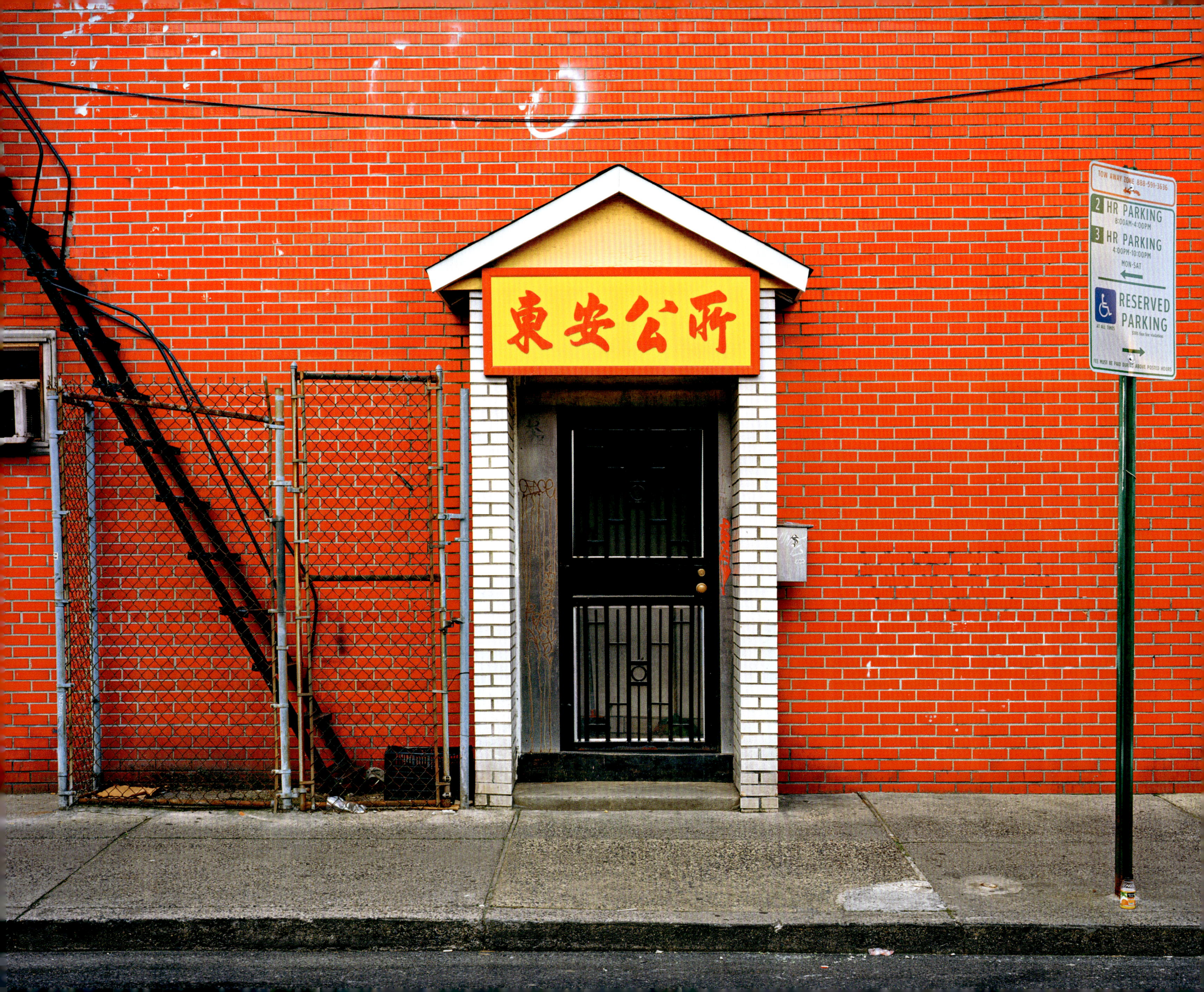
東安公所
TOW AWAY ZONE 888-591-3636
2 HR PARKING
8:00AM-4:00PM
3 HR PARKING
4:00PM-10:00PM
MON-SAT
RESERVED PARKING
AT ALL TIMES
$301 fine for violations
FEE MUST BE PAID DURING ABOVE POSTED HOURS

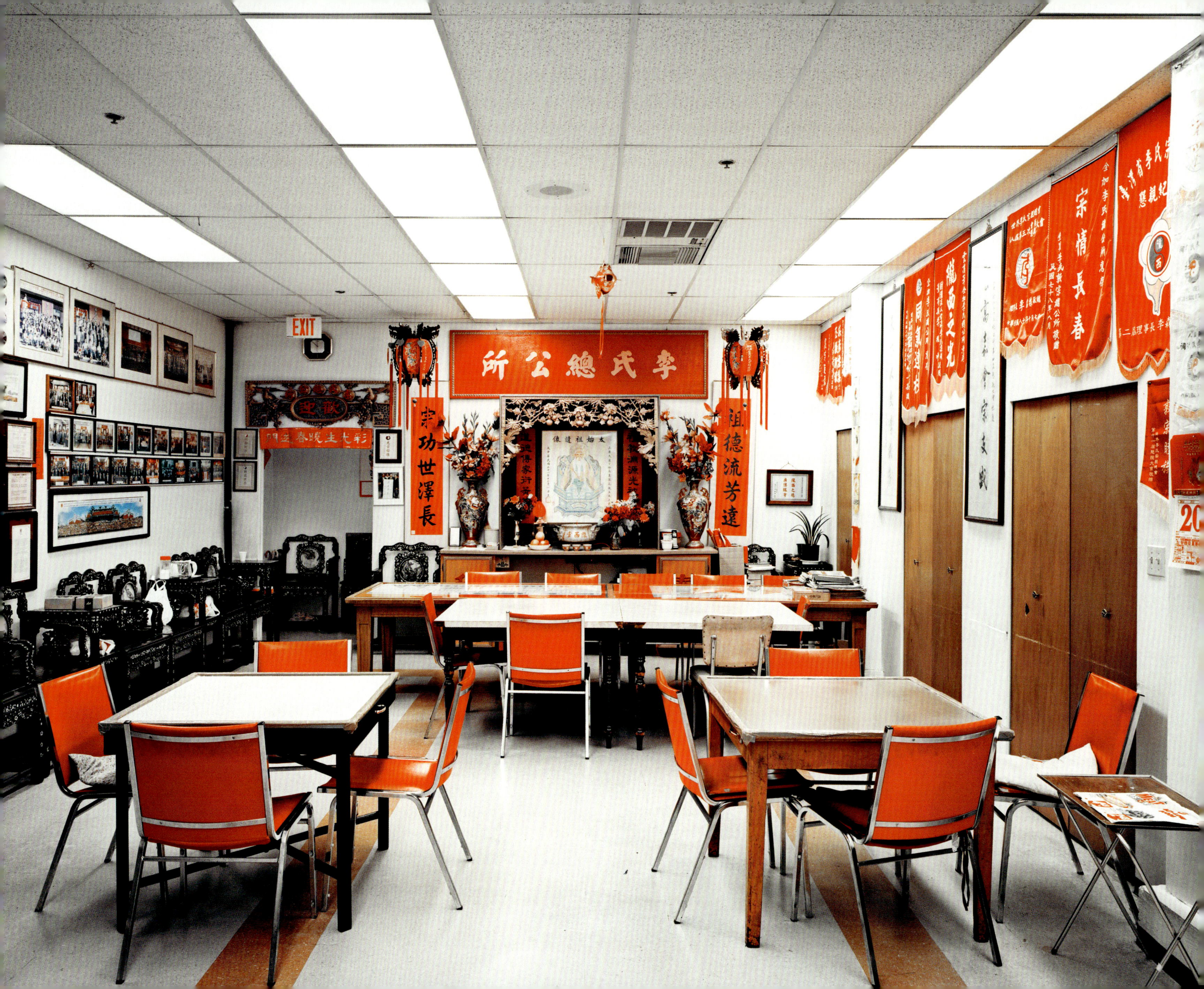

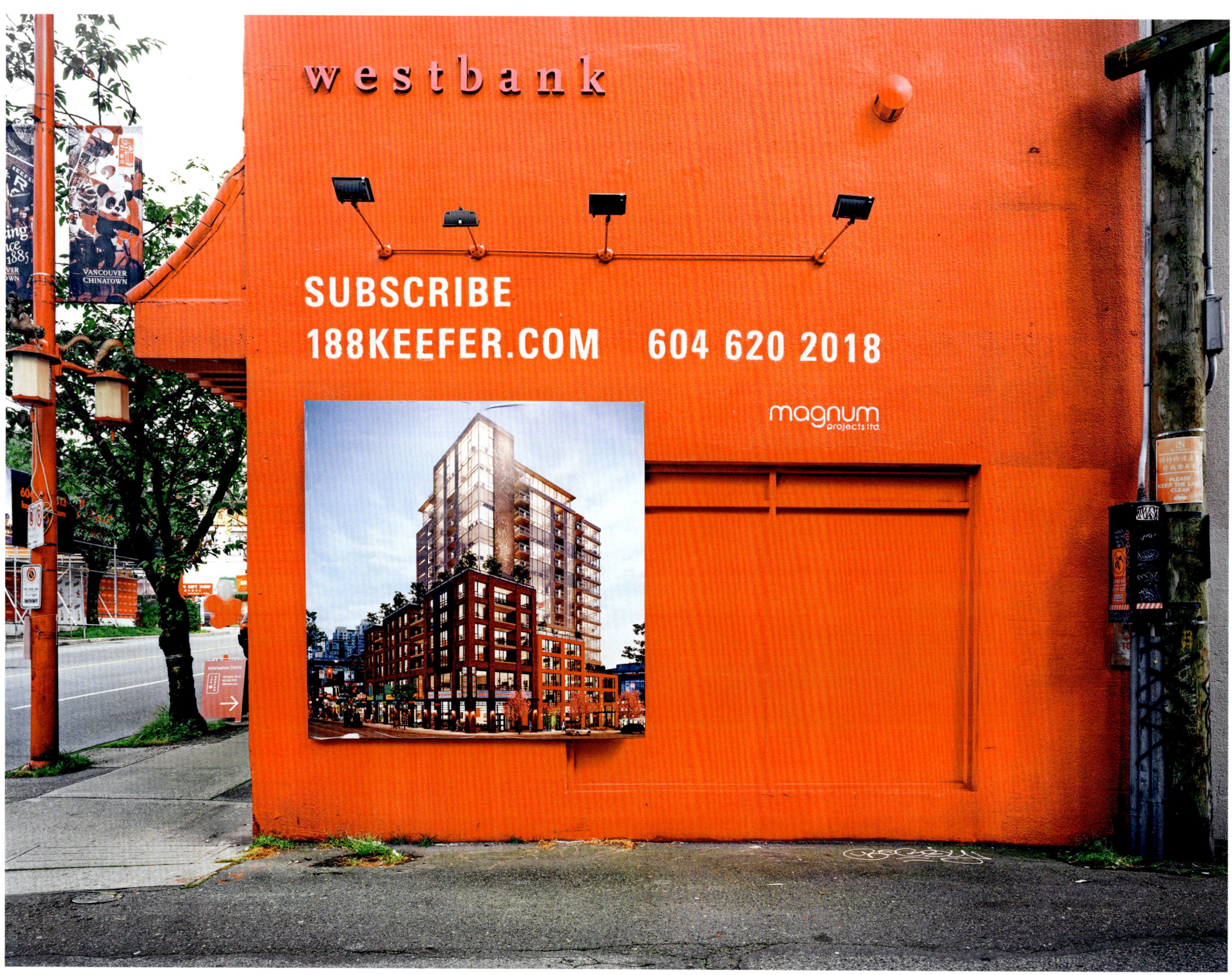

188 Keefer Street, Vancouver, 2013

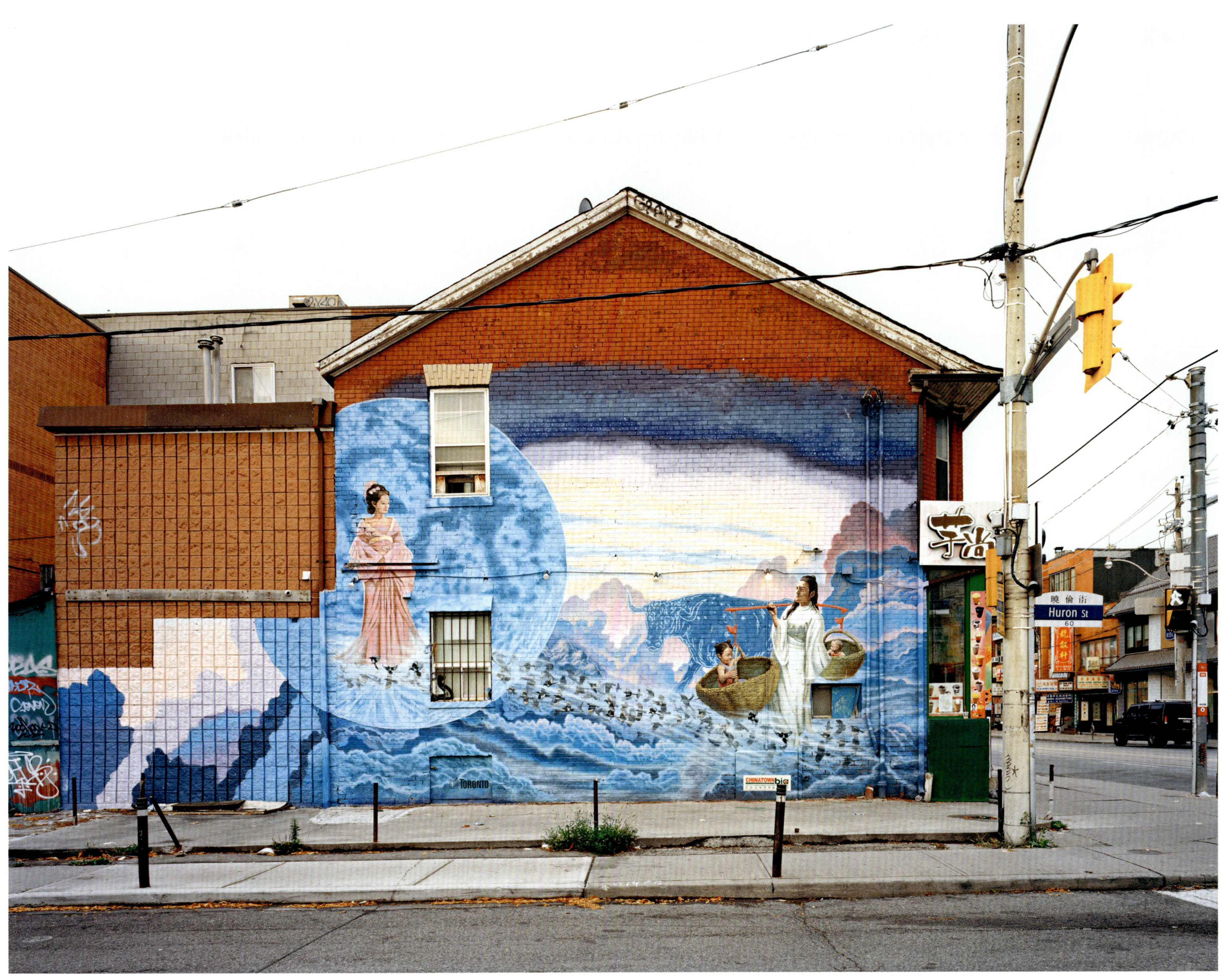

Milky Way Mural, Toronto West Chinatown, 2017 (designed and painted by Allan Bender, John Nobrega, Stacey Kinder; commissioned by Toronto Chinatown BIA)

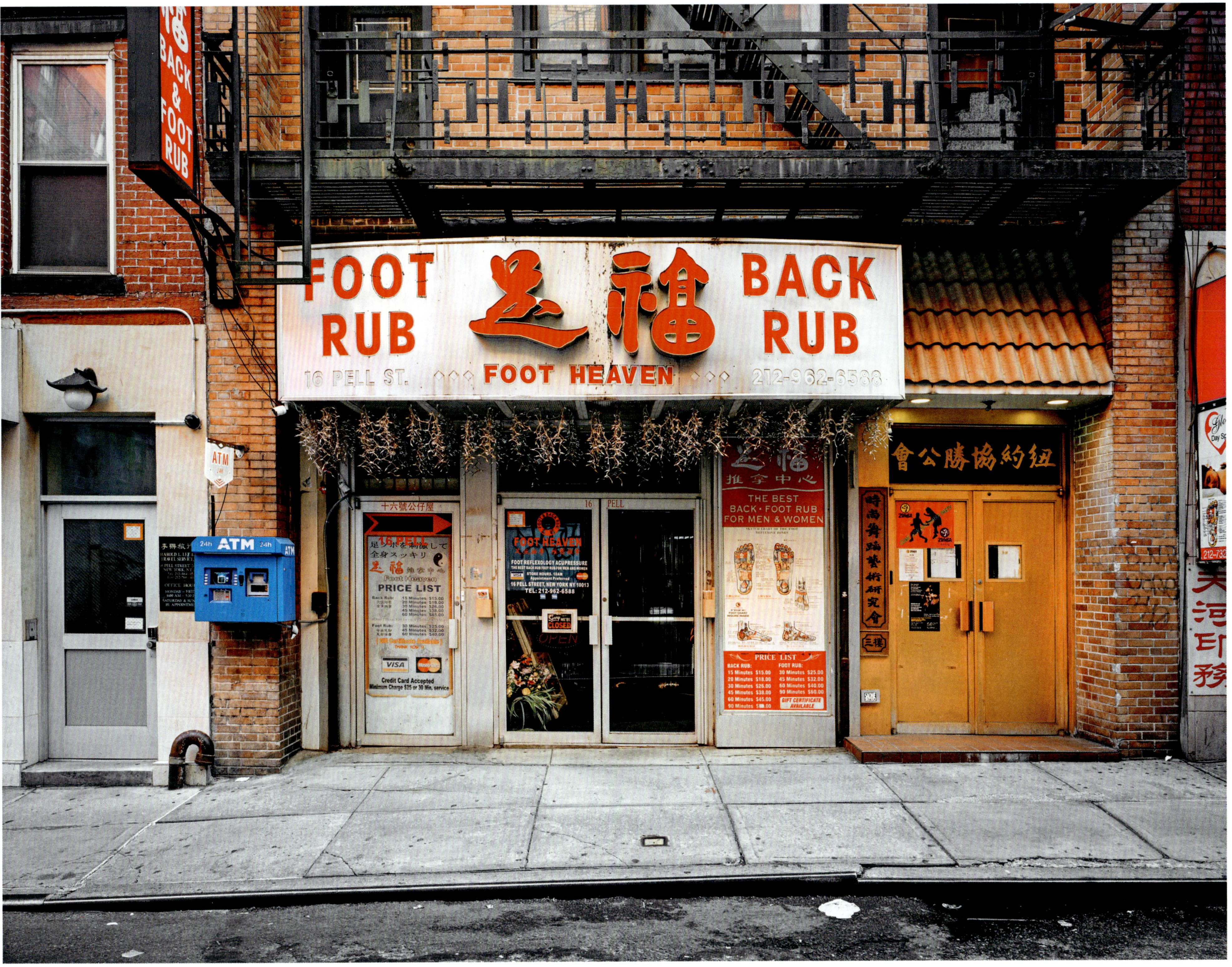

Foot Heaven, Manhattan, 2019

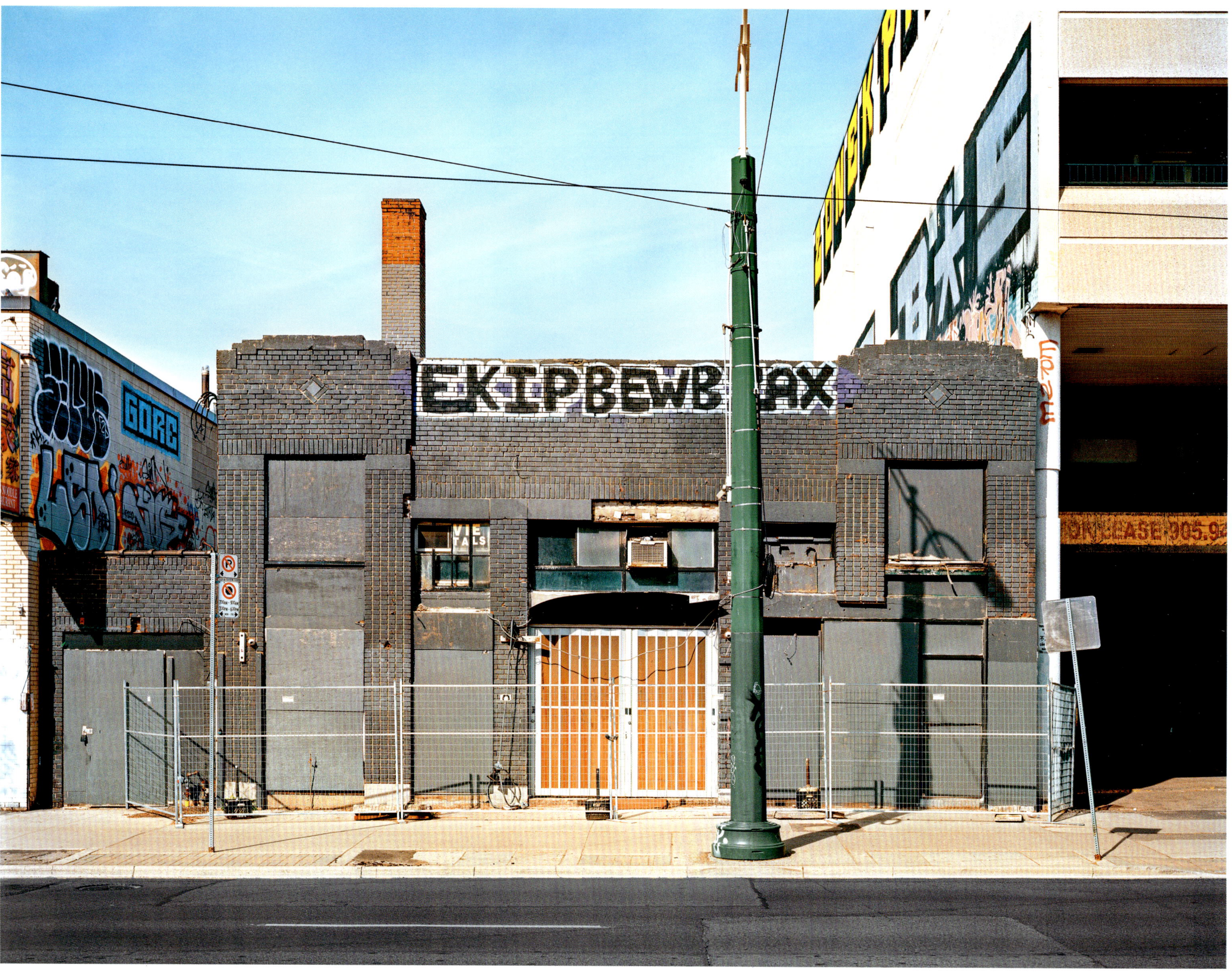

GORE
EKIPBEWBLAX
ON LEASE 905.9

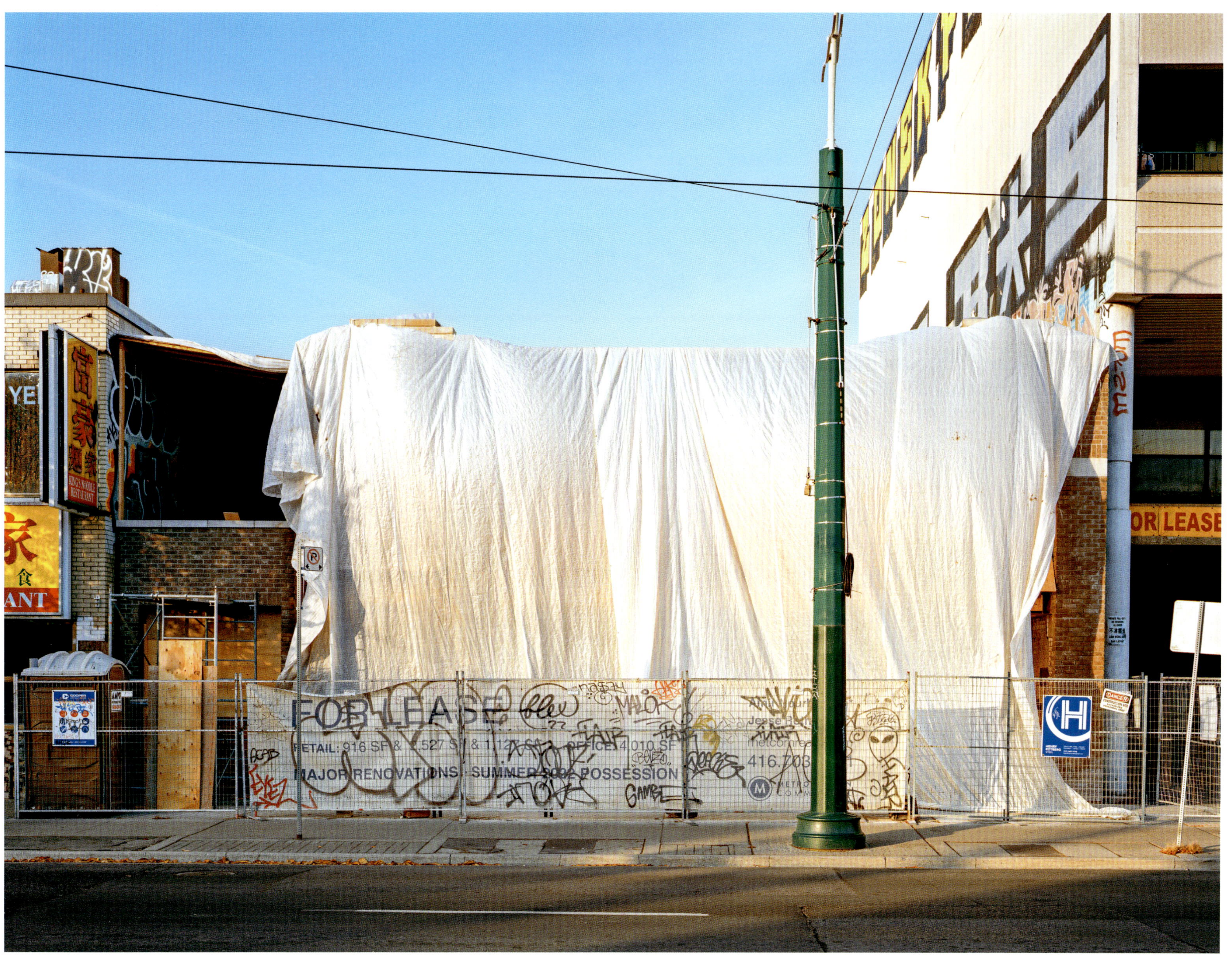

298 Spadina Avenue, Toronto West Chinatown, 2021, 2022 (diptych)

Fan Tan Alley, Victoria, 2013

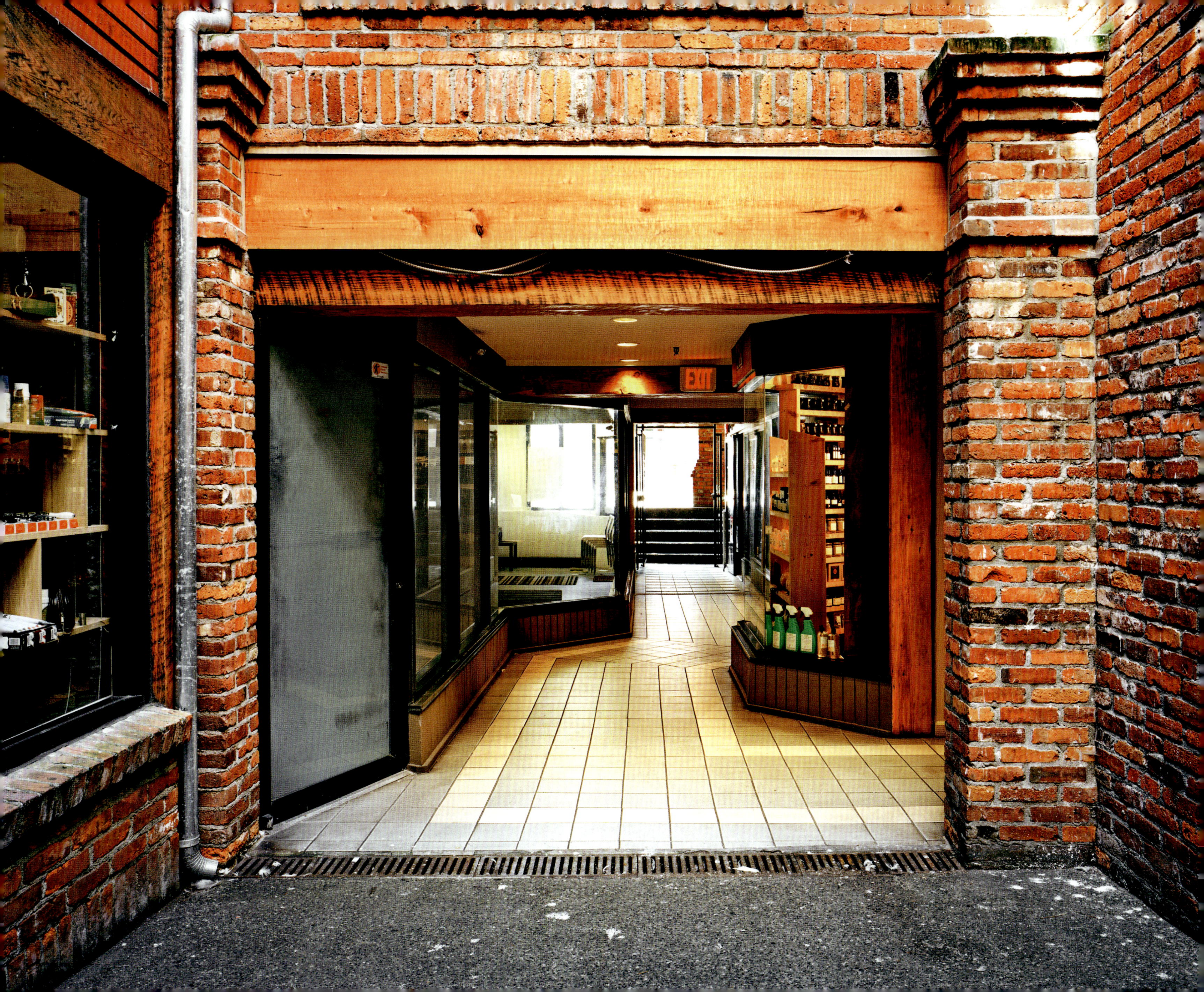

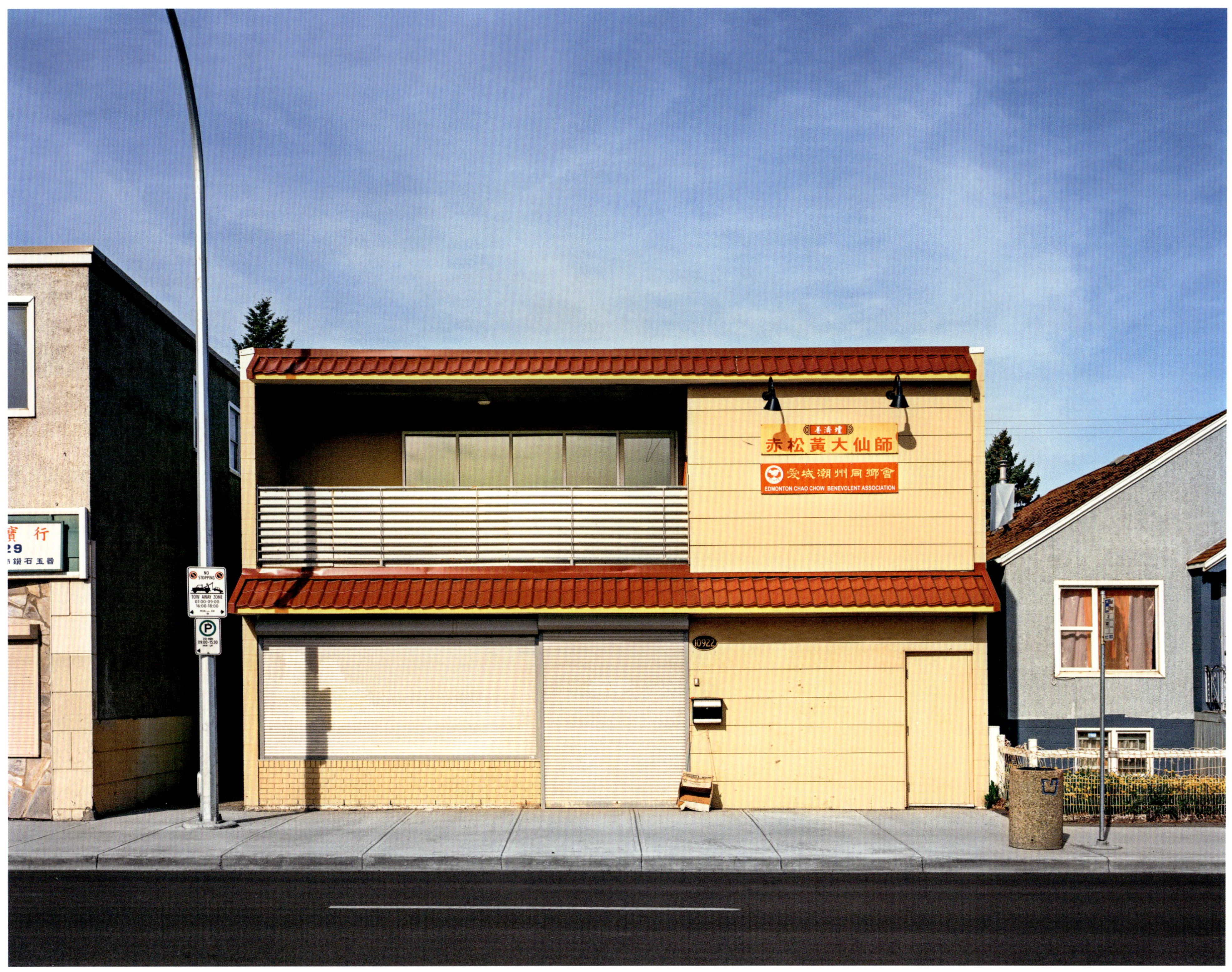

Edmonton Chao Chow Benevolent Association, Edmonton, 2015

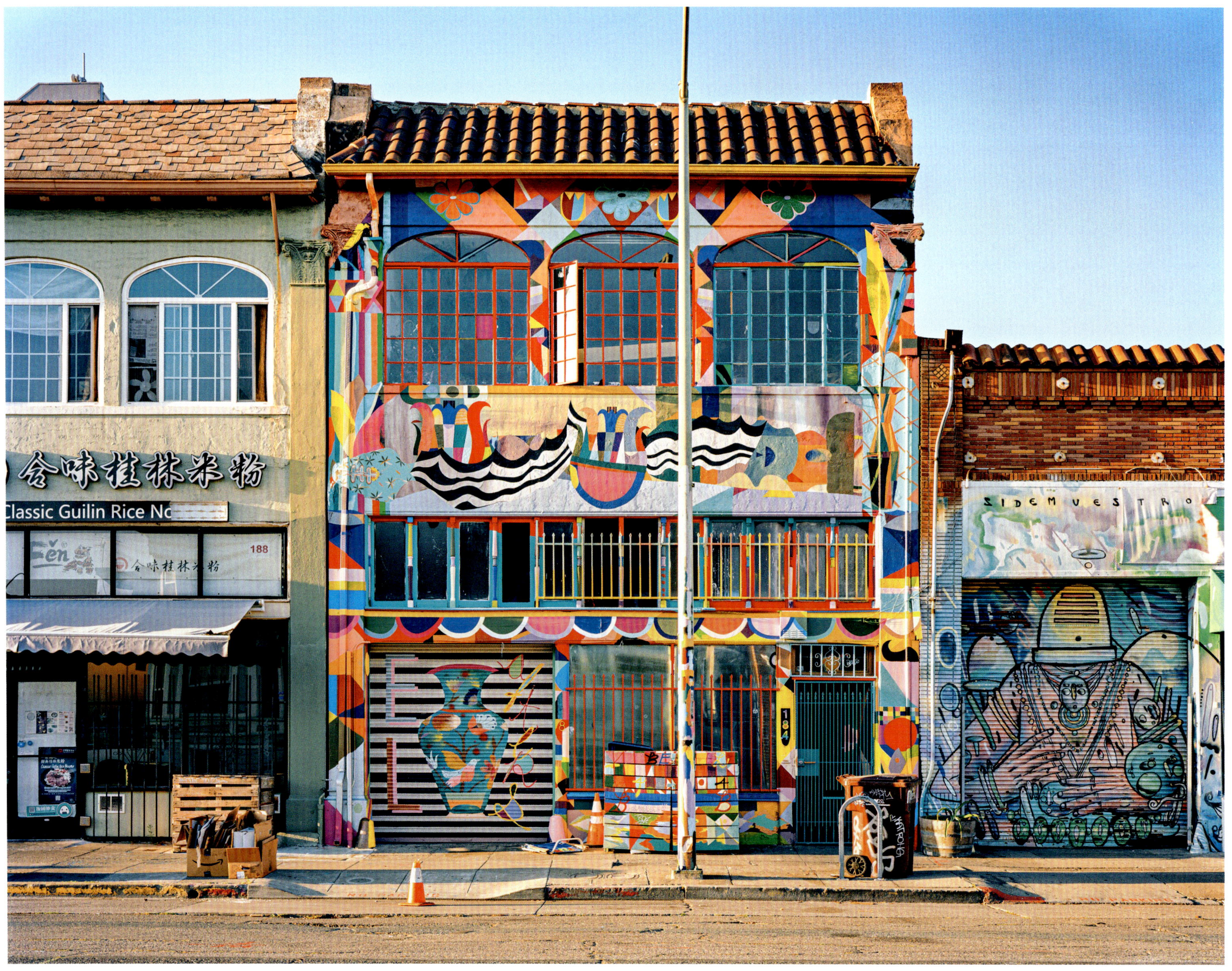

B4BEL4B Gallery, Oakland, 2023

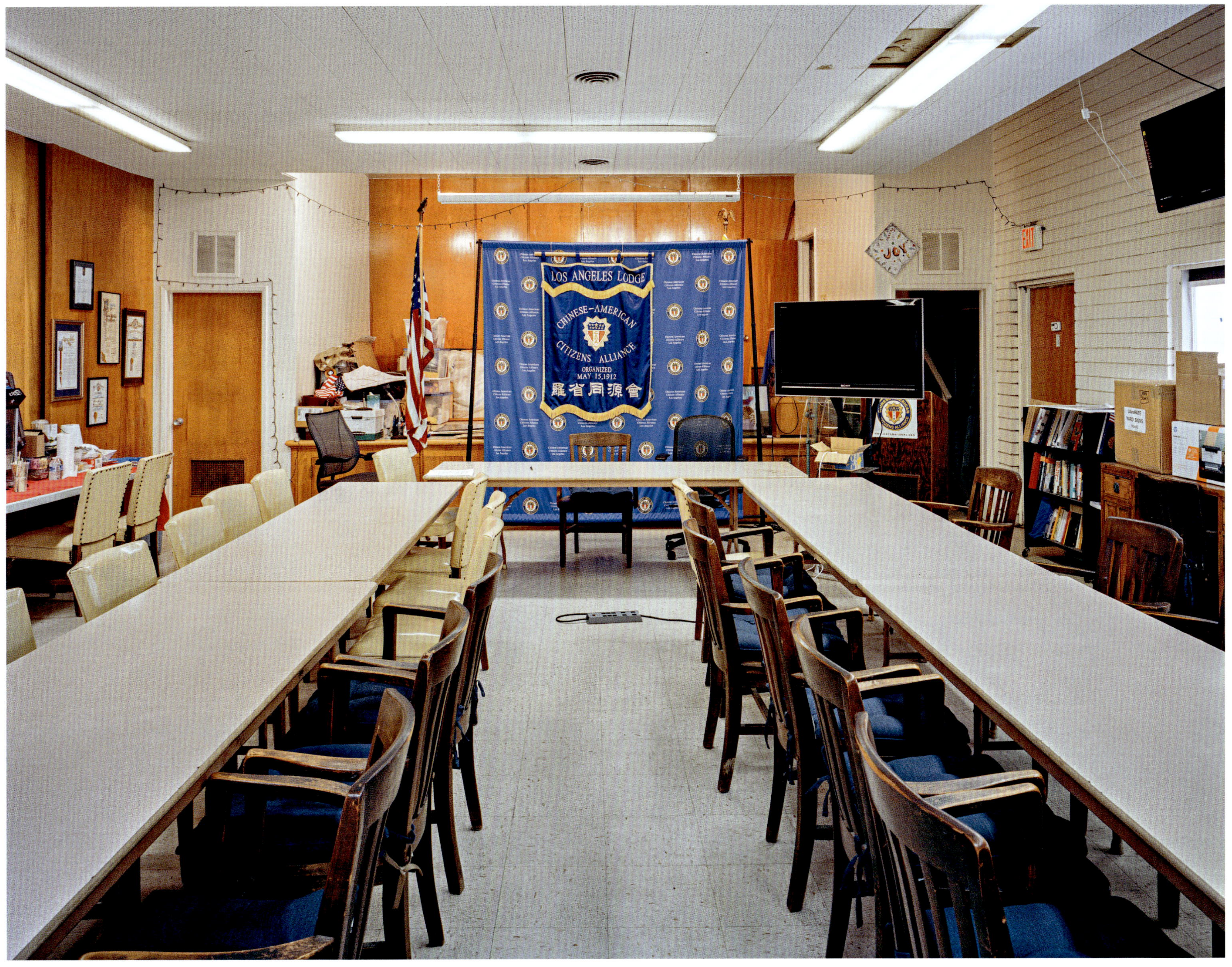

Chinese-American Citizens Alliance, Los Angeles, 2024

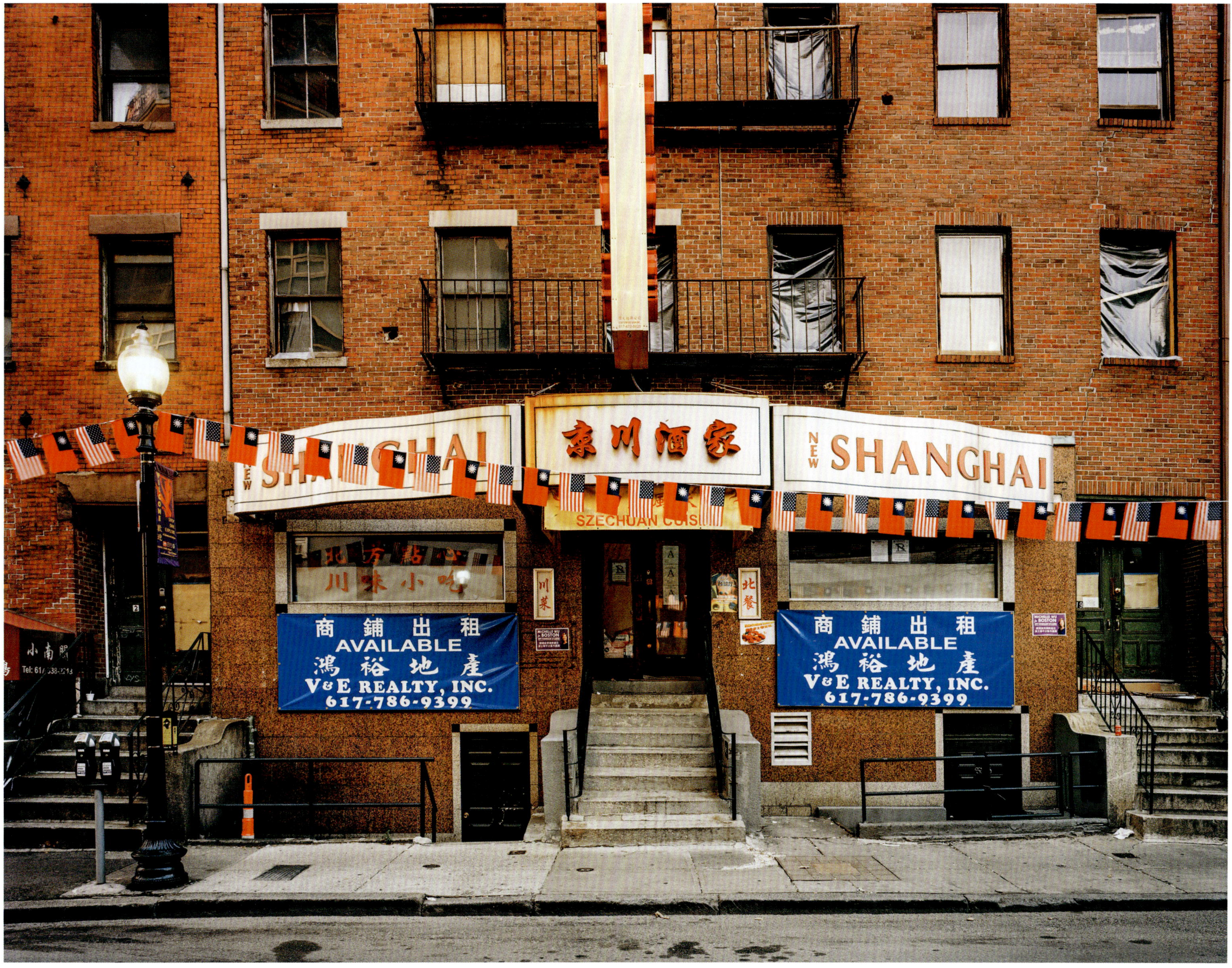

New Shanghai, Boston, 2019

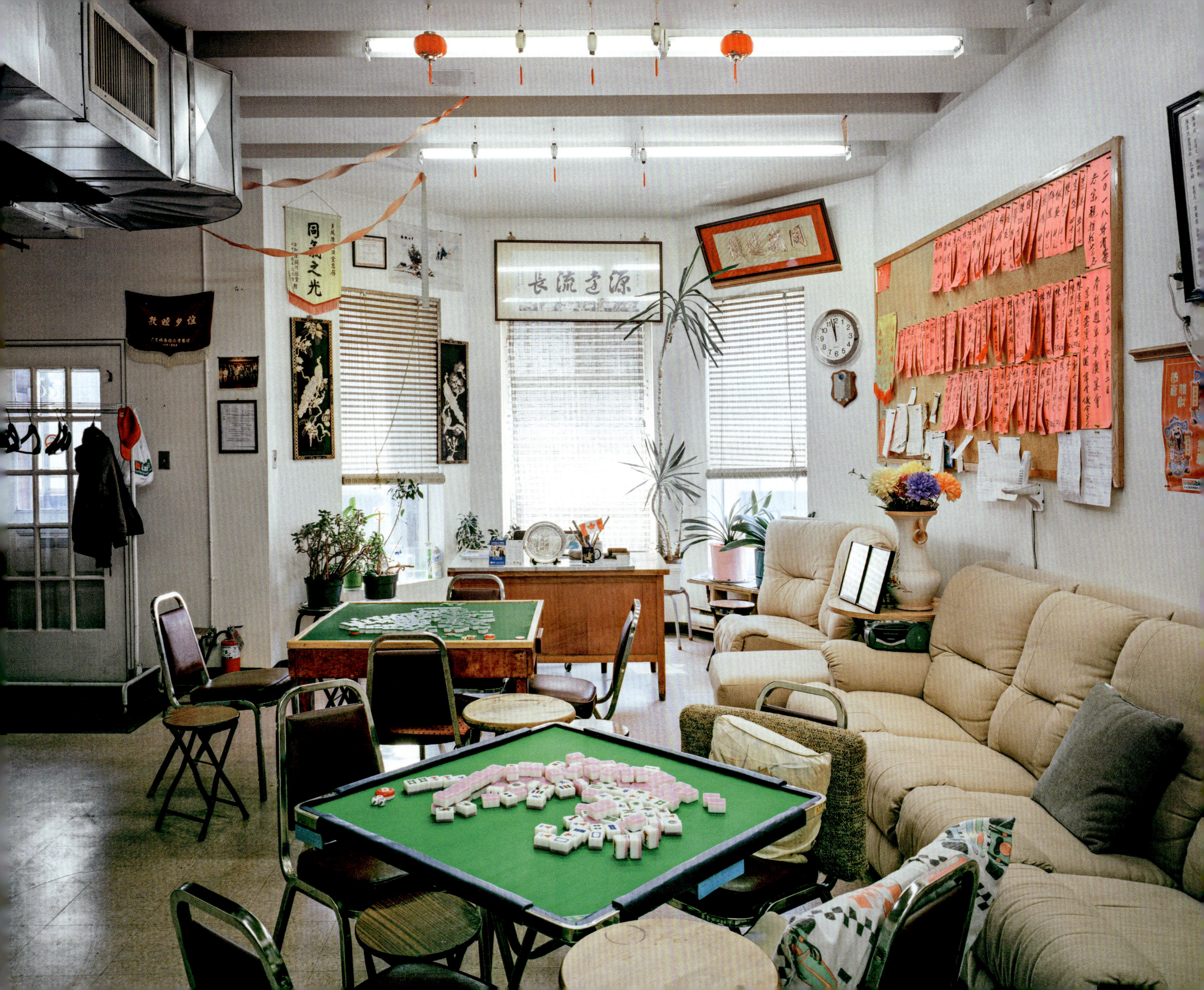

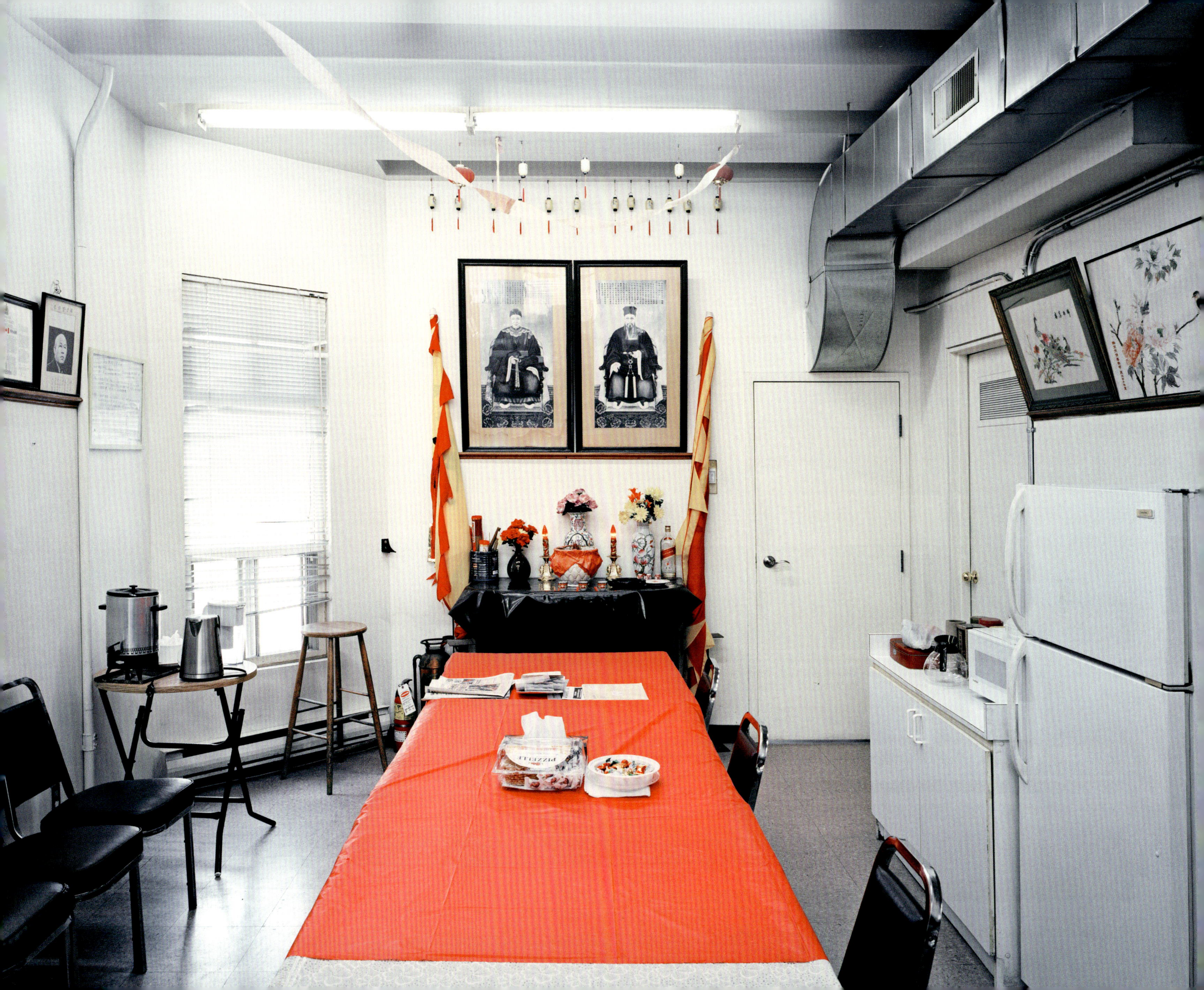

following spread
Yee Fung Toy Society of Canada, Vancouver, 2016, 2014 (diptych)

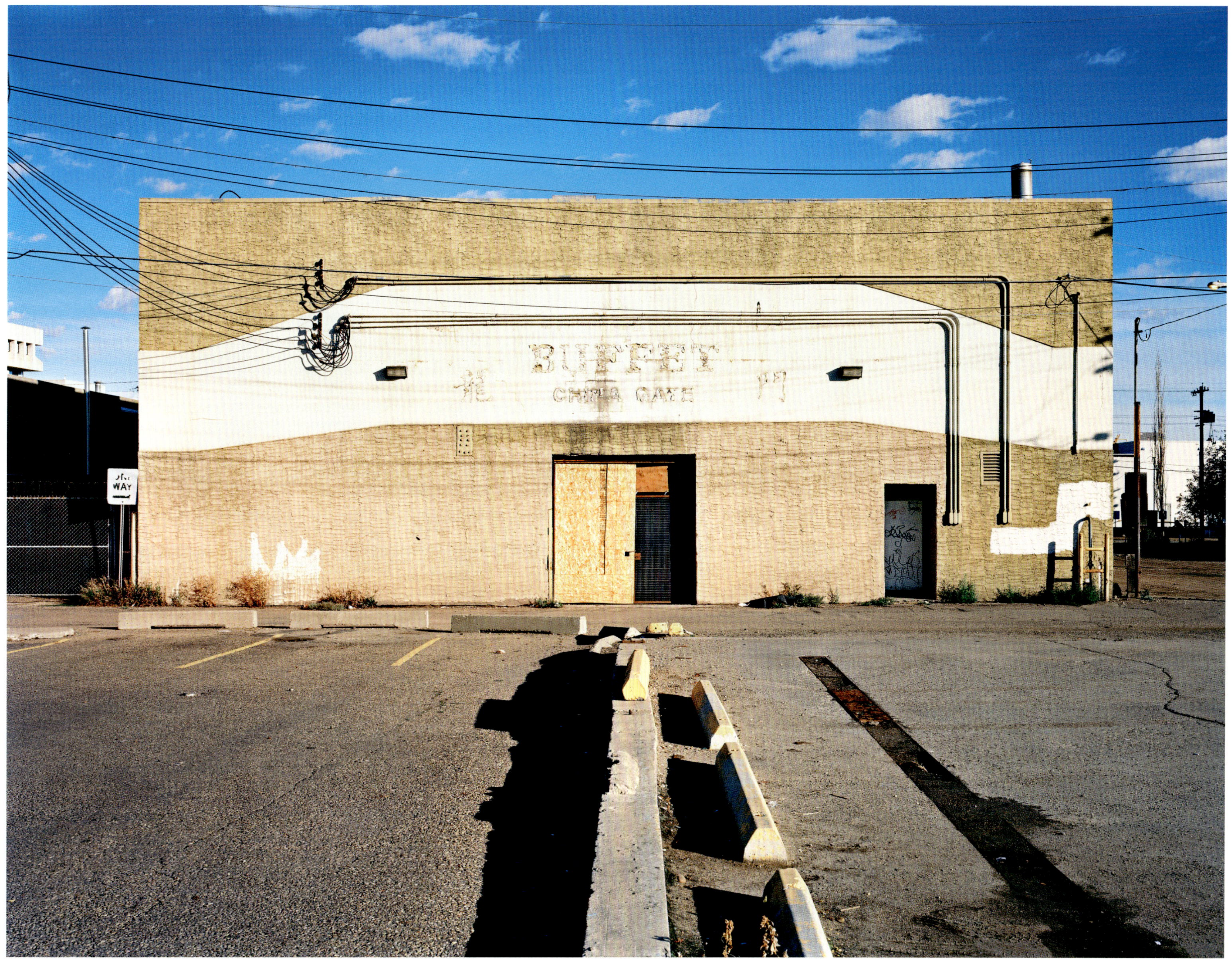

Buffet China Cafe, Edmonton, 2015

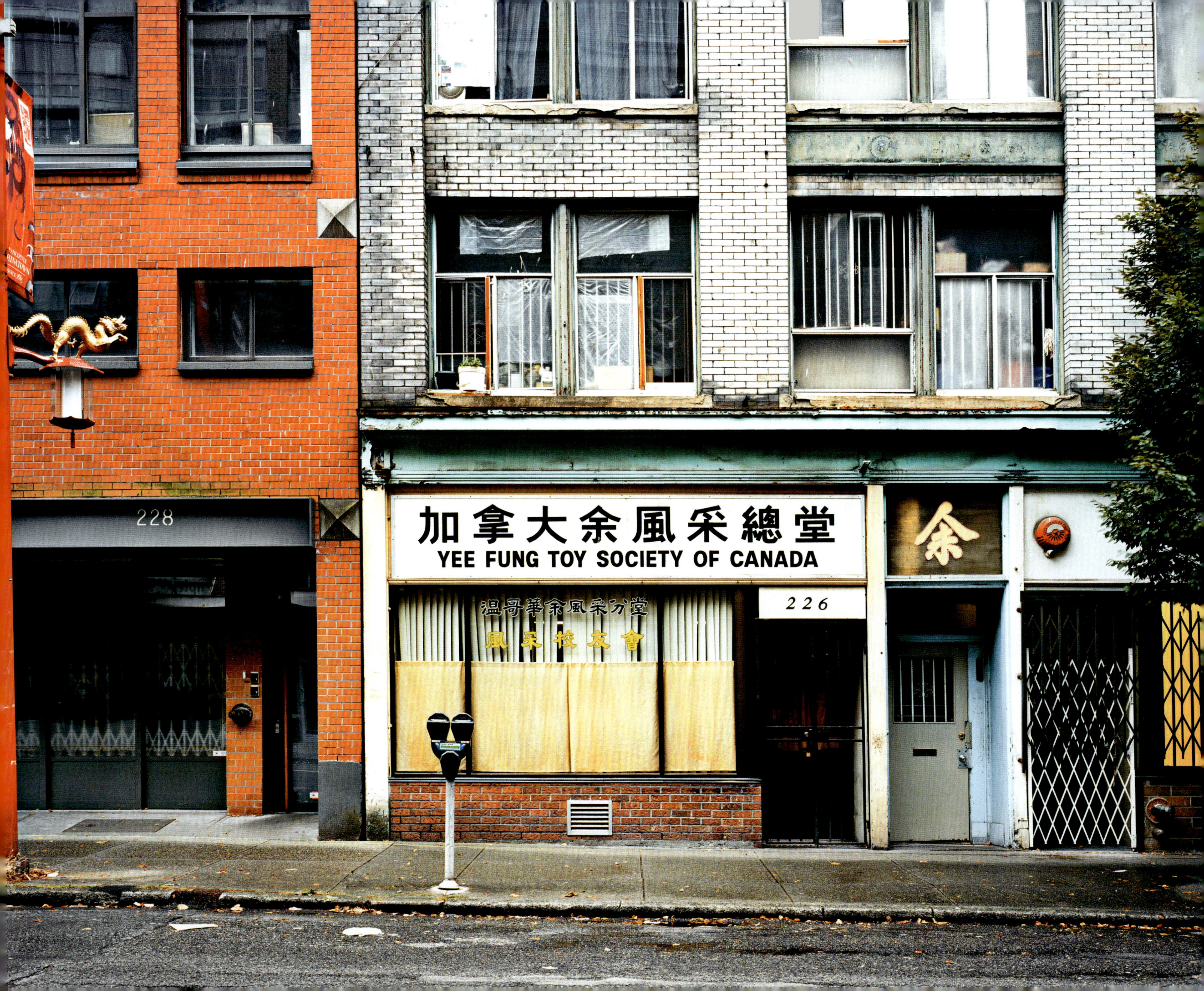
228
加拿大余風采總堂
YEE FUNG TOY SOCIETY OF CANADA
溫哥華余風采分堂
風采校友會
226
余

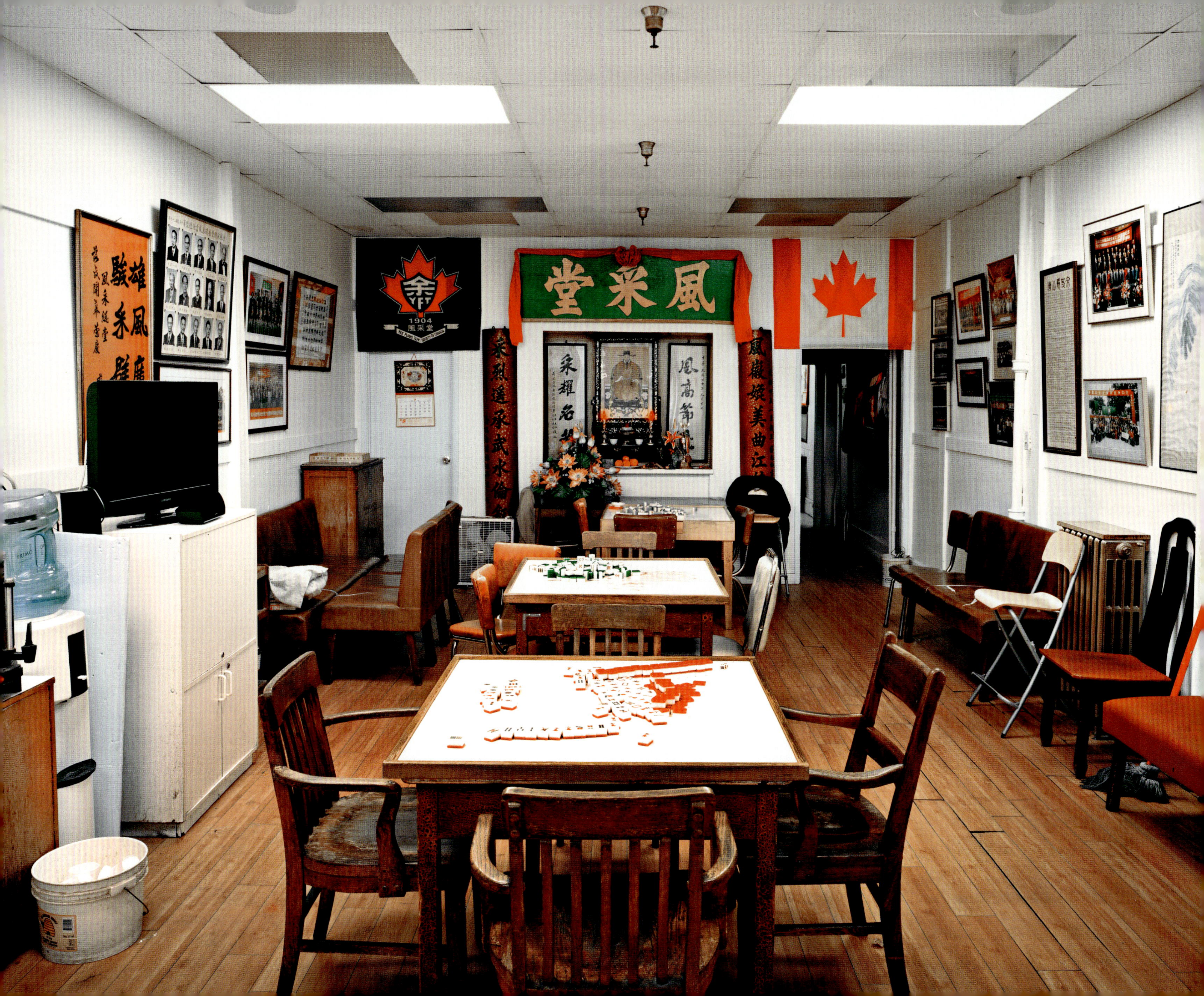

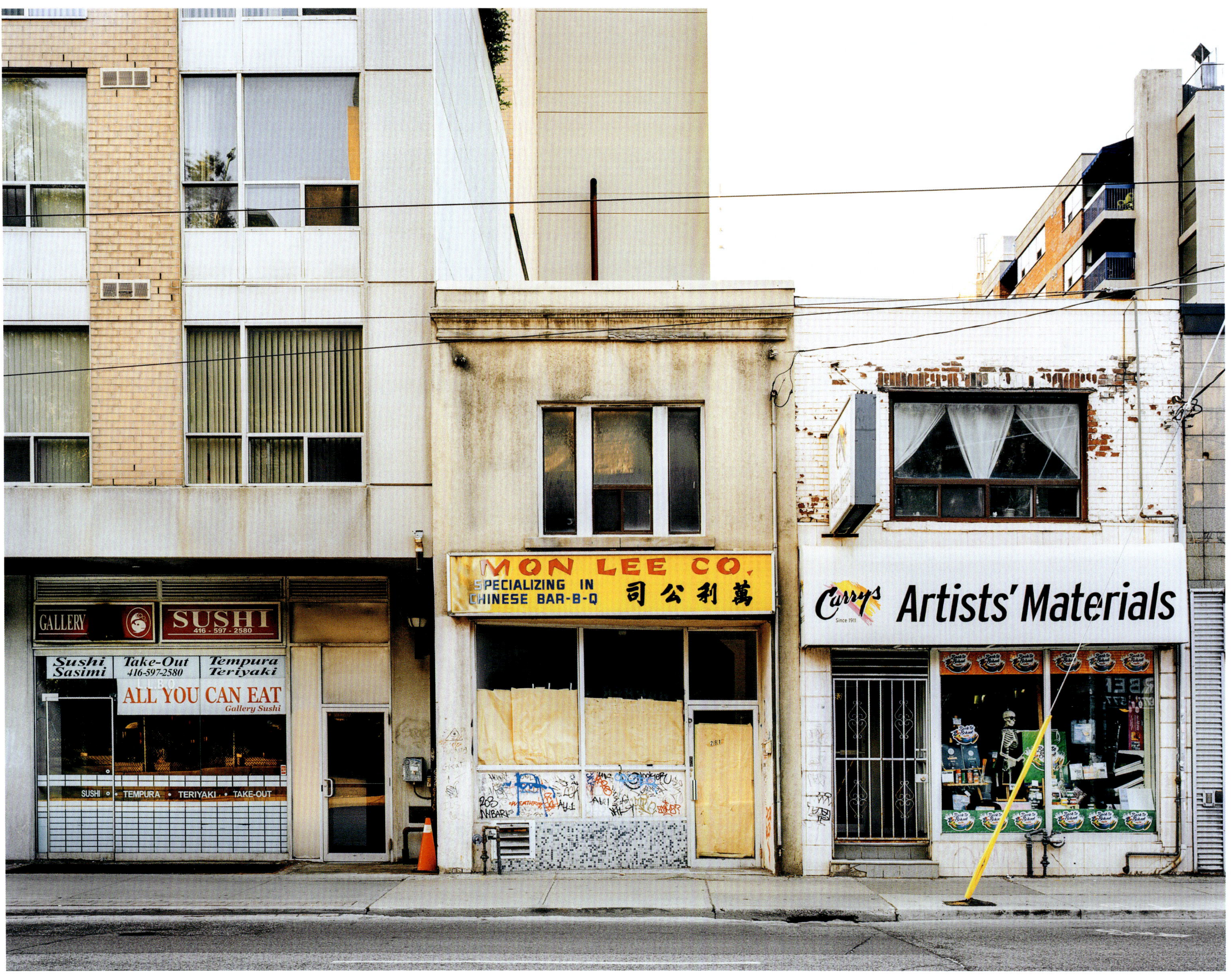

Mon Lee Co., Toronto West Chinatown, 2016

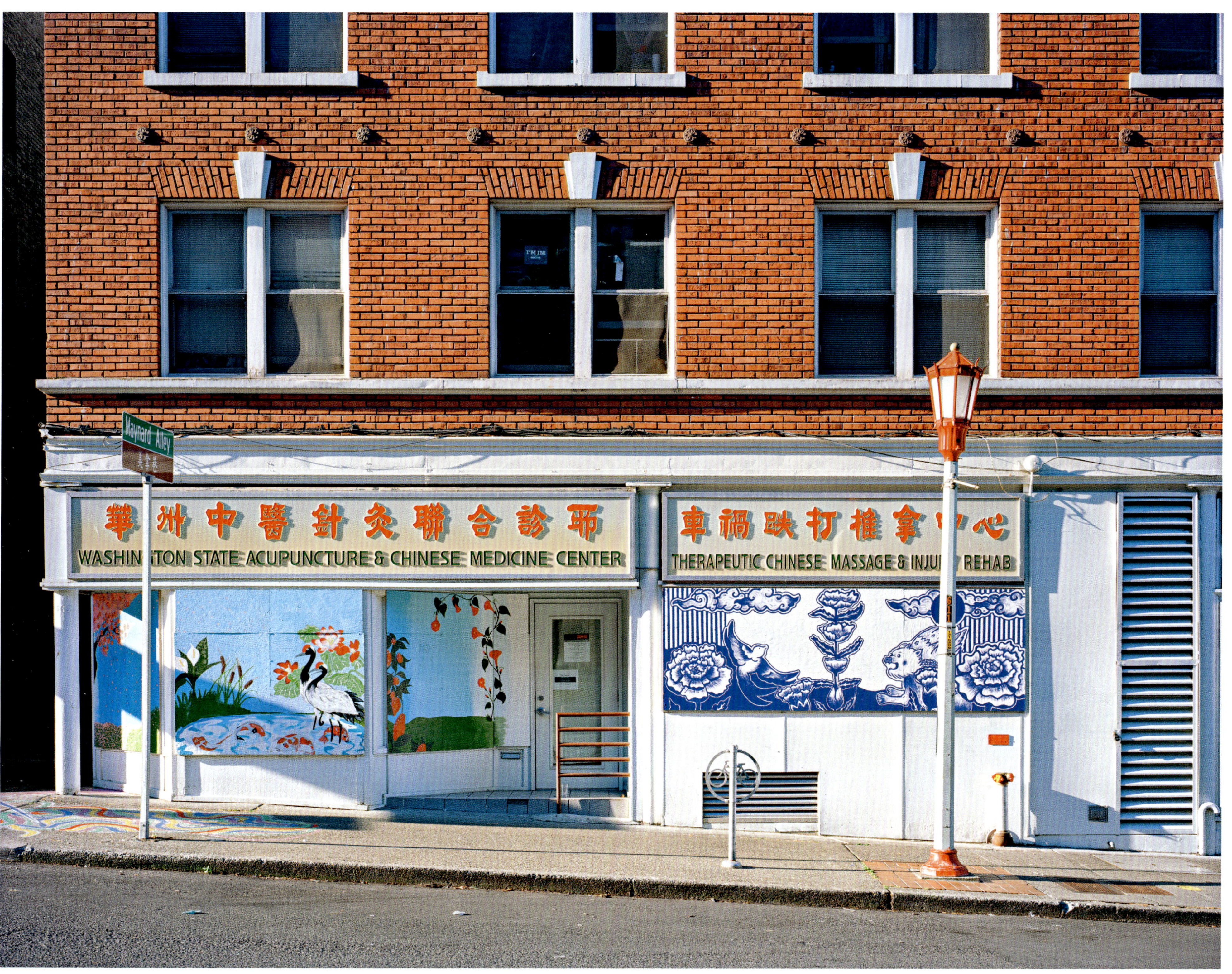

Washington State Acupuncture & Chinese Medicine Center, Seattle Chinatown–International District, 2022

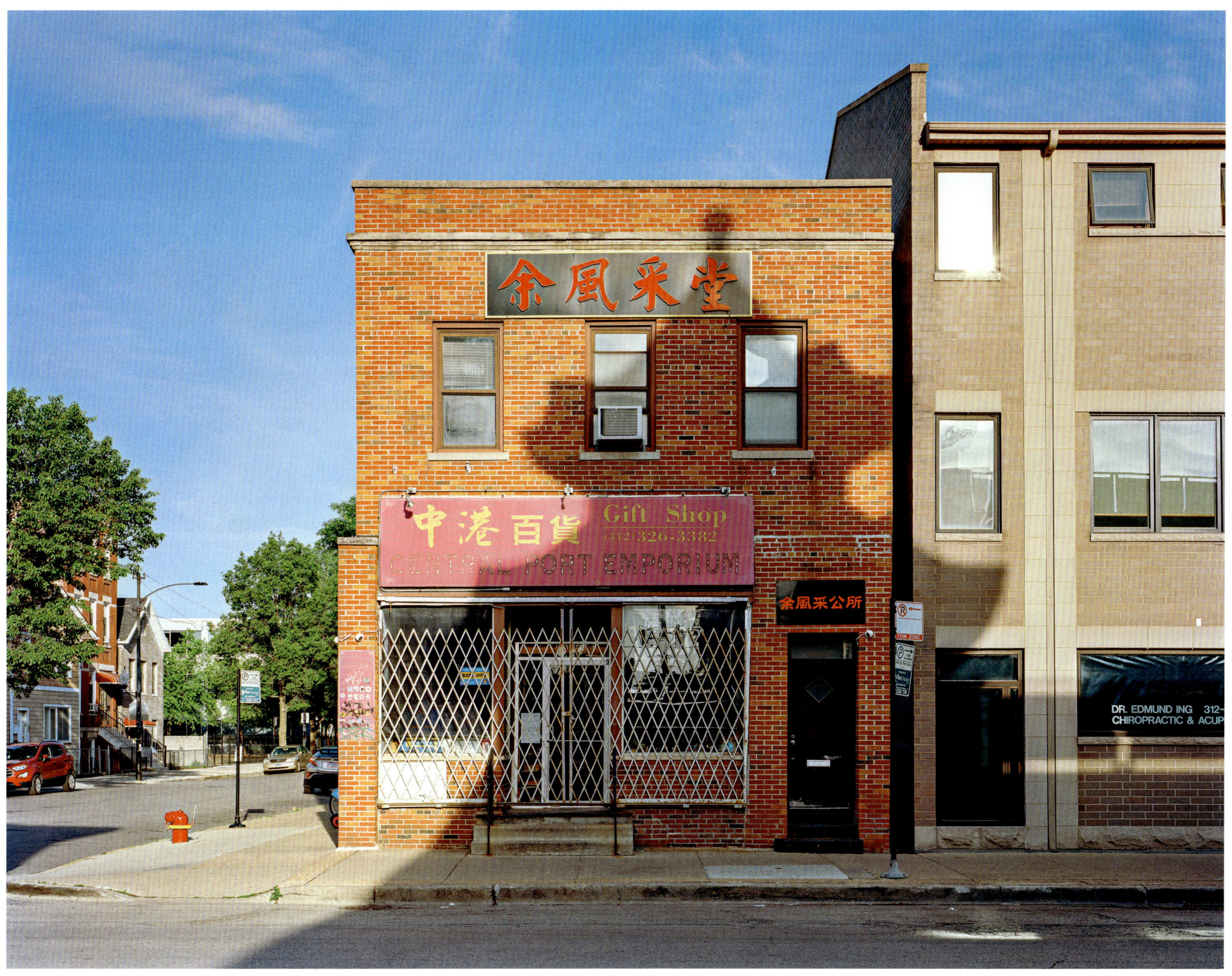

Central Port Emporium, Chicago, 2022

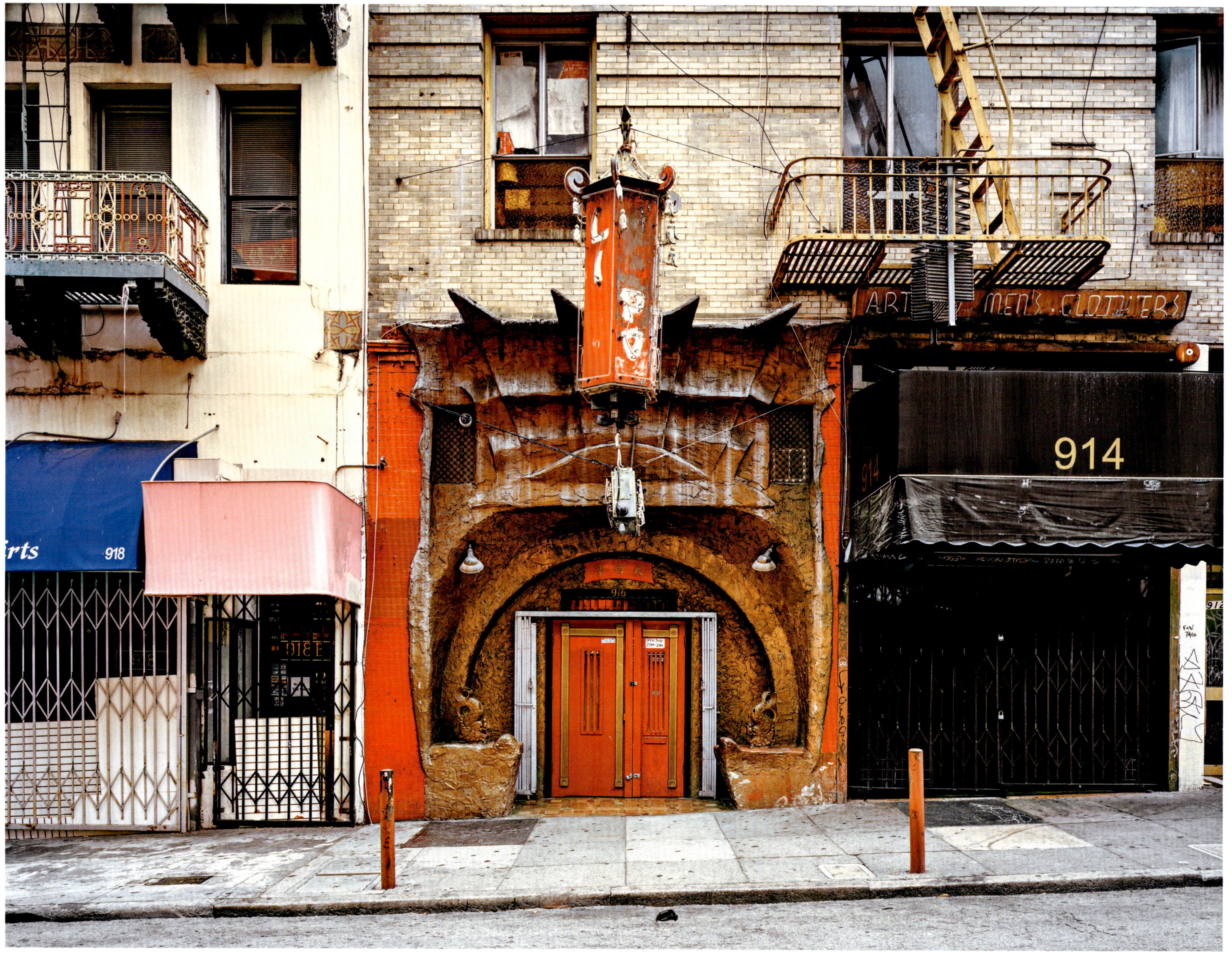

Li Po Cocktails, San Francisco, 2017

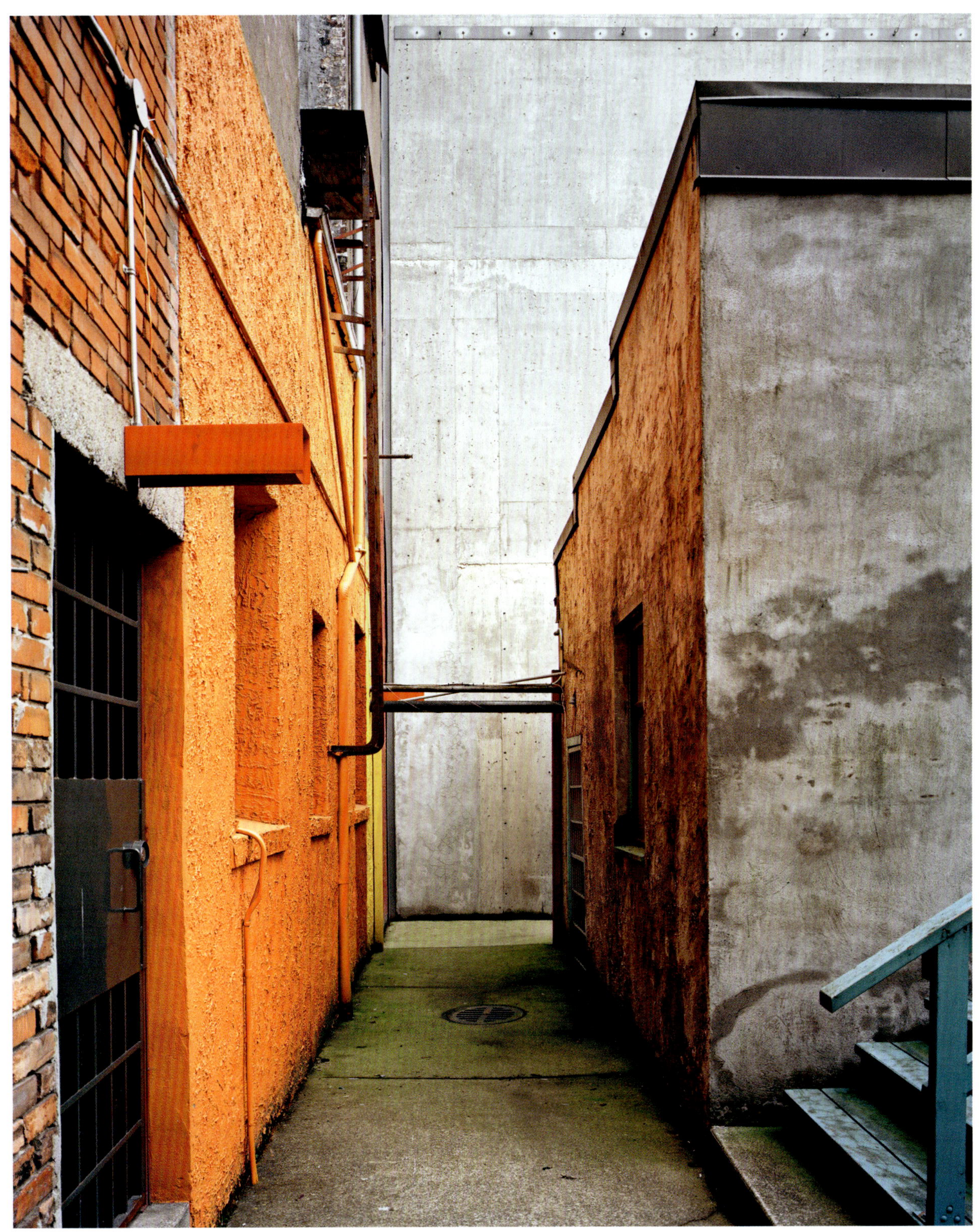

Courtyard Between East Pender Street, Market Alley, Carrall Street, Columbia Street (East View, Alley), Vancouver, 2013

Jane's Tea Shop, Vancouver, 2013

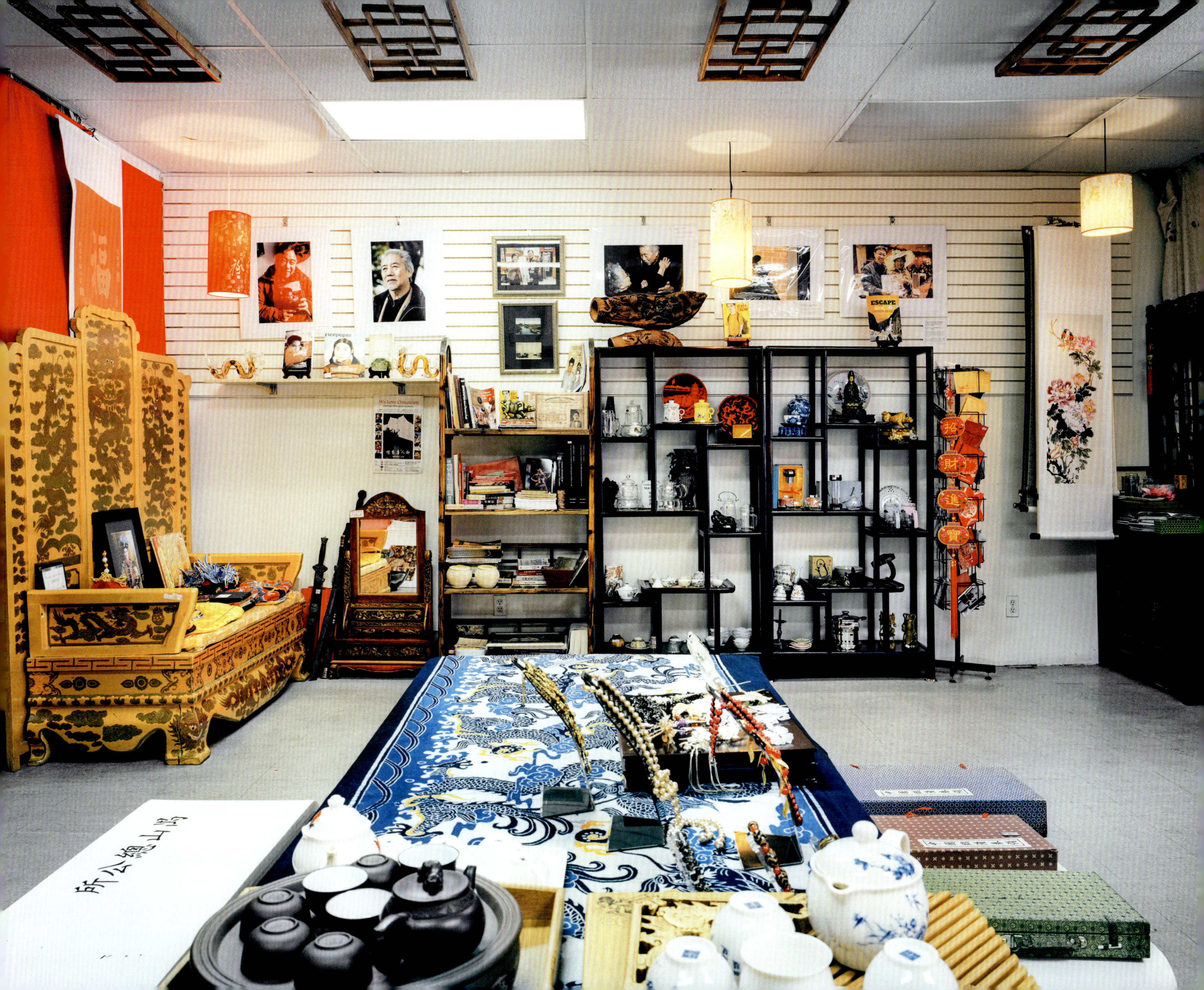

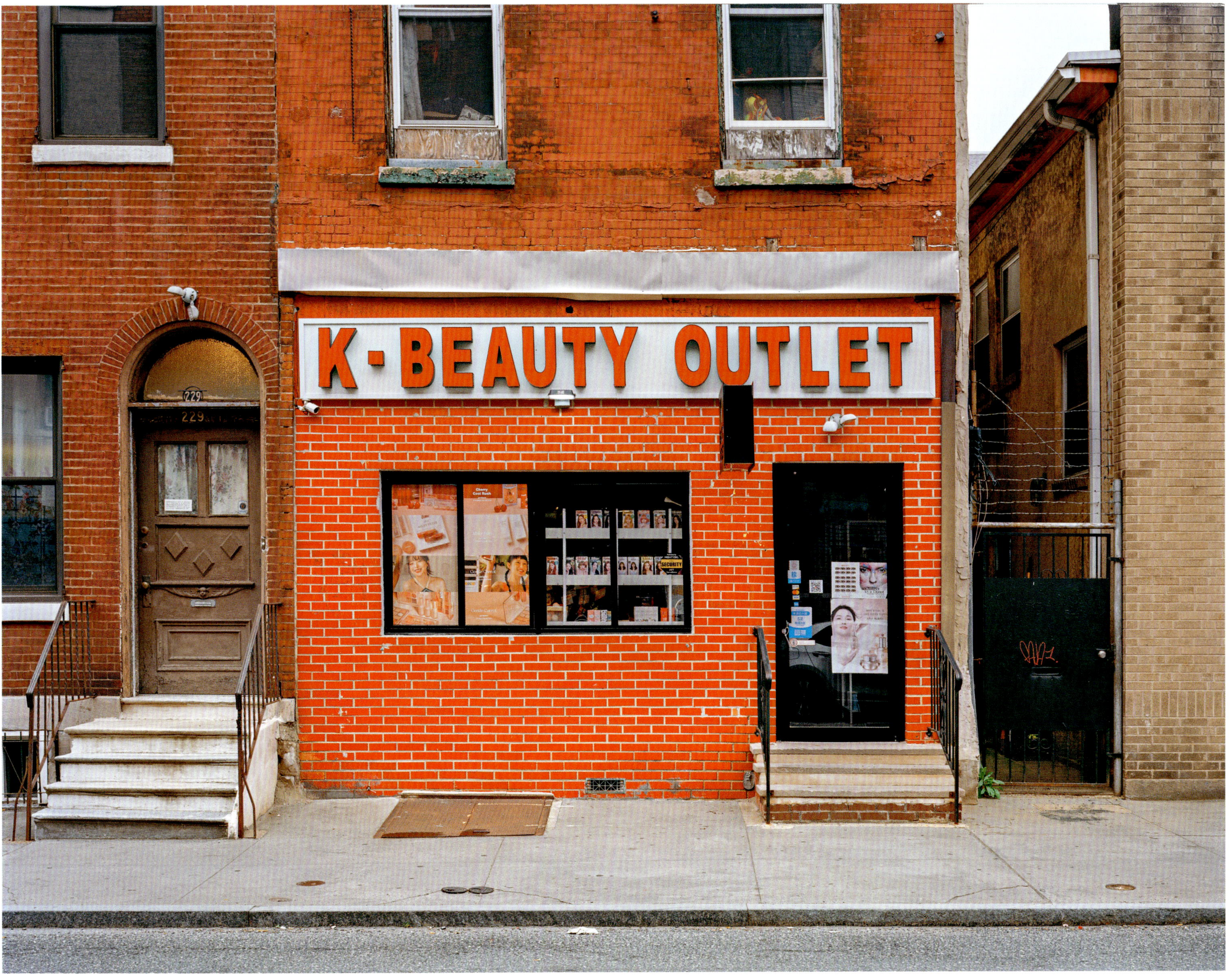

K-Beauty Outlet, Philadelphia, 2022

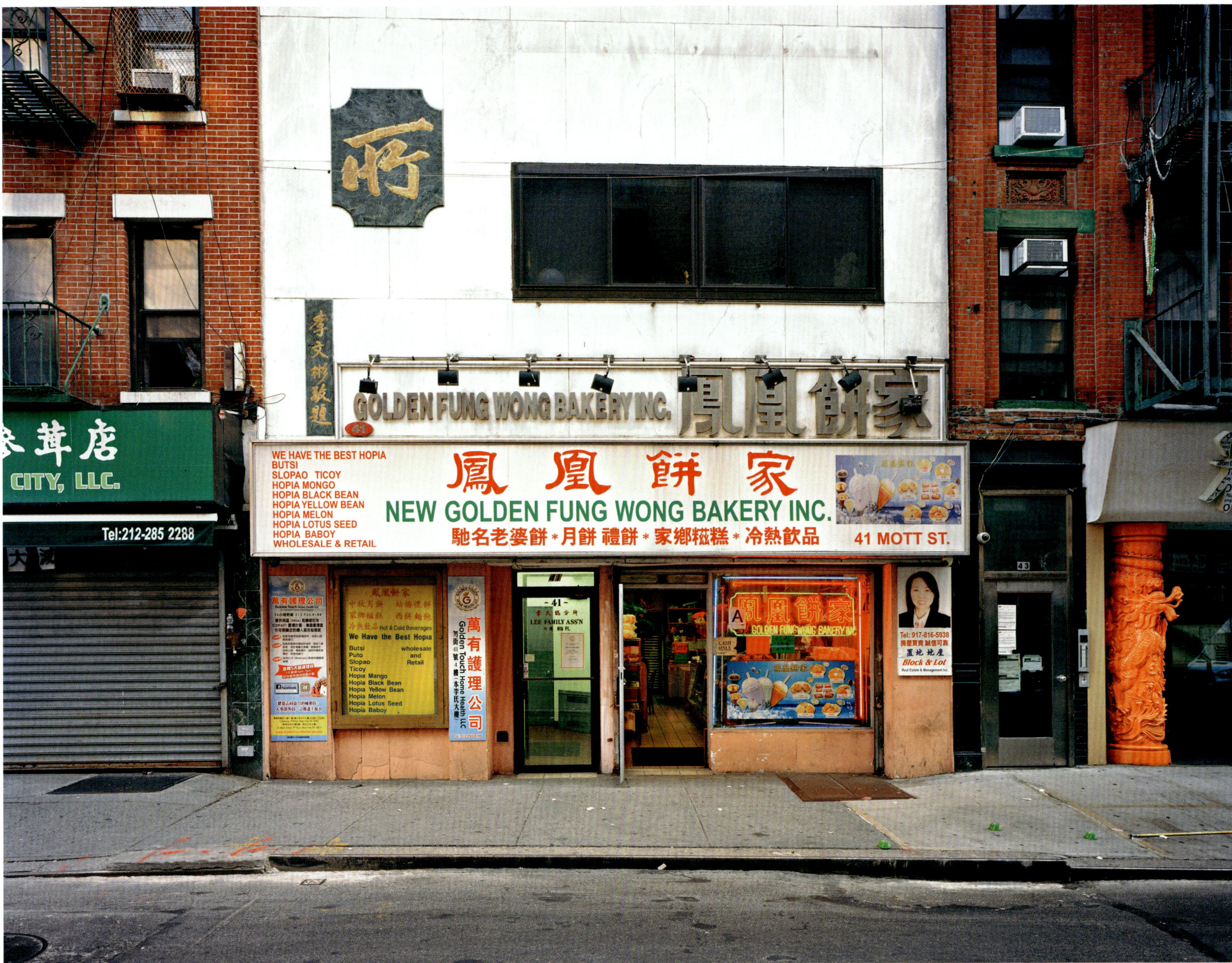

New Golden Fung Wong Bakery Inc., Manhattan, 2019

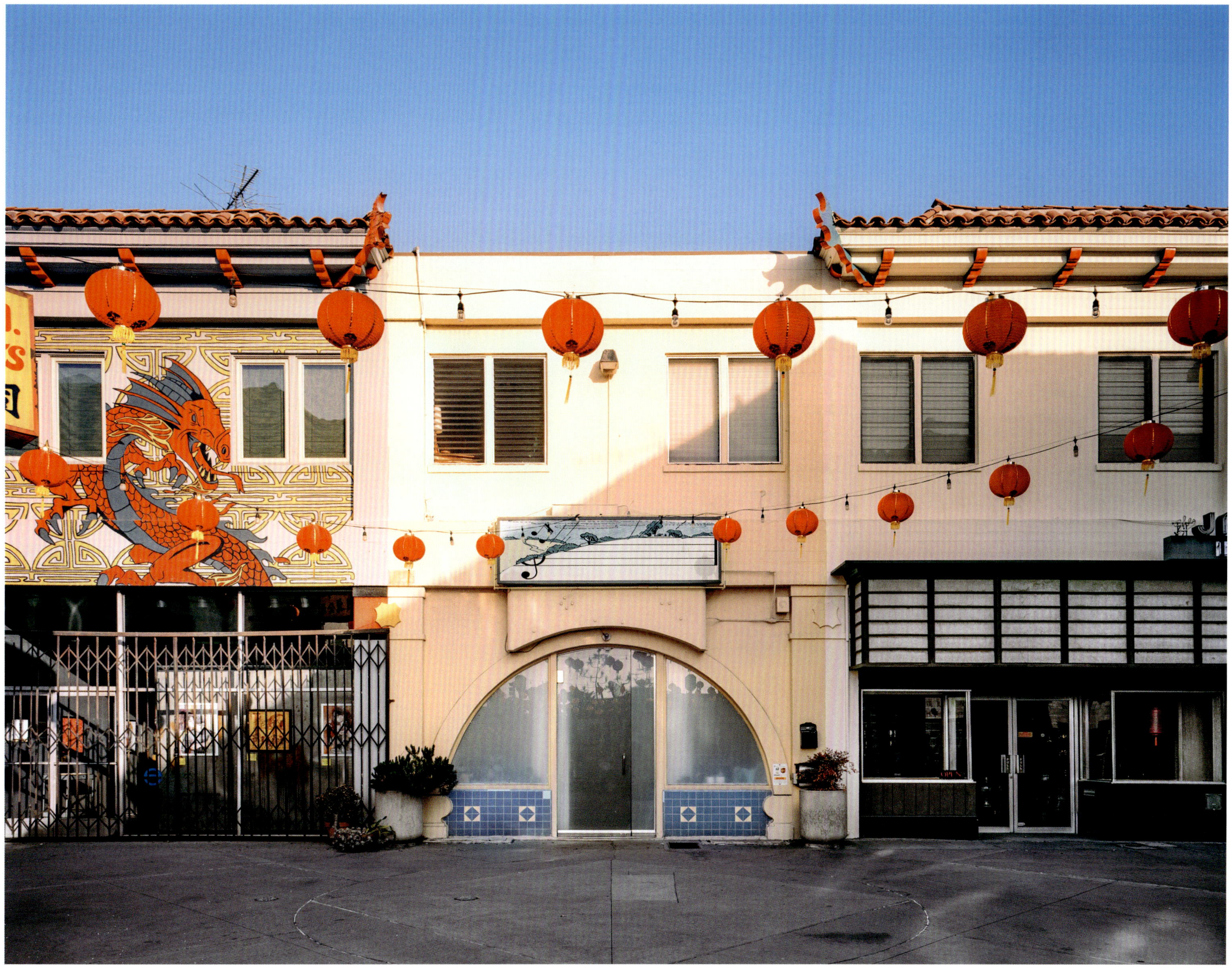

955 Chung King Road, Los Angeles, 2018

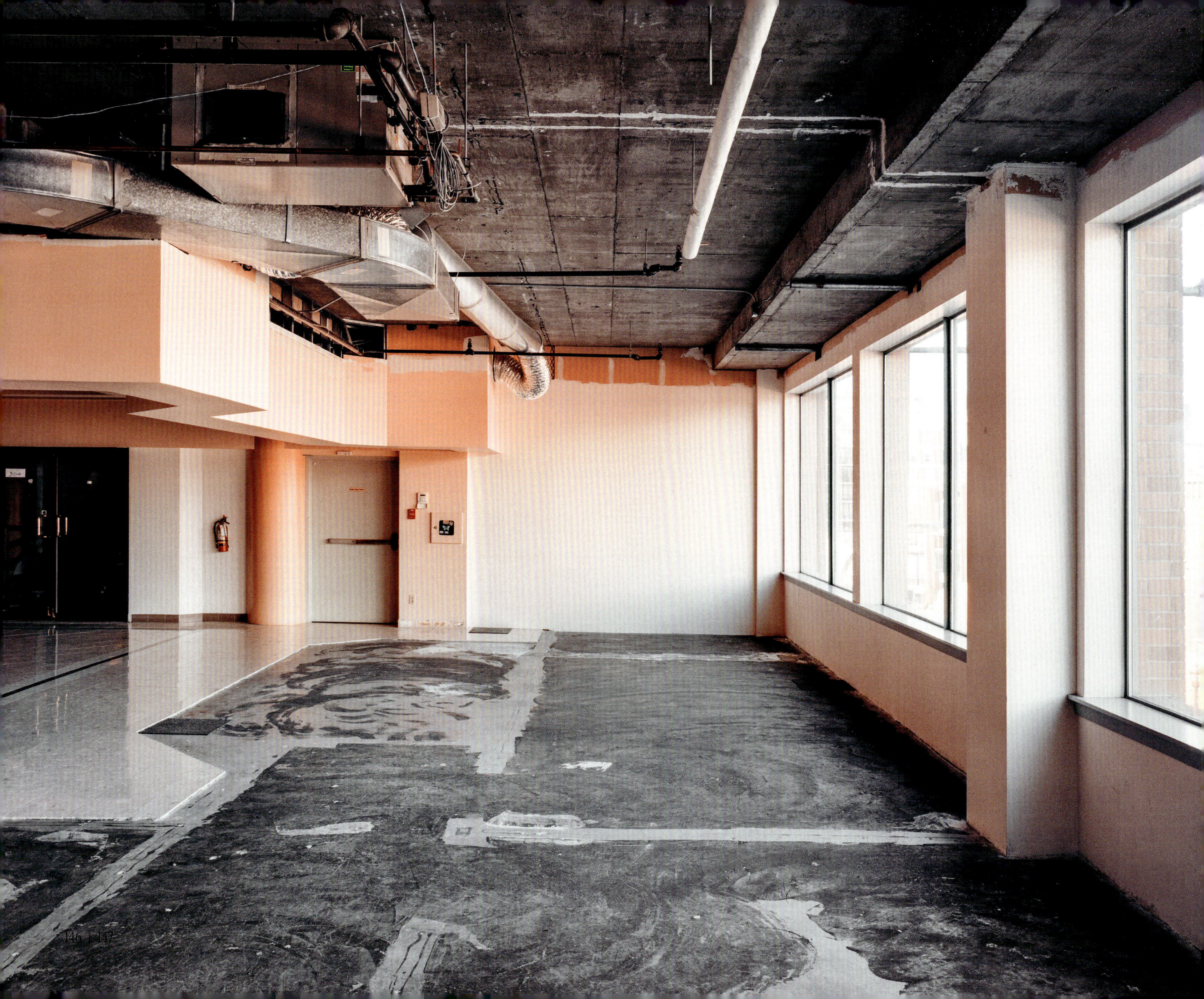

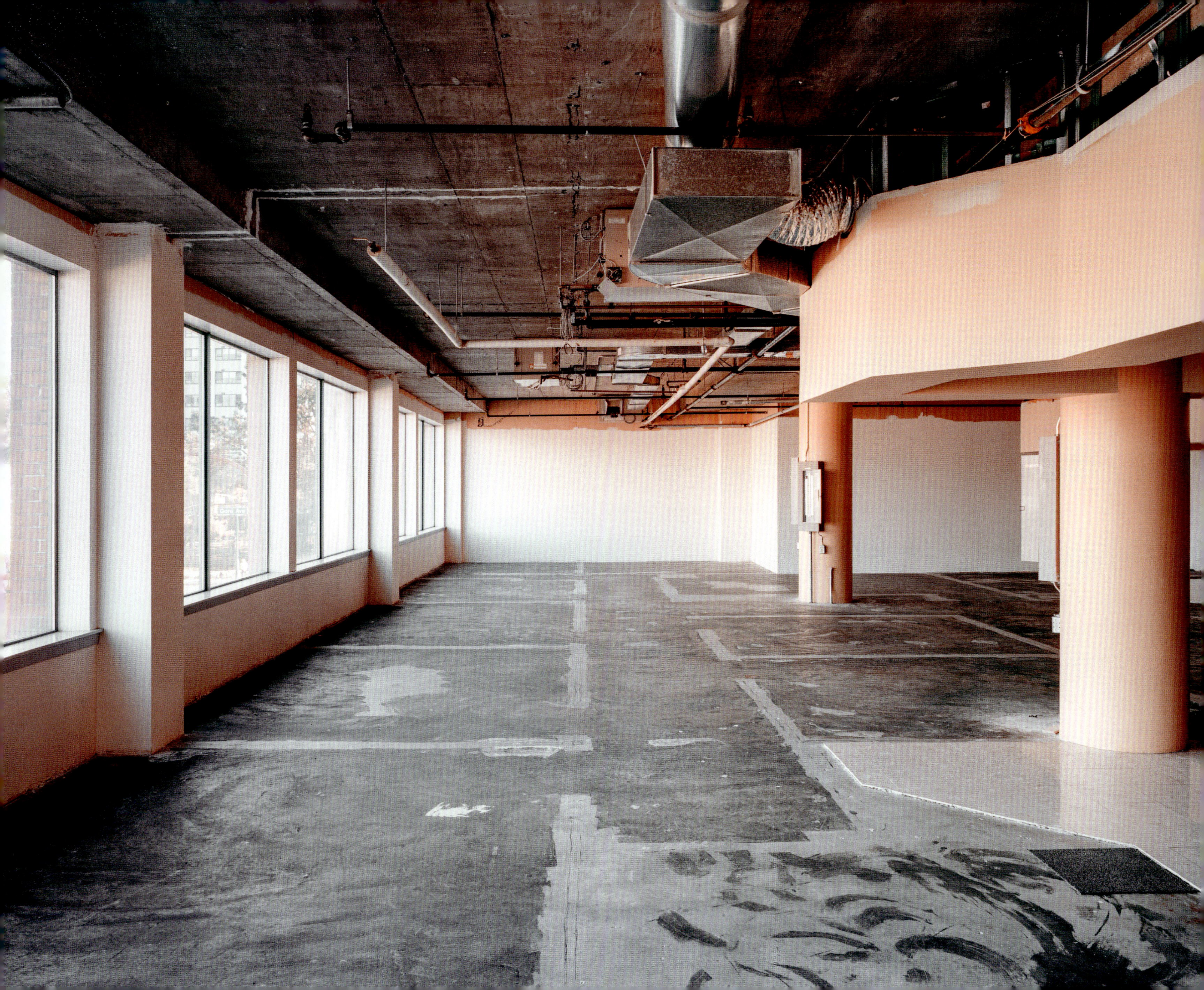

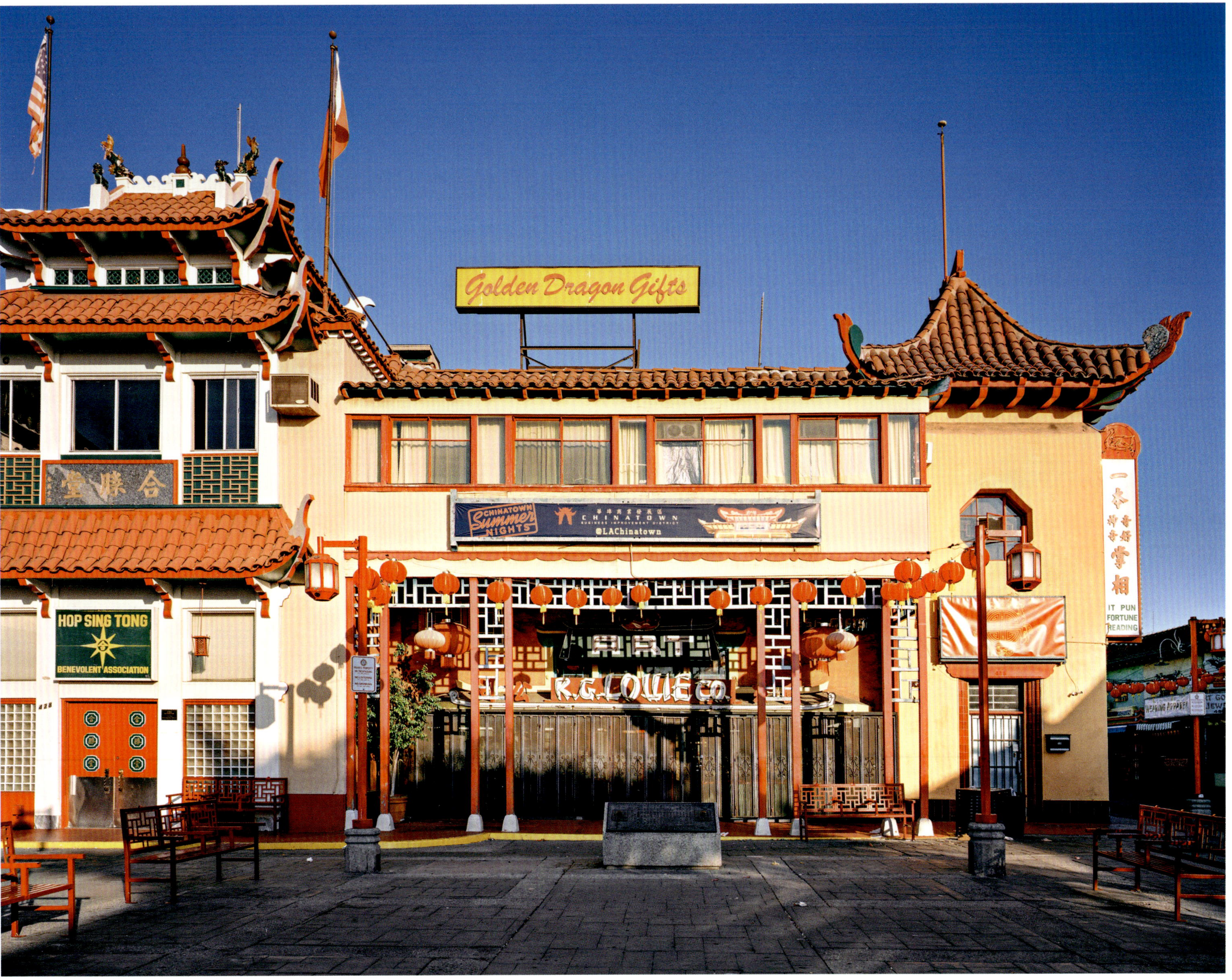

Gold Dragon Gifts, Los Angeles, 2018

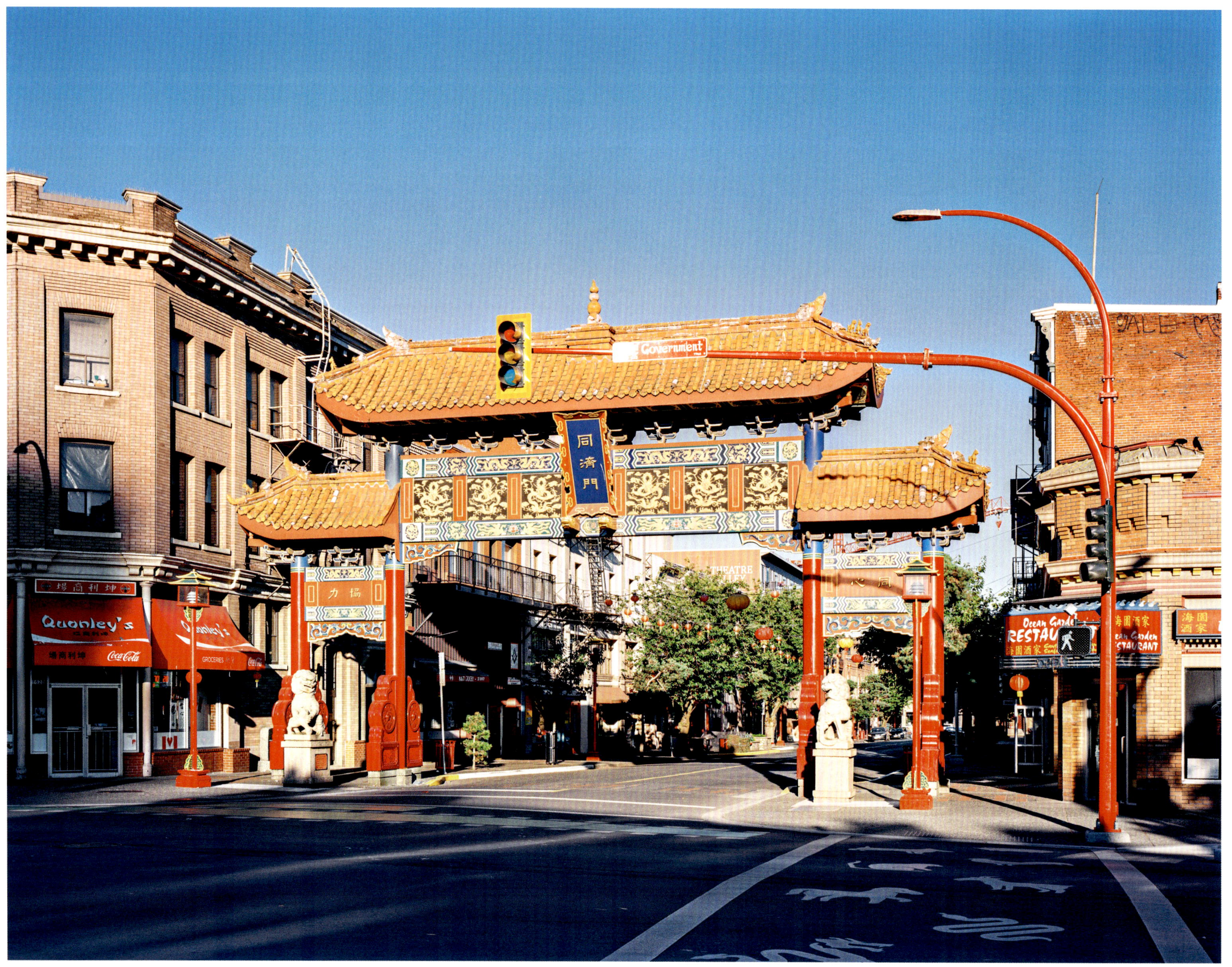

Gate of Harmonious Interest, Victoria, 2023

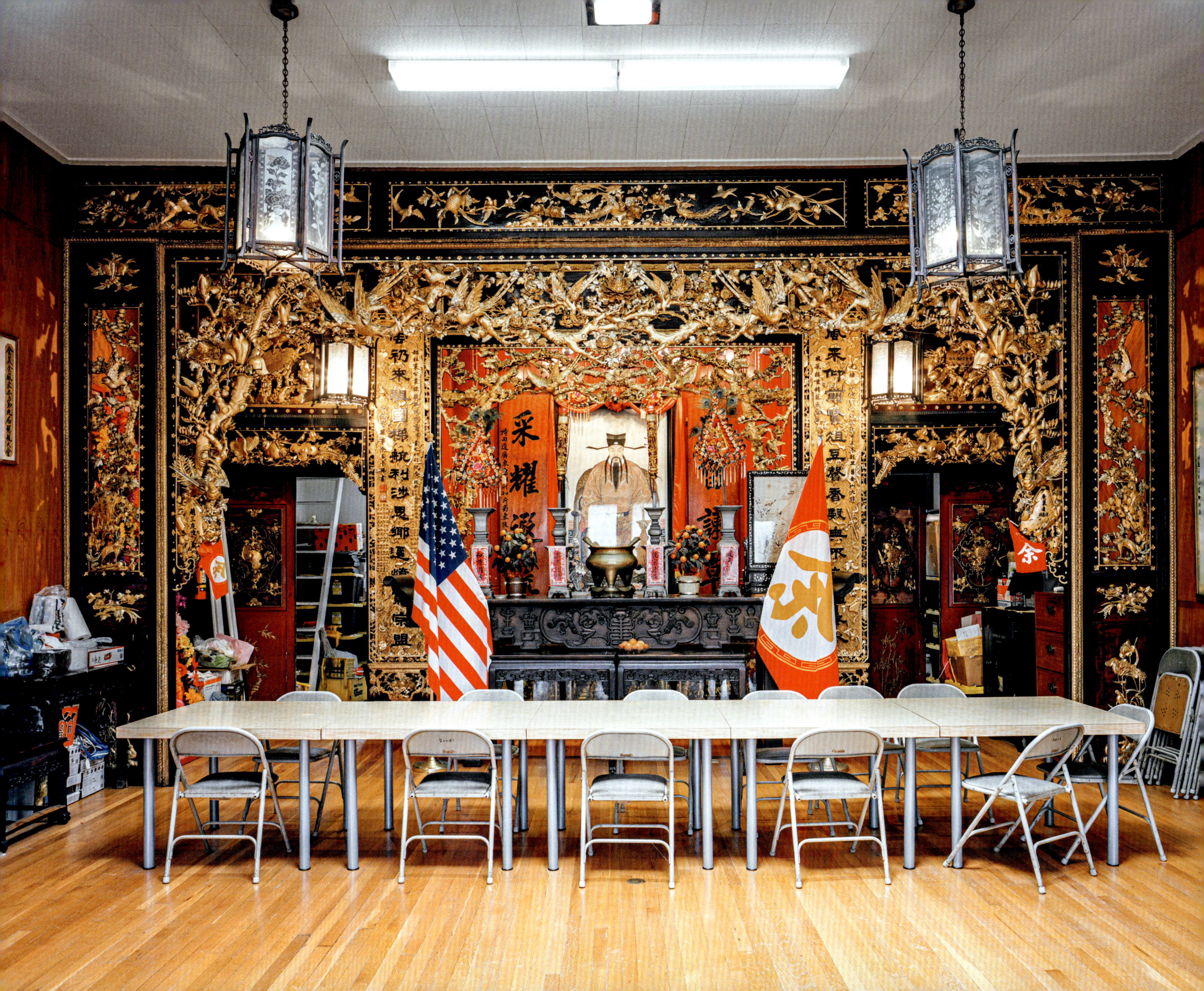

previous page
Yee Fung Toy Family Association, San Francisco, 2023

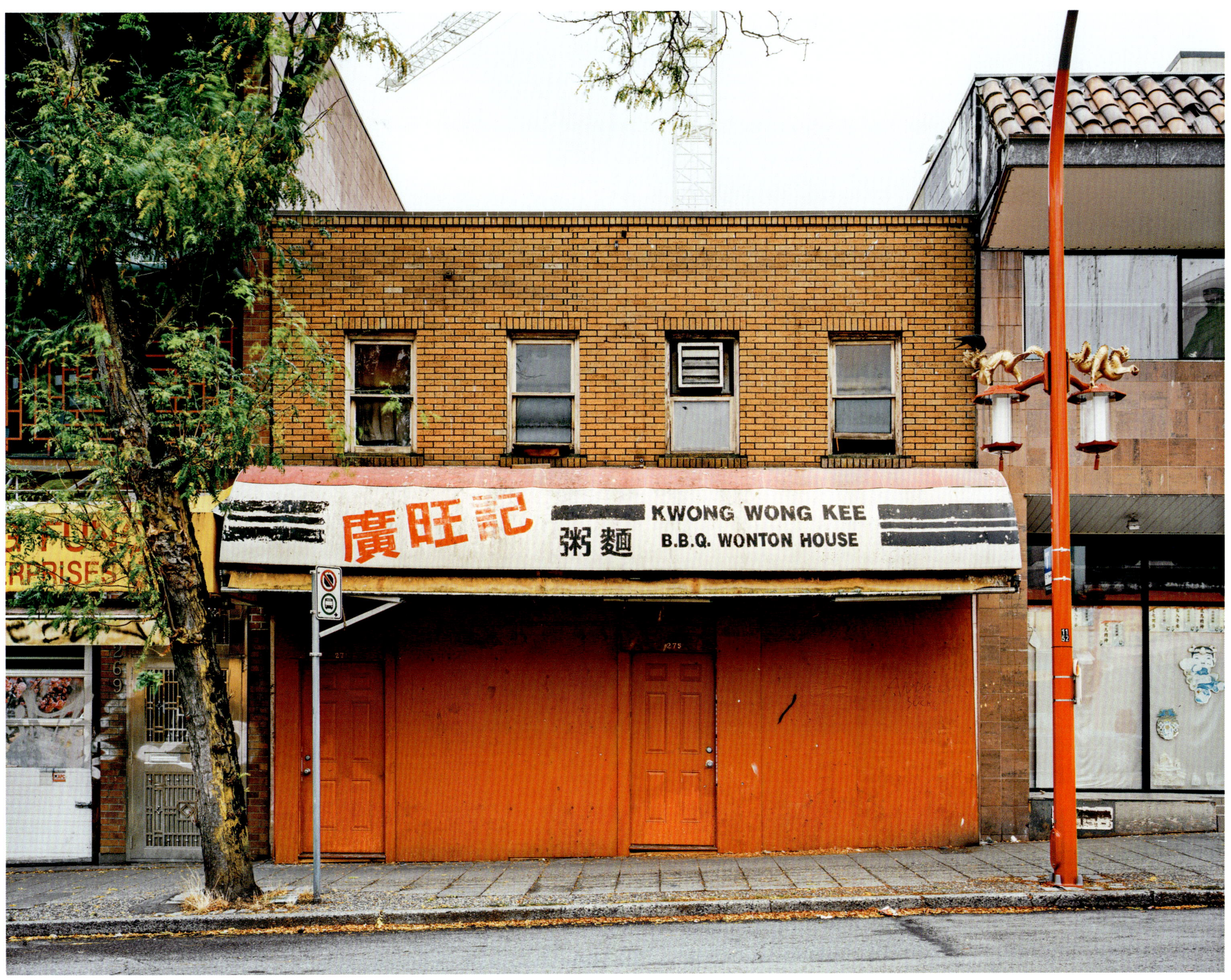

Kwong Wong Kee B.B.Q. Wonton House, Vancouver, 2017

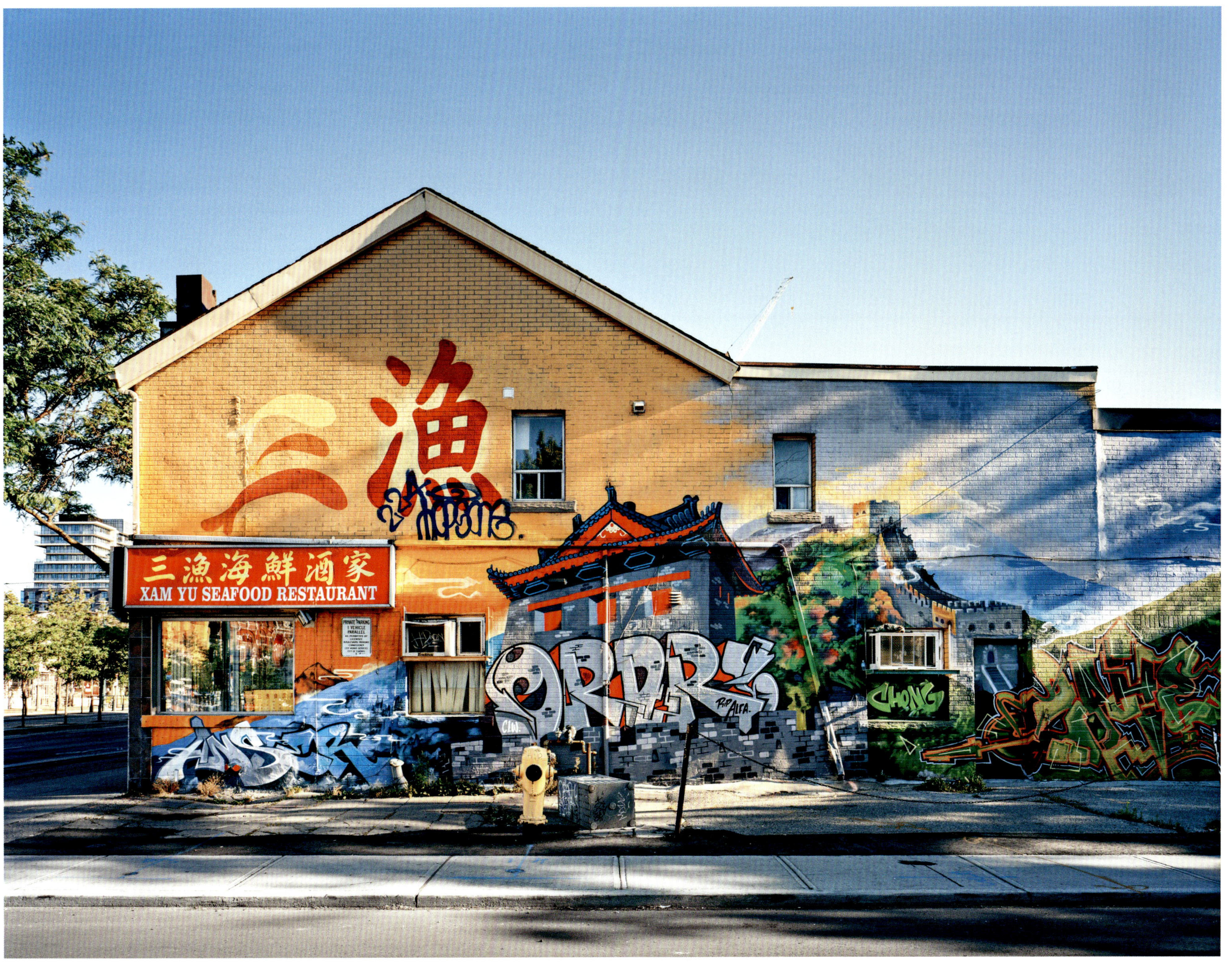

Xam Yu Seafood Restaurant, Toronto West Chinatown, 2016

Chinese Consolidated Benevolent Association of Chicago, Chicago, 2022

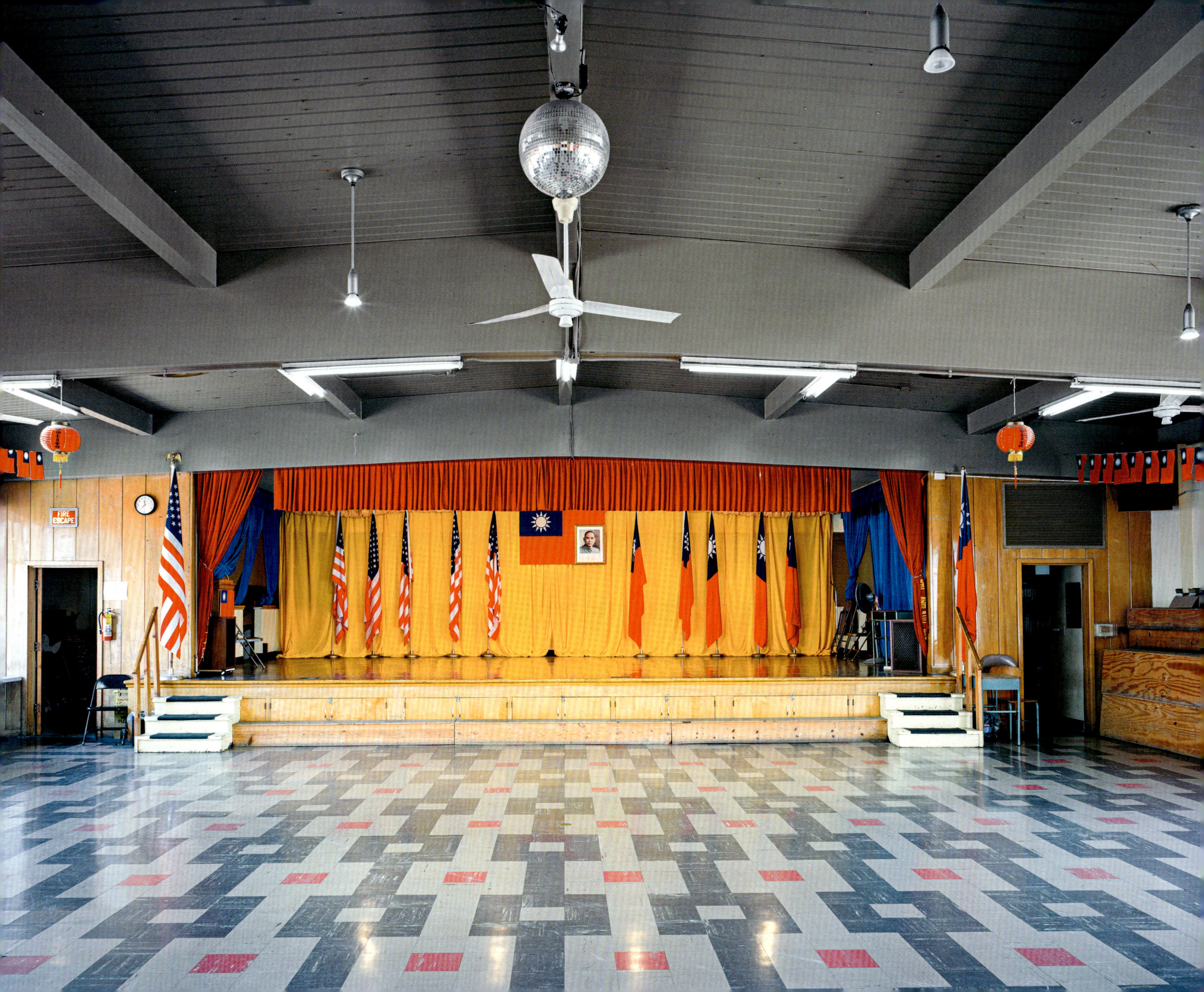

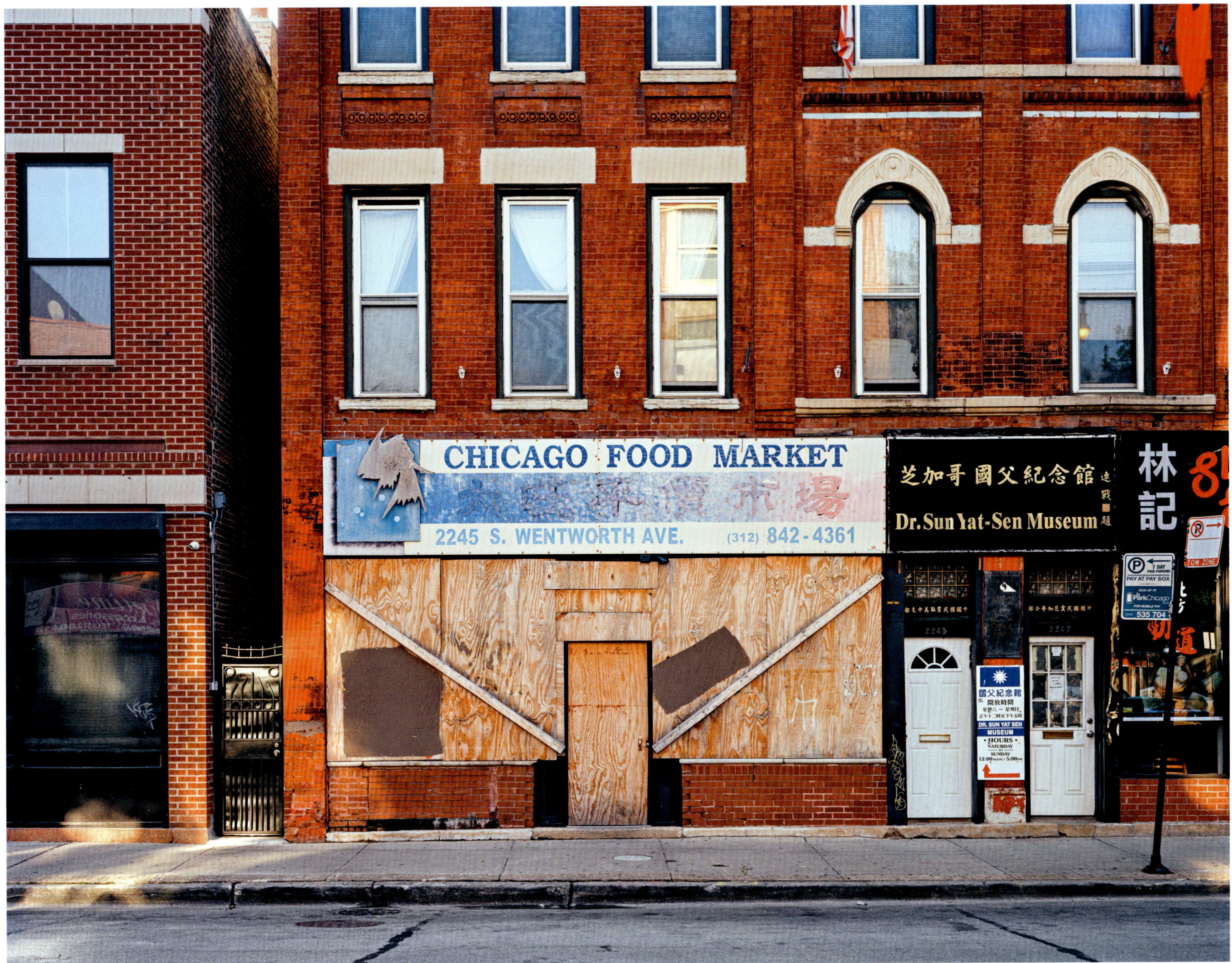

Chicago Food Market, Chicago, 2022

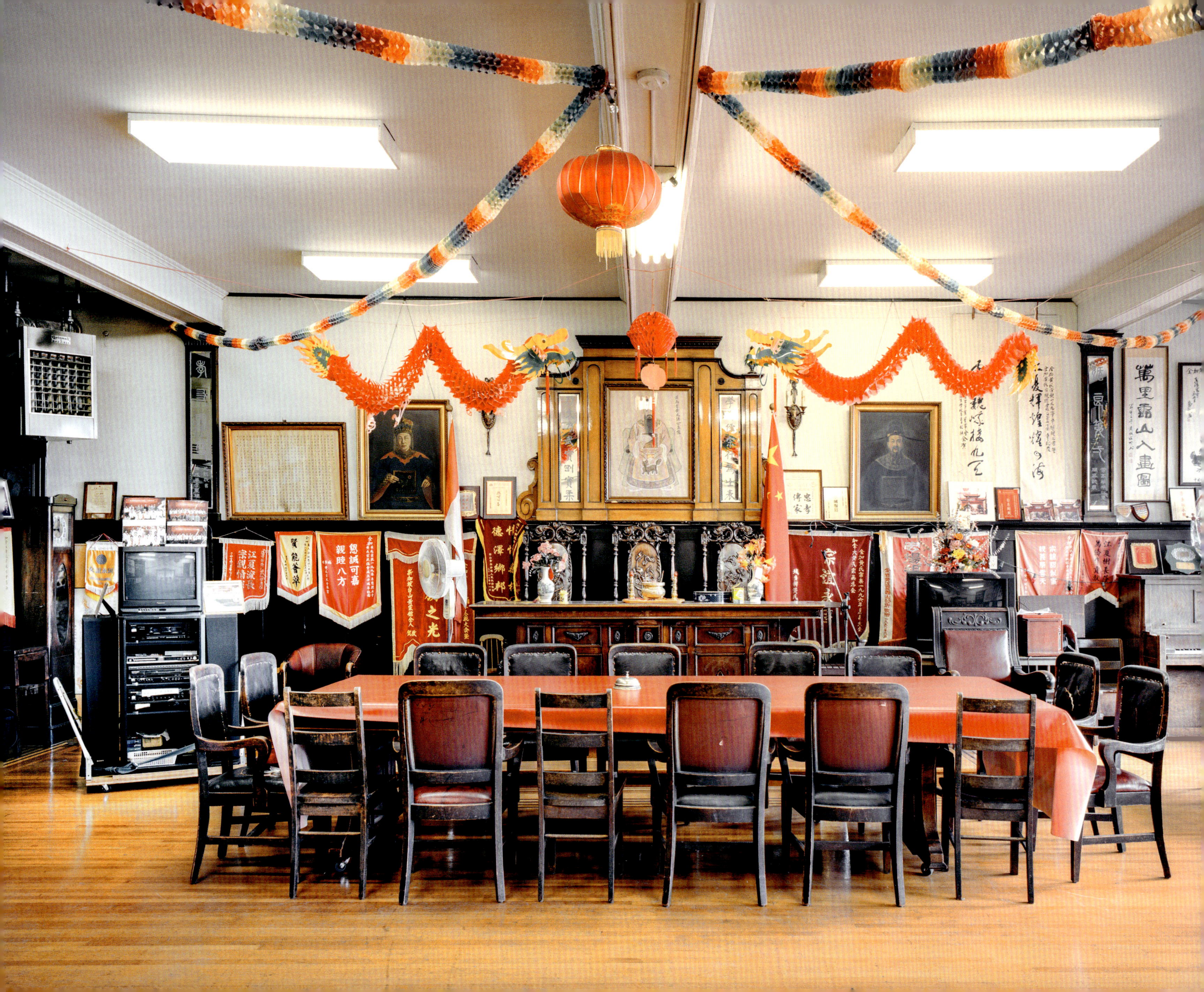

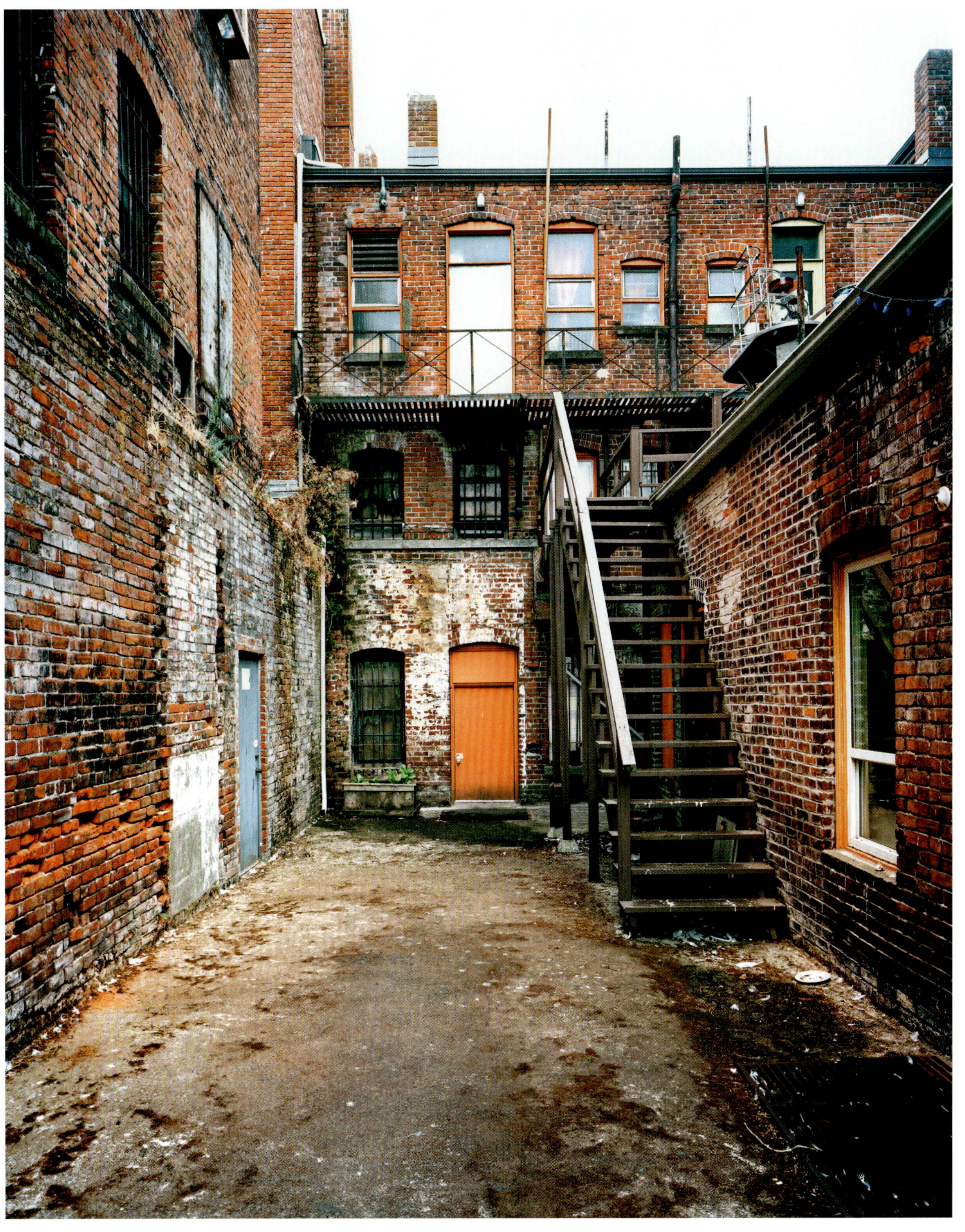

Wongs' Benevolent Association of Canada, Vancouver, 2017

Courtyard Behind Lee Block (South View), Victoria, 2014

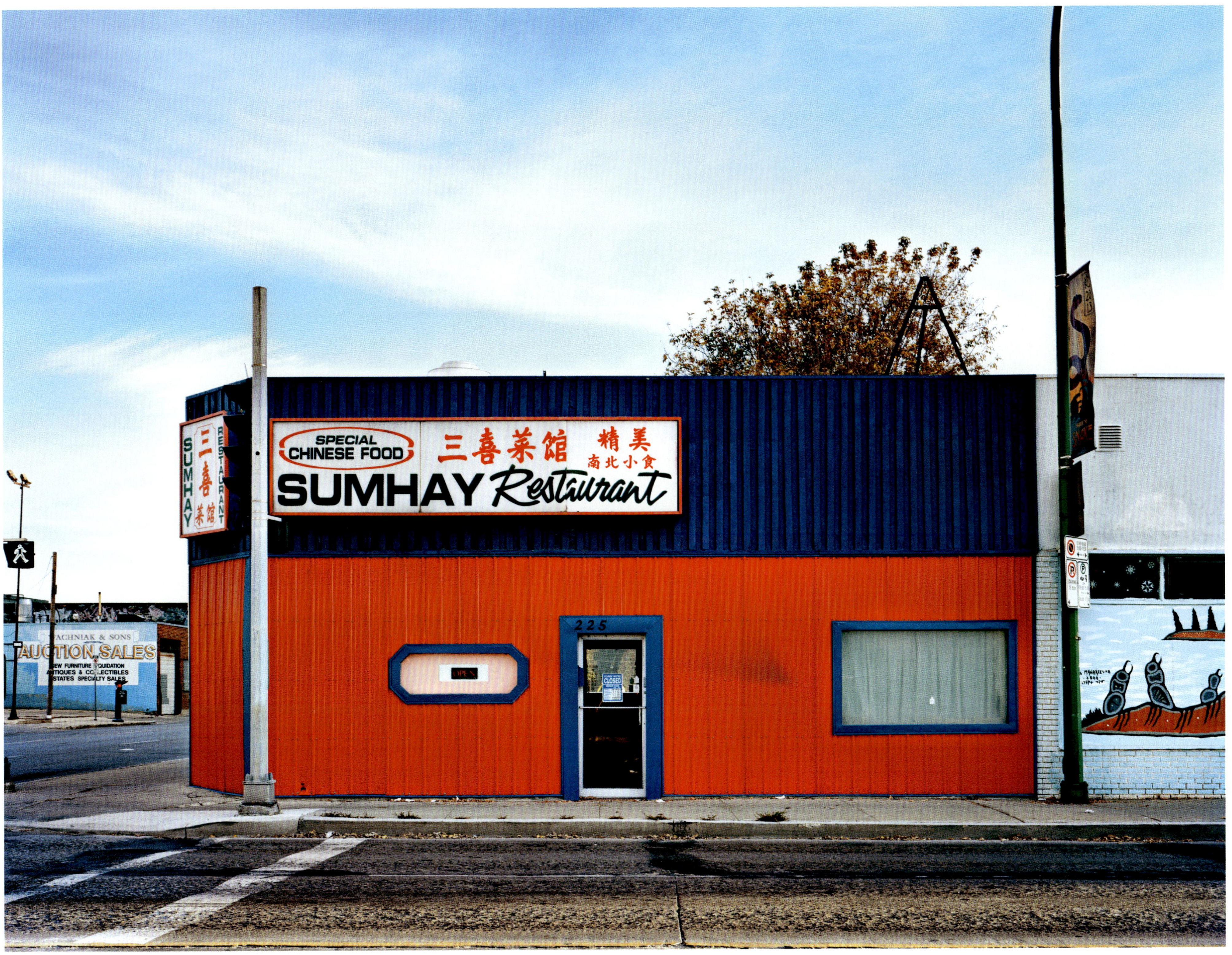

Sumhay Restaurant, Winnipeg, 2013

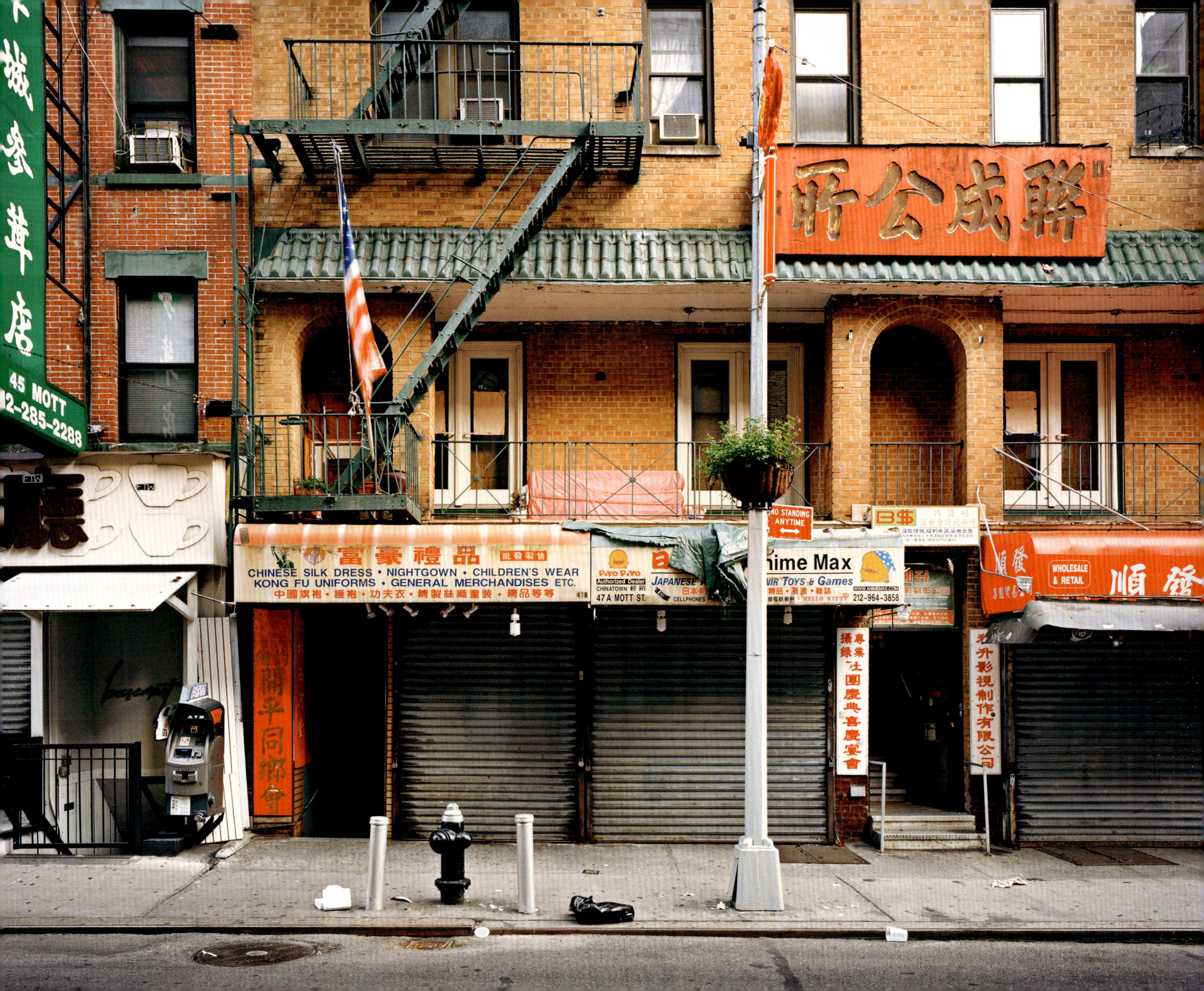
45 MOTT
2-285-2288
昕公成聯
富豪禮品
比發零售
CHINESE SILK DRESS • NIGHTGOWN • CHILDREN'S WEAR
KONG FU UNIFORMS • GENERAL MERCHANDISES ETC.
中國旗袍 • 睡袍 • 功夫衣 • 精製絲織童裝 • 精品等等
關平同鄉會
NO STANDING
ANYTIME
P yo P yo
Authorized Dealer
CHINATOWN 輕鬆
JAPANESE
日本
CELLPHONES
47 A MOTT ST.
hime Max
vir Toys & Games
WWW.ANIMEMAX.COM
• HELLO KITTY •
212-964-3858
日$
高瑞明
保險理財、福利申請、遷地出售
專業
攝錄
團慶典喜慶宴會
升
升影視制作有限公司
WHOLESALE
& RETAIL
順發
ATM

45–47 Mott Street, Manhattan, 2019

Montreal Chinese Association, Montreal, 2012

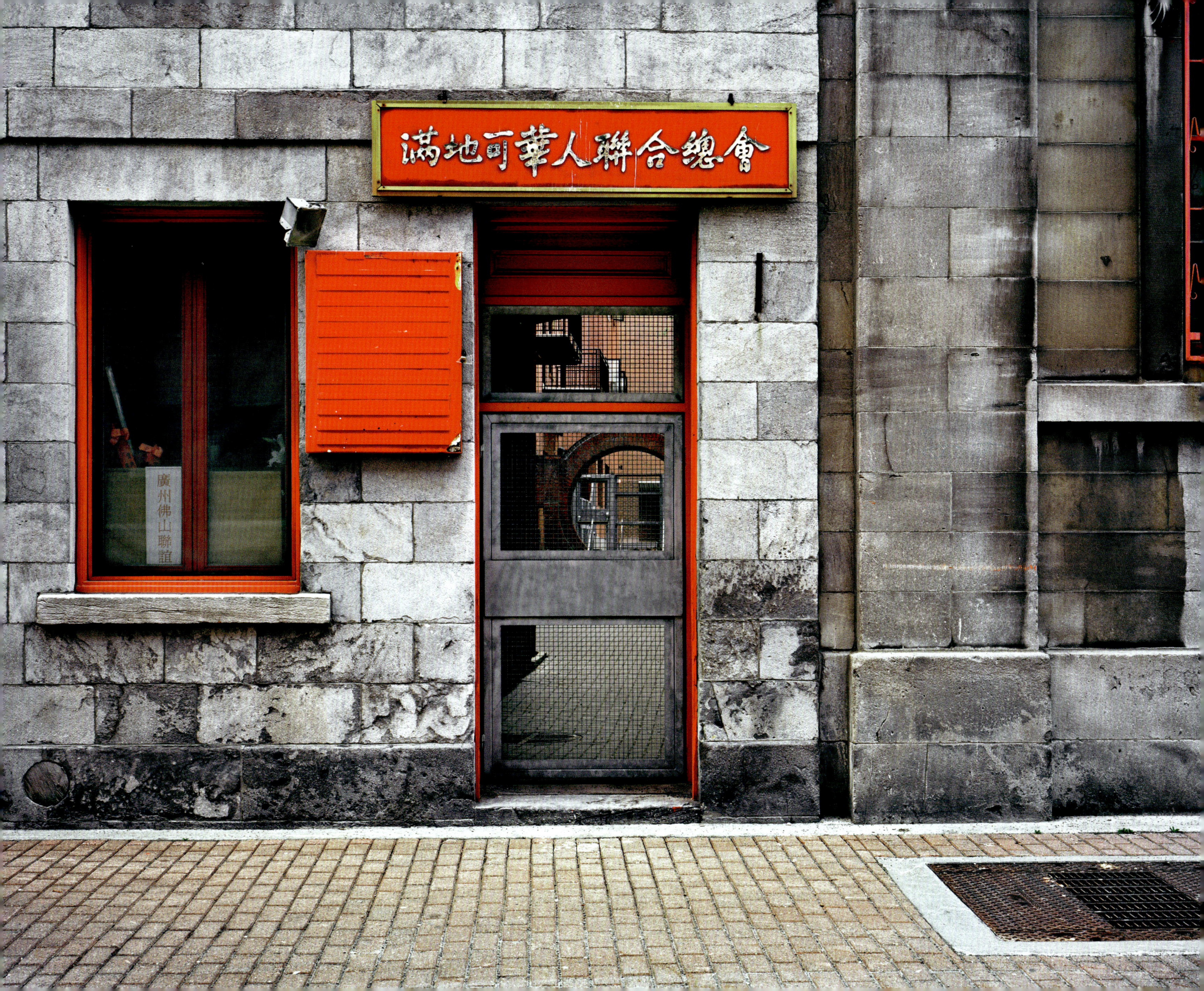

満地可華人聯合總會
廣州佛山聯誼

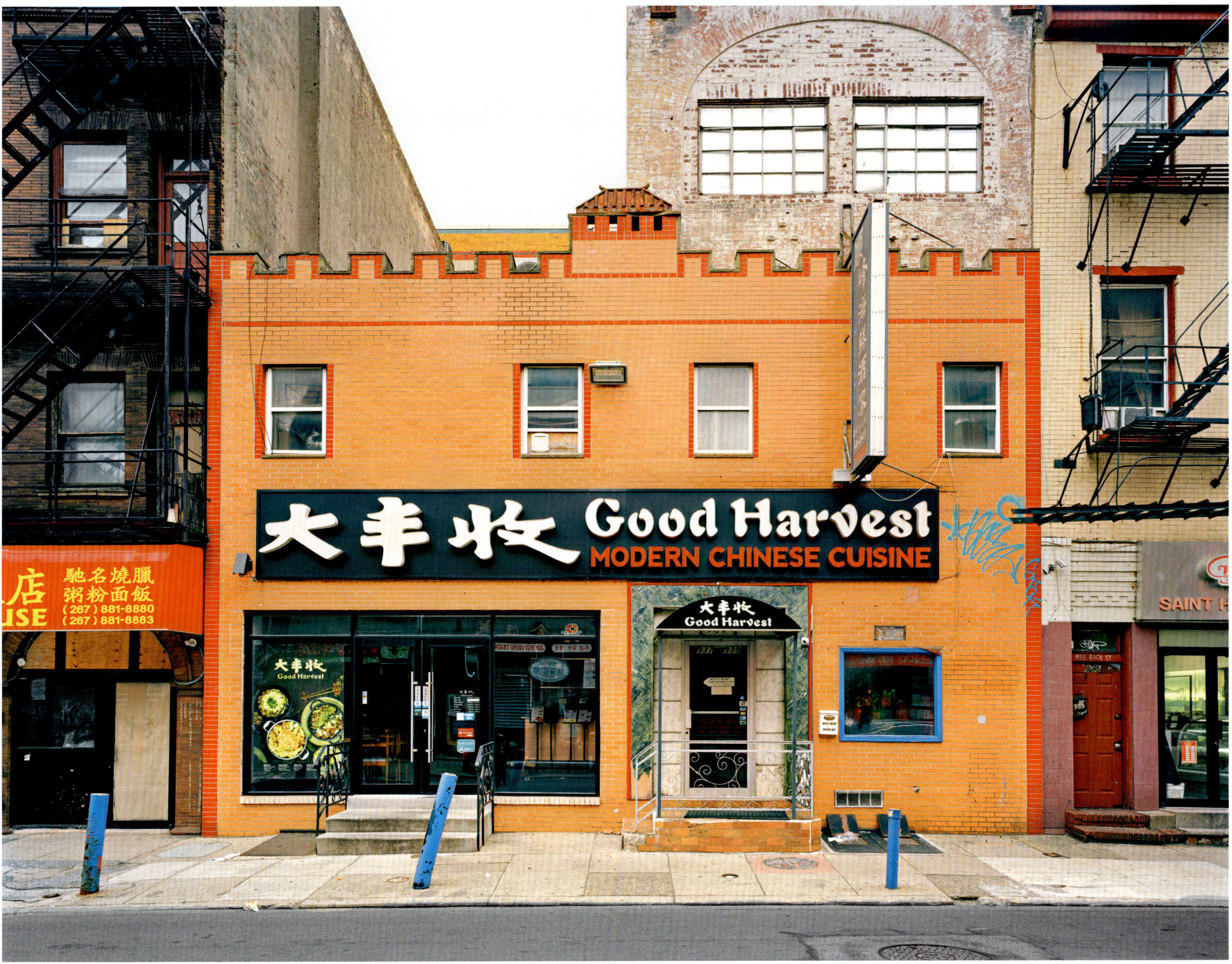

Good Harvest Modern Chinese Cuisine, Philadelphia, 2022

Lim Sai Hor Kow Mock Benevolent Association, Vancouver, 2014

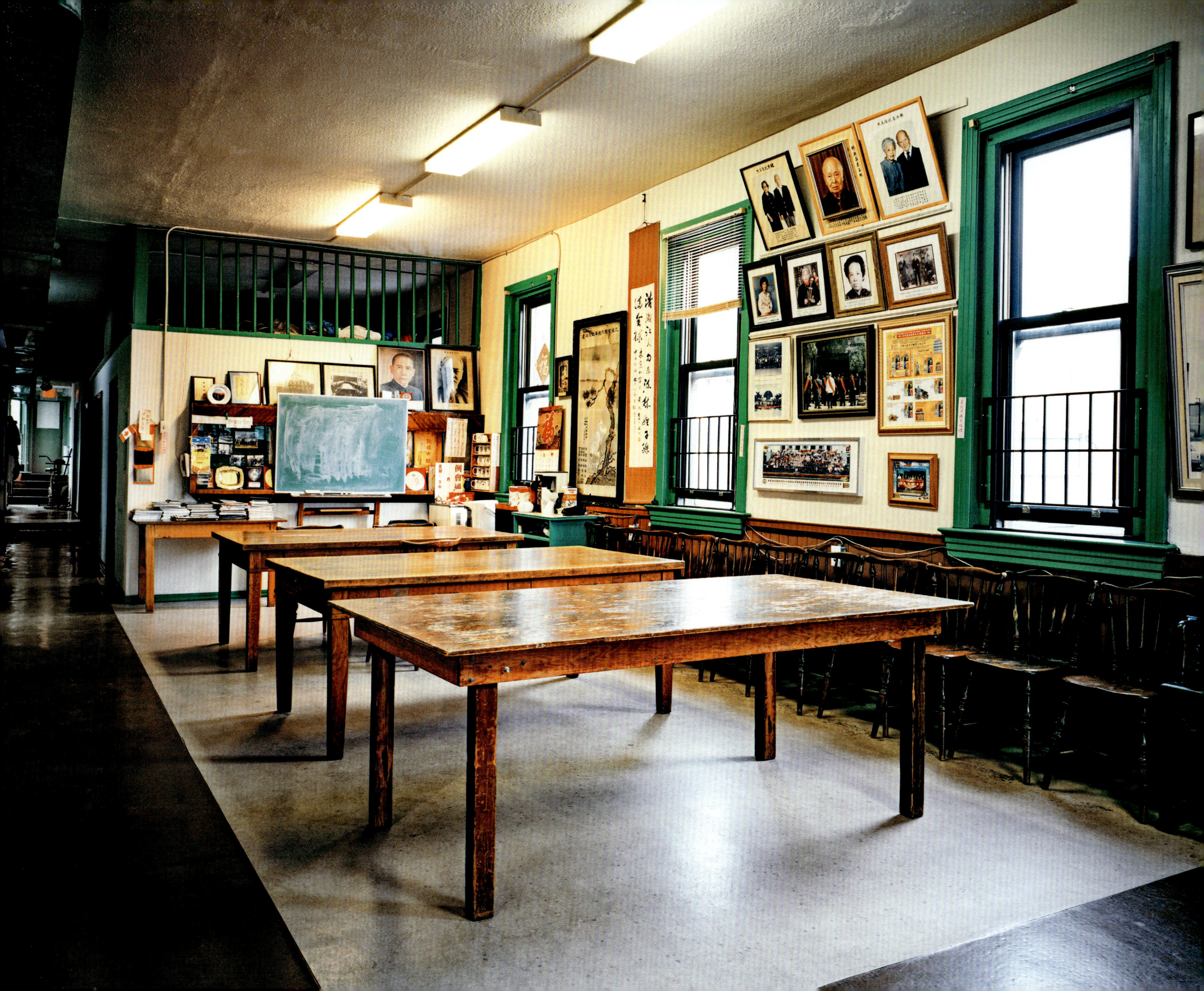

Hong Luck Kung Fu Club, Toronto West Chinatown, 2019

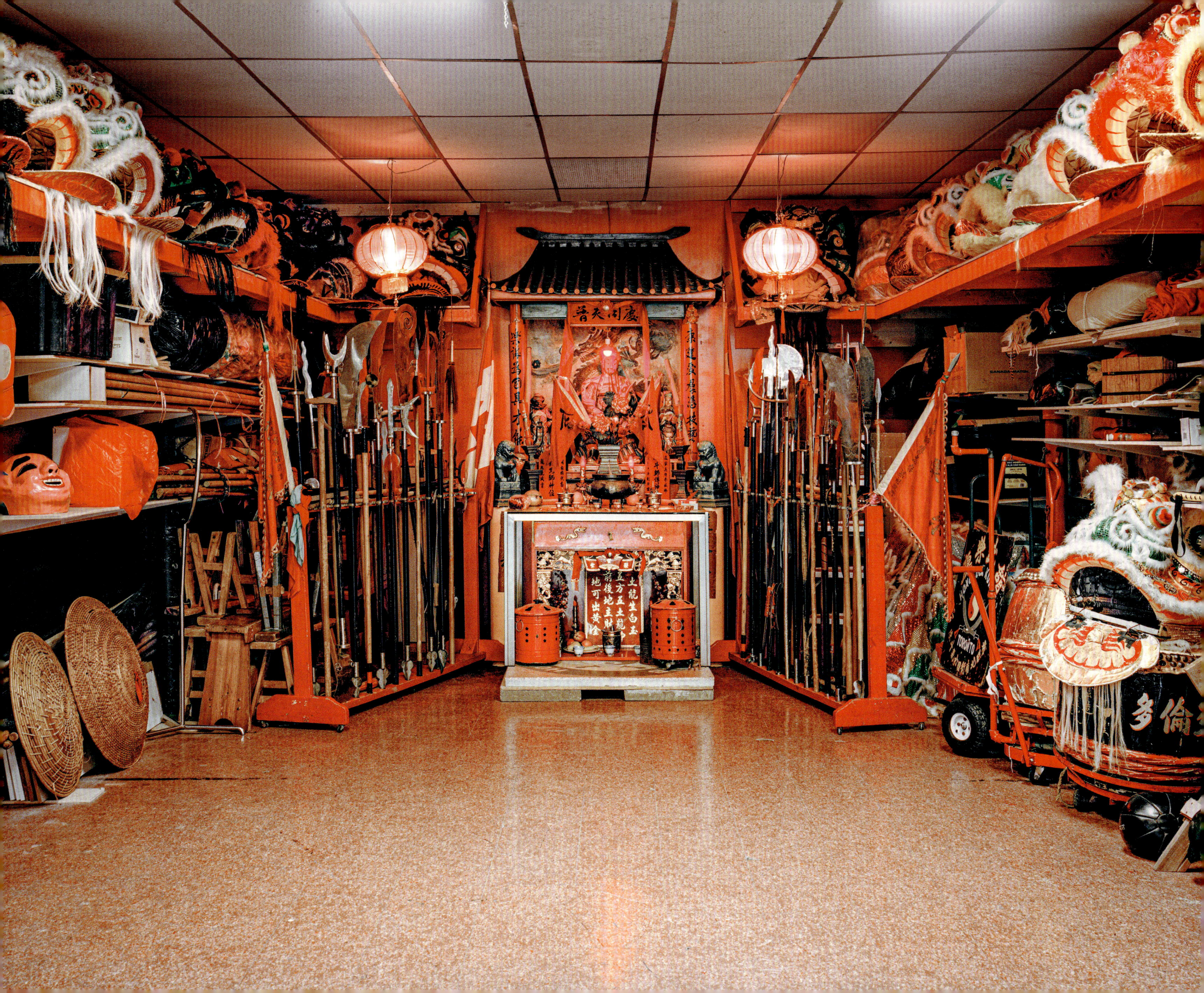

September 15, 2023

GABRIELLE MOSER I want to start by asking you about your research process: How do you identify locations for your Chinatown series?

MORRIS LUM When I started the project, I didn't have a focused way of thinking about Chinatowns. I knew I wanted to walk around and to get a sense of the different types of spaces within Chinatowns, but I was also interested in the aesthetic dimensions of a Chinese vernacular. So, for instance, the reappearance of archways and text, as well as the use of colour. The colours most associated with Chinese identity are red and gold and green, which provide a sense of good luck. Many businesses, particularly restaurants, use red and gold in their signage and in their interior decorations as well.

When I started to do site visits in 2011, I didn't have a specific sense of what I wanted to document. It was more instinctual, like "This looks interesting" or "This building has a particular architectural vernacular—an archway, or a triangular rooftop—that might be interesting as a photograph." As I met more people within the different Chinatown communities, that's when I really started to understand the different facets of Chinatown. For example, there is the commercial side, like restaurants and gift shops, and then there are legacy buildings, such as for clan or family associations. In my mind, that's how I started to organize the different types of spaces that I wanted to connect with and capture.

Now, after working on the project for more than a decade, when I visit a site, my choices are more about looking for places that I haven't captured yet. Part of my process is also about revisiting places that I've been to before and seeing shifts or changes. For instance, if a legacy business or mom-and-pop shop is closing because the owners want to retire, then I want to recognize that this particular place has been part of the community for a long time. I hope the photographs are able to prompt questions about change and as a result affect the dynamics of the community.

GM Could you say more about what you mean by that?

ML Chinatowns started off as working-class neighbourhoods. On the West Coast, the people who lived in Chinatowns were predominantly men who, after working on the railway, found work as labourers in agriculture, domestic service, or mining. In Canada from 1923 onward, the so-called Chinese Exclusion Act—the Chinese Immigration Act—essentially disallowed new Chinese immigrants from coming to Canada, and it put immigrants already in Canada in a precarious place: without citizenship or property or voting rights, until the act was repealed in 1947. During the exclusion period, the Chinese were told explicitly that they did not belong. Similar policies in the United States already embodied this pattern of exclusion. For Chinese people living in North America at the time, Chinatown was a safe haven, and it was really the only place where they could live and gather and find solace.

After the Chinese Immigration Act was repealed in Canada in 1947, after the Second World War, migration from China to Canada started to slowly happen again. And as a result, people from different parts of China moved to Chinatowns as their first destinations, bringing very different social classes to them than what existed at the time. Along with that influx came different languages, different dialects of Cantonese, and also different cuisines. Oftentimes there would be tensions between the existing community in a Chinatown and the new community, but at the same time, that also grew Chinatowns. From the 1950s onward, immigration increased, especially from Hong Kong in the 1990s in the lead-up to the UK's handover to China, ending British rule there. Then there was a later wave of immigration from Mainland China that brought a different language—more Mandarin-speaking people—different cuisines from all parts of China, and a different way of living. It has always felt like there are constant waves of rejuvenation in Chinatowns, culturally speaking, but these shifts also have a visual corollary: the spaces change as the needs of the Chinatown change.

GM The façades you capture then become a register of the different layers of social and cultural immigration that have changed the neighbourhood.

ML Yes, exactly. A really nice example is how on the one side of the street is a Cantonese-style restaurant that might have the word "Canton" in its name, and then, on the other side, another restaurant might contain the word "Shanghai," which is very Mandarin. These simple name choices reflect the very different styles of food coming into Chinatowns. It's a way of using the businesses to see different generations of immigration.

The research I do before shooting also involves meeting with elders, historians, writers, poets, artists, architects, and city planners who are born and raised in, or who have become part of, the community. Learning the stories and histories of community members has really enriched my own understanding of Chinatown[s]. I grew up in the suburbs and as an adult frequented Chinatown. Now I'm in Chinatown practically every day. My relationship to Chinatown is different from the lived experience of people who grew up there. They were part of a Chinatown history that I wasn't. When I was in Vancouver in 2013, I met Chinatown elder Jim Wong-Chu; he helped me understand the various components that make up a Chinatown. For instance, Jim was the one who took me to the hidden courtyards and alleys in Vancouver's Chinatown and explained how they formed and how they were integral during the time of exclusion to people's socializing and gathering. Jim educated me on the importance of these spaces.

GM What can you tell me about your working methods out in the field compared with the working methods you use in the studio? How much selecting and editing is happening in-camera, as opposed to the process of developing and printing the images?

ML I think the editing happens equally, both in the space of production and in the dark-room. When I get to a Chinatown I'm not familiar with, the first thing I do is just walk through it with a point-and-shoot camera. This is a very reactive, loose way of photographing. And I think that's a way for me to understand or unpack the nuances of each Chinatown. And then I prepare for the next day. The morning is when I usually bring out my four-by-five camera. The first couple of days are a bit explorative: I'm not totally sure what I should be shooting, but I am also interested in who's around and who's walking early in the morning.

Recently, when I was in the Chinatown in Oakland, California, I hung out at a large outdoor park that had a basketball court and slides and a table tennis, and a school close by, and when I was starting to photograph in the first couple of days, I noticed parents bringing their kids to the park before school. A few days later, I went to San Francisco, and it was very different in the mornings: that Chinatown is more a space you commute *through* to get to downtown if you're working in an office. It has a very different feeling in the mornings.

GM What drew you to the large-format camera—which is notoriously heavy to transport and complicated to set up—for street photography, so often imagined to be quick and of-the-moment?

ML I first started working with a four-by-five camera while doing my master's degree in documentary media at Toronto Metropolitan University, and at the time, film—that is, the manufacturing of film—was starting to disappear: Polaroid was going out of business, and it was feared Kodak would too. And Robert Burley, one of my professors, had done a project about these film-manufacturing plants closing. So I thought, maybe I should take advantage of the fact that there's still film I can purchase and start using my large-format camera. And, of course, film didn't die; if anything, the manufacturing of film is now ramping up again.

Many of my influences are also photographers who work with a four-by-five and shoot on film. People like Stephen Shore and Lynne Cohen, who document "(un)common spaces" (in Shore's words) in California or the desert or building interiors, using a large-format analogue camera, which brings to these spaces a presence and dignity. I think I wanted to share that quality by also using this type of camera in Chinatowns, to say that I believe these places have a strong historical importance to their respective cities. I wanted to reflect that and also pay respect to their history. I've been trying to do these spaces justice.

GM I can imagine the scene of you setting up the camera on the streets early in the morning, announcing that it's a landscape that you're capturing, since historically that's what the large-format camera—with its long exposure times—has been used for, and declaring to passersby that the scene is worthy of this sustained attention. There's something lovely about that contrast: of the spaces changing, sometimes very quickly, and you as an artist trying to capture that change through a cumbersome, labour-intensive process of observation.

You spoke already about the influence of landscape photographers like Stephen Shore and Lynne Cohen on your work, but I also see a conceptualist influence in your taking photographs of the same category of object but attending to the very small variations that make each building individual. You can have, as you do in this series, dozens of restaurant façades and they're all different, even though they are all, in a way, similar. There's a typological quality to the photographs, akin to Bernd and Hilla Becher's images of industrial infrastructure. Together, we've been looking too at the catalogue of the work of early-twentieth-century commercial Chinese photographer C.D. Hoy as we work on sequencing the images of Chinatown, and his are portraits of local residents in the Interior of British Columbia after the gold rush. Are there other photographers who have inspired your work?

ML I take references from many types of photography. New Topographics has definitely been an influence. But I also look to people who photographed inside Chinatown in street photography style, as a way of representing one's own culture. Jim Wong-Chu is one of those people, but also Corky Lee, who was a mainstay of Manhattan's Chinatown. Corky documented everything in this New York City Chinatown: labour movements, scenes that reflected what happened after 9/11, but also more subtle things about growing up in Chinatown. When I first began searching for photographs of Chinatowns, more than a decade ago, there weren't a lot of easily accessible resources. The spotlight on Chinatowns didn't exist then. And now there's so much more out there to draw inspiration from. I think it's amazing to see a new generation of storytellers focused on Chinatowns as a place of belonging.

GM What was your photographic training like, and how do you think about the question of genre in relation to these influences?

ML Ever since I was a kid, I've been interested in photography. I have a picture of myself with a toy camera, taking pictures. But my mom was the photographer in the family. She had an old Canon point-and-shoot camera, and I was fascinated by it—the way the flash popped up.

My uncle had a 35-millimetre single lens reflex camera, a Minolta X-700. He gave it to me to use in high school, and I started working with the lens more, focusing and considering composition, and then I also took darkroom classes. I brought what I learned in high school to my undergraduate program at the University of Toronto, where I started experimenting with a Hasselblad, a medium-format camera, and that was an interesting challenge because the film produces a square-format image.

Those early material experiments have stayed with me: I shoot only with available light, for both interior and exterior images, in the Chinatown series, for instance.

GM How do you choose which works are shown in the gallery as prints?

ML Sometimes it's about pairs of images that say something about a story. And those come forward fairly easily. Often it's about using individual photographs to show archetypes within the series. Depending on where the work is shown, sometimes it's more about a specific geographic focus in relation to the museum or gallery.

GM What was it like to work in the book format compared with the process of making prints for a gallery? Did that change your sense of scale within the project?

ML It did. In a book, the prints are often one size for consistency, whereas in a gallery there is more play with the final sizes. But because we're working in a book format, there's already the parameter of the size of the book itself and the reading experience. Playing with scale on a page, and the order of images from page to page—I found that experience really interesting.

There are some similarities in that, when you are in a gallery space, you can go up close to an image or pull back from it. For the book, I was trying to replicate the experience of looking at something from afar and then looking at something really closely.

GM Yes, there's a sense of intimacy that you can have with an image, which in some ways is intensified with a book because you can hold it in your hands and have it as part of your everyday domestic life. To me, this mirrors your relationship with Chinatowns as an artist: there is an embeddedness in the community and dedication to it, but also a kind of mournful tone to some of the images, especially when you're capturing something that has disappeared or fallen apart, or is on the verge of erasure.

ML Because Chinatowns are changing so much, and it's common now to see businesses closing down, I feel like I need to just photograph it. Then I'll have that shot scanned and stored as a digital file, and it might fall out of my conscious memory for a time. But when I revisit that site and see it is completely changed, that shot becomes relevant again. Sometimes it takes time for the story of a location to become a bit more whole: it's a way of collecting, because cities are not stagnant. They change. That has allowed me more freedom in some ways, because now I'm trying to capture everything, or as much as I can.

對話林耀基
Gabrielle Moser

2023 年 9 月 15 日

加比・莫澤（Gabrielle Moser）：我想先請你談談你的調研過程：你是如何為唐人街系列挑選拍攝地點的？

林耀基　在開始做這個項目的時候，我對唐人街並沒有特別明確的認識。我知道我想四處走走，感受唐人街裡各種不同的空間，我也對華人日常生活中的風土美學很感興趣。比方說，反復出現的拱門與文字以及對色彩的運用。紅色、金色與綠色是最能代表華人身份的色彩，這些顏色帶有吉祥的寓意。很多商家，尤其是餐廳，會在招牌和室內裝潢中使用紅色和金色。

我在 2011 年開始實地走訪，當時並不太清楚自己究竟想要記錄些什麼。更多時候是憑直覺行事，比如：「這個看起來很有意思」，或是「這棟建築上的風土元素很特別——一道拱門，或是三角形屋頂——或許會是一張很有意思的照片。」隨著與各類唐人街社群的接觸逐漸深入，我才開始真正理解唐人街的不同面向。比方說，有商業性的那一面，像餐廳和紀念品店；也有歷史性的建築，例如宗親會或家族會館。就這樣，我開始在腦海裡把那些我想理解與捕捉的空間分門別類。

現在，這個項目已經進行了超過十年。每當我走訪一個現場，我會更傾向於選擇那些尚未捕捉過的地方。同時，我的創作過程也包括重訪曾經去過的地點，觀察那裡是否出現了什麼變化。比方說，如果一間歷史悠久的老店，或是一間由夫妻經營的小鋪，因為店主退休而將歇業，那麼我就要讓這個地方長久以來在社區中的角色被看見。我希望這些照片能引發人們對變化的思考，並促動社區內部的動態關係。

莫　你可以再展開說一下你指的是什麼嗎？

林　唐人街最早是作為勞工階層社區而形成的。在西岸，居住在唐人街的人主要是男性，他們在修建鐵路後，轉而從事農務、家庭雜役或礦工等體力勞動。在加拿大，自 1923 年起，所謂的「排華法案」——即《華人移民法》——根本上全面禁止新的華人移民入境，也讓已經身在加拿大的華人處境岌岌可危：沒有公民身份、無法擁有地產，也沒有投票權，直到 1947 年該法案被廢除。在排華時期，華人被明確告知他們「不屬於這裡」。而在美國，更早已有類似的政策體現了這種排華模式。對當時生活在北美的華人而言，唐人街是一處避風港——幾乎是唯一能夠居住、聚集、尋求慰藉的地方。

1947 年，第二次世界大戰結束後，加拿大正式廢除了《華人移民法》。從那時起，來自中國的移民開始慢慢重新進入加拿大。來自中國不同地區的人們會把唐人街作為初抵加拿大時的首個落腳點，也給原有的唐人街社群帶來截然不同的社會階層。與之一起湧入的，還有多種語言，不同的廣東方言，以及來自不同地區的菜系。唐人街原有社群與新來移民之間，往往會出現一些張力，但同時，這樣的互動也推進了唐人街的發展。從 1950 年代起，移民人數逐漸增加，尤其是 1990 年代，在英國終結對香港的統治並將其管治權移交給中國前夕，來自香港的移民。後來又出現一波來自中國大陸的移民潮，他們帶來了不同的語言——主要是普通話——也帶來了大陸各地不同的菜系，以及不同的生活方式。從文化層面來看，唐人街總讓人感受到一種不斷的新生，而這些變化也常常在視覺上有所呼應：隨著需求的改變，唐人街的空間也隨之轉變。

莫　那麼，你所捕捉的那些建築立面就成了一種紀錄，標記了不同層面社會與文化移民如何改變了這些街區。

林　對，正是如此。舉個很貼切的例子：馬路一邊有家粵菜館，店名裡出現「廣東」兩個字；而在馬路另一邊，則是一家店名裡帶有「上海」字樣的餐廳，明顯偏向普通話語系。這些簡單的命名選擇，反映了不同菜系在唐人街的流入。透過這些店家，我們可以看見不同世代移民所留下的痕跡。

　　我在拍攝之前的調研，也包括與社區中的長者、歷史學者、作家、詩人、藝術家、建築師以及城市規劃師的交流——他們有些是在唐人街出生長大，有些則是在後來成為這個社區的一份子。了解這些社區成員的故事與歷史真正豐富了我對唐人街的理解。我自己是在市郊長大的，成年後才開始常來唐人街。現在，我幾乎每天都在唐人街出沒。我與唐人街的關係與那些從小生活在那裡的人並不一樣——他們本身就是唐人街歷史的一部分，而我不是。2013 年，我在溫哥華認識了唐人街長者朱藹信（Jim Wong-Chu），他幫助我理解構成唐人街的各種要素。比方說，是他帶我走進溫哥華唐人街那些不為人知的內院與小巷，並向我解釋這些空間是如何形成的，以及在排華時期，它們如何成為人們社交與聚會的重要場所。他讓我學會如何看待這些空間的重要性。

莫　你能談談外景拍攝時的工作方式與在工作室裡有何不同嗎？有多少挑選與編輯的決定是在拍攝當下完成的，而不是留到影像沖洗與印製階段再處理的？

林　我覺得編輯這件事是等同的，既發生在拍攝現場，也發生在暗房裡。當我來到一個還不熟悉的唐人街時，我做的第一件事就是拿著一台傻瓜相機走一圈。這是一種非常直覺、也比較隨性的拍攝方式。我認為這是我用來理解並梳理每個唐人街細微差異的方法。接著，我會準備隔天的拍攝。早晨通常是我使用 4×5 大畫幅相機的時段。最初幾天是比較探索性的：我還不太確定該拍些什麼，但同時也會留意周圍有什麼人、是誰在一大早走上街頭。

　　最近我在加州奧克蘭的唐人街時，曾在一個大型戶外公園裡待著，那裡有籃球場、滑梯、乒乓球桌，旁邊還有一所學校。剛開始拍攝的那幾天，我注意到有家長會在上學前帶孩子來公園。幾天後我去了舊金山，那裡的早晨就完全不同：如果你是在市中心辦公樓上班的人，那個唐人街更像是一個清晨「穿行」的通勤空間。那裡早晨的氛圍非常不同。

莫　是什麼吸引你選擇用大畫幅相機進行街頭攝影？這類相機一向以笨重、操作繁瑣著稱，而街頭攝影通常給人的印象則是快速而即興的。

林　我最初開始用 4×5 大畫幅相機，是在多倫多都會大學（Toronto Metropolitan University）讀紀實媒體碩士的時候。那時，膠片——也就是膠片的生產——正在逐漸消失：寶麗來（Polaroid）當時即將倒閉，大家也擔心柯達（Kodak）可能撐不下去。我的導師之一羅伯特・伯利（Robert Burley），剛完成一個關於膠片工廠關閉的攝影項目。於是我想，也許應該趁著還能買到膠片的時候，利用這個機會，開始用我的大畫幅相機。當然，膠片最後並沒有真的消失；反而這幾年，膠片生產又開始回溫了。

　　許多對我產生影響的攝影師也都用 4×5 大畫幅相機，並用膠片拍攝。像是史蒂芬・肖爾（Stephen Shore）和琳恩・柯恩（Lynne Cohen），他們會用這種膠片相機記錄加州的「（非）尋常空間」（用肖爾的說法），或是沙漠，或是建築物的內部空間。這類相機為這些空間帶來一種存在感與莊嚴感。我想，在拍攝唐人街時，我也希望透過這樣的器材，表達我所堅信的：這些地方對其所在的城市具有深厚的歷史意義。我希望能夠呈現出這一點，同時也向這些地方的歷史致敬。我一直努力讓這些空間獲得應有的重視與尊重。

莫　我可以想像你一大早在街上架設相機的畫面，彷彿在宣告你所捕捉的是一幅風景——畢竟，大畫幅相機歷來多用於拍攝風景，能進行長時間曝光——同時也向路人表明，這個場景值得專注的凝視。這種對比很動人：一方面是空間本身可能迅速變化，另一方面，作為藝術家的你，卻選擇以這種笨重且費力的觀察過程，去試圖捕捉這些變化。

　　你剛才提到像史蒂芬·肖爾和琳恩·柯恩這類風景攝影師對你創作的影響，不過我在你的作品中也看到觀念派的影響——你拍攝的是同一類型的物體，但特別關注其中細微的差異，讓每一棟建築都成為獨特的個體。就像在這個系列中，你拍了許多餐館的外立面，它們在某種意義上都很相似，卻又各自不同。這些照片具有類型學的特質，很像貝歇夫婦（Bernd and Hilla Becher）拍攝工業設施的影像。我們在整理這些唐人街影像的排序過程中，也一起翻閱了二十世紀初華人商業攝影師周耀初（C.D. Hoy）的作品集。他的作品是在淘金熱之後，為卑詩省內陸地區的在地居民所拍攝的肖像。除了這些攝影師，你還受到其他人的啟發嗎？

林　我會參考許多不同類型的攝影。「新地景攝影」（New Topographics）對我肯定有影響，但我也借鑒那些用街頭攝影風格記錄唐人街的人，作為自身文化表達的方式。朱藹信就是其中之一，還有紐約唐人街的代表人物李揚國（Corky Lee）。李揚國幾乎記錄了紐約唐人街的各個方面：從勞工運動，到反映 9/11 之後生活的場景，再到那些唐人街長大的細膩日常。十多年前我剛開始搜尋有關唐人街的攝影作品時，並沒有多少可以輕易獲取的資料。那時候，唐人街還不是大家關注的主題。而現在，可以讓人汲取靈感的資源越來越多。看到新一代敘事者將唐人街視為一種歸屬之地來關注，讓我感到欣喜。

莫　你的攝影訓練過程是怎麼樣的？面對這些影響，你怎麼看待「類型」（genre）這個問題？

林　我從小就對攝影很感興趣。我有一張照片，是我拿著玩具相機拍照的樣子。不過，家裡真正的攝影師是我媽媽。她有一台老式的佳能傻瓜相機，我對那台相機非常著迷——特別是閃光燈彈起時的樣子。

　　我舅舅有一台 35 毫米的單鏡反光相機——美能達（Minolta）X-700。他在我高中時把這台相機借給我用，於是我開始有更多機會接觸鏡頭的操作、對焦，以及思考構圖。那時候我也開始上暗房課。後來，我把高中時累積的這些經驗帶進多倫多大學的本科課程，並開始嘗試使用哈蘇（Hasselblad）的中片幅相機。這對我來說是一個很有趣的挑戰，因為這種膠片會產生方形畫幅的影像。

　　那些早期對物料的實驗經驗，一直以來都跟隨著我。舉例來說，在我的「唐人街」系列中，無論是拍攝室內還是室外，我都只依靠自然光。

莫　你是如何挑選那些會被印製出來、在畫廊展出的作品的？

林　有時候，是因為某些圖像的配對組合能夠講出一個故事，那些作品就比較容易出挑。更多時候，則是以單張照片來代表整個系列中的各種典型。再有，根據作品的展出地點，選擇會更多地取決於美術館或畫廊所在地的具體地緣脈絡。

莫　與為畫廊空間準備印製作品的過程相比，將作品以書本形式呈現，是一種怎樣的過程？這是否會改變你對整個項目的尺度感？

林　確實有改變。在書本裡，為了整體的一致性，印刷品通常都是統一尺寸的；而在畫廊展出時，則可以在作品的最終尺寸上有更多變化。但因為我們這次是以書本形式呈現，書本本身的尺寸以及閱讀的體驗就已經構成了一種框架。我開始想像如何在頁面上玩轉尺度，以及影像在每一頁之間的排序——我覺得這整個過程非常有趣。

　　其實這當中也有某種共通性。當你身處畫廊空間時，可以走近看一張照片，也可以退後觀看。而在書本的空間裡，我會試著複製那種從遠處觀看某個東西，再靠近細看、觀察的經驗。

莫　是的，觀看影像時會產生一種親密感，而在某種程度上，書本的閱讀經驗會進一步強化這種感受，因為你可以把它捧在手裡，讓它成為日常家居生活的一部分。在我看來，這也對應了你作為藝術家與唐人街之間的關係：你完全融入了這個社群，並投身其中。但在某些影像中，也帶著一種哀悼的意味，尤其是當你捕捉到那些已經消失、破敗，或即將被抹去的事物時。

林　因為唐人街的變化實在太大了，現在店家關門歇業已經很常見，我總覺得自己必須先把它拍下來。之後我會把照片掃描，並存成數位檔案，可能有一段時間不會特別去想它。但當我某天再回到那個地方，發現它已經徹底改變時，那張照片又重新變得重要。有時候，一個地方的故事需要時間才能慢慢完整——這也是一種收集的方式。因為城市不是靜止不動的，它會不斷變化。在某種程度上，這也讓我有了更多自由，因為我現在試著去捕捉一切，或至少盡我所能地去記錄它們。

I would like to dedicate this book to the community members from Chinatowns across what is known as North America and Turtle Island. As an immigrant and settler with roots in both Trinidad and Tobago and China, I have been on a journey to find oneself that I never would have imagined or expected. While the road of this journey is far from unfolded, I would like to take this moment as a time to thank Lily and Gabrielle and to reflect on the generosity of so many who have welcomed me with open arms (usually with an offering of tea or a snack). This selection does not include all the wonderful places I've photographed; it does represent my first offering (of many) of the larger body of work from my *Tong Yan Gaai* photography series. My journey wouldn't have been possible without the wisdom and guidance of the generations that have come before and are continuing to grow the Chinatown community today. It feels impossible to express my gratitude to everyone who has embraced me along the way. To the community that makes up Chinatowns—the clan associations, mom-and-pop business, artists, historians, and friends.

—Morris

LILY CHO 曹美寶 is Associate Professor of English at York University. She is the author of *Eating Chinese: Culture on the Menu in Small Town Canada* (2010) and *Mass Capture: Chinese Head Tax and the Making of Non-citizens* (2021).

GABRIELLE MOSER is Associate Professor of Art History and Research Chair and Director of the Gail and Stephen A. Jarislowsky Institute for Studies in Canadian Art at Concordia University in Montreal. She is the author of *Projecting Citizenship: Photography and Belonging in the British Empire* (Penn State University Press, 2019).

MORRIS LUM is a Trinidadian-born photographer and artist whose work explores the complex hybridity of the Chinese-Canadian experience through photography, form, and documentary practices. His work delves into the representation of Chinese history in both media and archival materials, highlighting how these narratives are shaped and communicated. Lum's work has been exhibited and screened across Canada and the United States. Currently, he is focused on a cross–North American project examining the transformation of Chinatowns, capturing the evolving architectural and cultural landscapes of these communities.

Published in 2025 by
WORK BOOK and DelMonico Books • D.A.P.

WORK BOOK is a publishing collective led by
Robyn Lew and Jim Shedden.

DelMonico Books
available through ARTBOOK | D.A.P.
75 Broad Street, Suite 630
New York, NY 10004
artbook.com
delmonicobooks.com

ISBN: 9781636811796

Library of Congress Control Number: 2025936413

Printed and bound in Belgium
10 9 8 7 6 5 4 3 2 1

DESIGNER
Gilbert Yu-Bun Li 李耀彬

IMAGE EDITORS
Gabrielle Moser and Morris Lum

MANAGING EDITORS
Robyn Lew and Jim Shedden

RESEARCHERS
Arlene Chan and Shawn Tse

TRANSLATOR
Yan Wu 吳彥

COPY EDITOR
Judy Phillips

PROOFREADERS
James Harbeck and Yan Zhou 周琰

PRE-PRESS
Paul Jerinkitsch

PRINTING & BINDING
Type A Print Inc.

TYPEFACES
Editorial New by Pangram Pangram Foundry
Fāng Zhèng Shū Sòng by FounderType
Tempel Grotesk by Production Type
Zed by Typotheque

PAPER STOCK
150 g/m² Magno Satin

FRONT AND BACK COVER
Doyers Street, 2019 (diptych)

END PAGES
Studio Session with Gabrielle Moser, 2025

BOOK FUNDERS
Photography Network Project Grant
Burtynsky Grant, CONTACT Photography Festival

PROJECT FUNDERS
Canada Council for the Arts
Ontario Arts Council

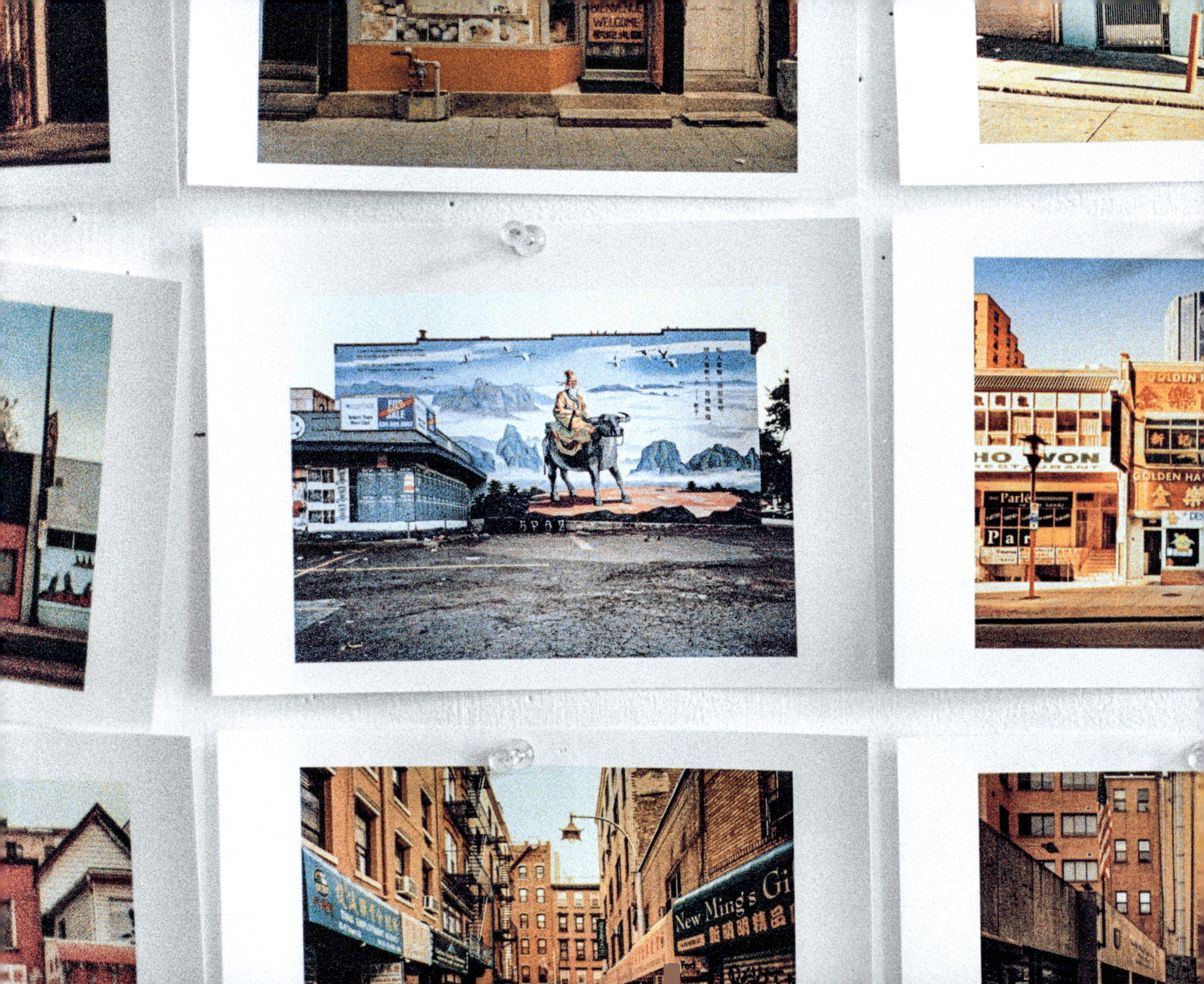